Courthouses of California

AN ILLUSTRATED HISTORY

Courthouse in Bridgeport, Mono County

Courthouses of California

AN ILLUSTRATED HISTORY

Edited with an Introduction by Ray McDevitt
Foreword by Chief Justice Ronald M. George

CALIFORNIA HISTORICAL SOCIETY • SAN FRANCISCO CALIFORNIA
HEYDAY BOOKS • BERKELEY CALIFORNIA

Published by Heyday Books in conjunction with
the California Historical Society

Library of Congress
Cataloging-in-Publication Data

Courthouses of California : an illustrated history
/ edited with an introduction by Ray McDevitt ;
foreword by Chief Justice Ronald M. George.
    p. cm.
 ISBN 1-890771-49-X
 1. Courthouses--California. I. McDevitt, Ray,
1943- II. California Historical Society.
 NA4472.C2 C68 2001
 725'.15'09794--dc21

    2001002632

Cover and Interior Design: Mark Shepard

Orders, inquiries and correspondence should be
addressed to:
Heyday Books
P.O. Box 9145, Berkeley, CA 94709
(510) 549-3564, fax (510) 549-1889
www.heydaybooks.com

Printed in Singapore by Imago

10 9 8 7 6 5 4 3 2 1

Contents

The California Historical Society thanks the
following donors, whose generous support
helped make this book possible.

Hanson Bridgett Marcus Vlahos & Rudy, LLP

The Upjohn Fund of San Francisco

Cotchett, Pitre & Simon

The Daily Journal Corporation

Neil Falconer, San Francisco

Farella Braun & Martell, LLP

Patrick Miyaki, San Francisco

O'Melveny & Myers, LLP

Mary Elizabeth Pike, Pasadena

University of San Francisco, School of Law

In Memory of Sidney H. Arden, Valley Glen

Valerie J. Armento, Sunnyvale

David Baer, San Rafael

Hon. Kenneth R. Barr, Judge, San Bernardino Superior Court

Jacquelyn Garman Beeman, Ross

Timothy J. Blackwood, San Jose

Hon. Richard Breiner, Judge (Ret.), San Rafael

Geraldine Brown, Merced

Michael J. Burke, San Francisco

Hon. Kenneth Mark Burr, Judge, Alameda Superior Court

William J. Bush, San Francisco

Elizabeth J. Cabraser, San Francisco

California Supreme Court Historical Sciety

Robert F. Carlson, Carmichael

Thomas H. Carlson, Palo Alto

James N. Casey, San Mateo

Robert A. Champlain, San Francisco

Boren Chertkov & Anne Bailey, Sacramento

Hon. Kenneth Lee Chotiner, Judge, Los Angeles Superior Court

Christopher E. Cobey, Atherton

Hal & Inez Cohen, San Francisco

Prof. Marsha Cohen, Hastings College of Law

Richard J. Collier, Berkeley

Jack Conneely, San Mateo

Joyce Cook, Los Angeles

Hon. John S. Cooper, Judge (Ret.), Berkeley

Hon. Lee E. Cooper, Jr., Judge (Ret.), Mammoth Lakes

Newton A. Cope, San Francisco

David J. Cowan, Los Angeles

Eleanore Dailey, La Crescenta

Hon. Vincent DiFiglia, Judge, San Diego Superior Court

Hon. Vincent N. Erickson, Judge (Ret.), Palm Desert

Hon. Charles D. Field, Judge, Riverside Superior Court

James M. Flack, San Francisco

James Fousekis, San Francisco

James & Louise Frankel, San Francisco

Robert & Leslie Frates, Hayward

Hon. Richard O. Frazee, Sr., Judge, Orange Superior Court

Gil Garcetti, Los Angeles

Jerry J. Goldstein, Laguna Niguel

Prof. Brian Gray, Hastings College of Law

Carol Gray, Mill Valley

Prof. Joseph Grodin, Hastings College of Law

Hon. Walter H. Harrington, Jr., Judge (Ret.), Woodside

Robert K. Hillison, Fresno

Debra Faraone Hodges, Campbell

Elizabeth and J.T. Holmes, Palo Alto

Hon. Francis J. "Jack" Hourigan, Judge, Los Angeles Superior Court

Thomas R. Hudson, Upland

Hon. Thomas M. Jenkins, Judge (Ret.), San Carlos

Hon. Michael M. Johnson, Judge, Los Angeles Superior Court

Hon. Robert F. Kaster, Judge, Siskiyou Superior Court

Hon. Thomas W. Kelly, Judge, Butte Superior Court

Hon. Thomas Kongsgaard, Judge (Ret.), Napa

Hon. Quentin Kopp, Judge, San Mateo Superior Court

Richard J. Krech, Oakland

Hon. Marlene A. Kristovich, Judge, Los Angeles Superior Court

Stephen A. Kronick, Sacramento

Ted Krumland, Orinda

Hon. John Letton, Judge, Trinity Superior Court

Alan Lilly, Sacramento

Tiberio P. Lizza, Belvedere

Hon. William T. Low, Judge (Ret.), La Jolla

John P. Lynch, San Francisco

Hon. James T. Marchiano, Associate Justice, Court of Appeal

Barry Martin, Sacramento

L.J. Chris Martiniak, Berkeley

Deborah Miller, Saratoga

Mortimer Lawyers & Counselors, San Francisco

Hon. Philip Moscone, Judge, San Francisco Superior Court

Lynn Tracy Nerland, Walnut Creek

Stephen G. Opperwahl, Pleasanton

Jack Owens, Modesto

Helen C. Page, San Francisco

Hon. Charles L. Patrick, Judge (Ret.), La Jolla

Pahl & Gosselin, LLP, San Jose

James Pfeiffer & Bonnie Rose Haugh, Novato

Jay & Joyce Powell, Visalia

Process Server Institute, San Francisco

Hon. Timothy Reardon, Associate Justice, Court of Appeal

Hon. Maria Rivera, Judge, Contra Costa Superior Court

Michael Satris & Bonnie M. Jones, Bolinas

Carolyn J. Schauf, Downey

Hon. Joseph Sneed, Judge, U.S. Ninth Circuit Court of Appeals

Dick & Joanne Spotswood, Mill Valley

Hon. & Mrs. Donald Umhofer, San Luis Obispo

Hon. Judith Vanderlans, Judge, Los Angeles Superior Court

Hon. Brian R. Van Kamp, Judge, Sacramento Superior Court

John Vlahos, Kensington

Robert J. Wade, Lake Elsinore

Paul R. Ward & Maureen J. Arrigo, Redlands

Donald B. Webster, Red Bluff

Timothy White, Los Angeles

Hon. Charles A. Wieland, Judge, Madera Superior Court

Hon. Raymond D. Williamson, Jr., Judge (Ret.), San Francisco

Joshua G. Wilson, Esq., Shafter

Hon. Robert W. Zakon, Judge, Los Angeles Superior Court

This book is dedicated to the memory of Raymond L. Sullivan with affection, admiration and gratitude.

Raymond L. Sullivan (1907–1999)
Born in San Francisco; educated at the University of San Francisco and at its Law School;
Attorney; Associate Justice and Presiding Justice, California Court of Appeal, First District,
Division One (1961–66); Associate Justice, California Supreme Court (1966–77); Professor of
Law, University of California, Hastings College of the Law (1978–93).

Foreword

Ronald M. George, Chief Justice of California

Every history is a serious undertaking, but histories of California can be especially formidable. With this welcome volume, Ray McDevitt contributes a missing chapter in the extraordinary story of the Golden State and gives us a comprehensive survey of what are quite likely our most significant public buildings—the courthouses of California.

In concise county histories laced with curious and sometimes startling anecdotes, *Courthouses of California* gives us a new perspective on state history. Here, for example, are stories of early statehood and the rivalries between pioneer communities for designation as county seats and as sites of the first courthouses. We learn of the countless fires, floods, and earthquakes that took their toll on what we now rightly regard as our architectural heritage. But of even greater effect is the underlying pressure of growth that is so much a part of California and that demanded—and demands to this day—continuous expansion, remodeling, and reconstruction of court buildings around the state.

It is in the photographs presented in this volume that the history of these buildings and the communities they served truly comes alive. Winston Churchill once remarked, "We shape our buildings, and afterwards, our buildings shape us." I believe this is especially true of our courthouses. In this rich and unprecedented collection, the story of the state unfolds in its architecture—from Spanish colonialism to statehood to postwar internationalism. The wedding of architecture and justice has resulted in buildings that have much to say about the values and aspirations of our citizens over the years.

I have some personal knowledge of the scope of the task of compiling the collection for this book. In 1996, my first year as Chief Justice, I resolved to visit the courts in each of our state's 58 counties. Over the ensuing year I traveled to every region of our state to meet with court, bar, and community leaders in each county. It was an invigorating and inspiring enterprise, one that gave me the opportunity to meet many of the committed men and women working in the courts and serving their communities.

I also had the occasion to visit most of the courthouses included in these pages that still serve the public. Based on those visits and combining interests in art and history, my wife, Barbara, began to research some of the historic courthouses that still survive. As her enthusiasm grew, so did the collection of images. After a year and countless inquiries to state libraries, local historical societies, individual collectors, and researchers, including Mr. McDevitt, she completed an impressive exhibit of photographs representing every county in the state, a record of the remarkable buildings dedicated by the people of our state to the administration of justice. The collection now hangs in the Judicial Council Conference Center in San Francisco, headquarters for the state's judicial branch.

Courthouses of California traces the line of history from the buildings in this exhibit back to the first courthouses of the new state and forward to the latest construction in the new century. I applaud Mr. McDevitt's diligence and commitment to preserving the history of what are, in the words of one judge at the turn of the last century, "our temples of justice."

Ronald M. George
Chief Justice of California
April 2001

Introduction

By Ray McDevitt

Courthouses have been constructed in each of the 58 counties in California and during each of the 15 decades since the state was created. The invention of photography roughly coincided with California's admission to the United States. Talented photographers (George Fardon, Carleton Watkins and Eadweard Muybridge among them) journeyed to California to record the Gold Rush and its aftermath. While few photographs exist from the Mexican California era, it is possible to assemble a visual history of California stretching back nearly 150 years. Thus, we can trace the evolution of courthouses from modest, even rustic, buildings in a state of 200,000 people to ornate Renaissance celebrations when the state reached 6 million, to massive complexes when California's population passed 30 million.

In the process, aspects of the state's history, not otherwise evident, are revealed. We can see, for example, the decline of the mining industry and the rise of agriculture during the 1870s in the relocation of county seats (and, therefore, courthouses) from foothill towns to new communities on the floor of the Central Valley. We can see the successive waves of architectural fashion from the austere Greek Revival of the 1850s and 1860s to the glass-walled rectangles of the International Style of the 1950s and 1960s and can gauge how powerful is the force of fashion by the similarity in styles of the courthouses constructed anywhere in the state during any given decade. And we can see the impact of the automobile after World War II as courthouses, like so many other types of buildings, were relocated away from their traditional downtown venues to sprawling government centers at the very edge of town. Along the way, we can observe the changing fashions in clothing, furniture, technology and social customs, all recorded by ubiquitous photographers.

In short, a photodocumentary history of California courthouses is also a pictorial history of California itself—a "family album" of one branch of the California family.

THE COURTHOUSE: AN ICONIC AMERICAN BUILDING

When former Vice President Al Gore announced his campaign for the Democratic Party's nomination for president, he stood on the steps of the Smith County courthouse in Carthage, Tennessee. The choice was no accident. Mr. Gore hoped to associate himself with values that the county courthouse can evoke: patriotism, traditional small-town virtues, the rule of law.

But law is a complex social institution and courthouses are complicated icons. Mr. Gore could certainly not have foreseen that his campaign for the presidency would end in a welter of lawsuits in courthouses ranging from humble buildings in rural Florida counties to the august structure that houses the Supreme Court of the United States in Washington, D.C. The involvement of the judiciary in the 2000 presidential electoral process provoked a heated national debate about the proper role of the courts in a democratic society, a debate that has persisted since the earliest days of the Republic. The spectrum of opinion about law and courts finds a parallel in the multiple perspectives through which we view courthouses themselves. There is no official roster of these perspectives, of course; in compiling this book I have encountered the following.

The Courthouse as Temple

Courthouses are freighted with society's aspirations: peaceful resolution of disputes between private parties; protection of the individual against oppressive abuse of governmental power; and due punishment of wrongdoers, coupled with vindication of the innocent.

The way in which these functions are performed is itself held to demanding standards:

- Equality before the law, with judgments unaffected by favoritism or bias
- Respectful attentiveness to all participants—providing each person his or her "day in court"

These are high ideals. Builders have tried to convey the courts' seriousness of purpose and dedication to principle through architecture. Conceiving of the courthouse as a temple is by no means simply a metaphor; it has specific historical roots. When Thomas Jefferson served as ambassador of the United States to France (1784–89), he visited Roman ruins in the south of France. He was much impressed with one temple in particular, the Maison Corrée at Nimes. His design for the Virginia capitol building in Richmond appropriated elements of the Maison Corrée's temple front. These

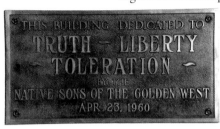

have since become identified with courthouses—the monumental staircase leading to a row of classical columns that support a triangular pediment. Later courthouse designers also incorporated a dome, echoing more recent temples such as St. Paul's Cathedral in London, designed by Sir Christopher Wren.

By the mid–20th century, California courthouses designed in the International Style no longer employed these features, nor the statues and stained glass windows that 19th-century courthouses also borrowed from ecclesiastic architecture. But they still proclaimed the ideals to which they are dedicated, in text carved into granite or forged in bronze.

Dedications on two courthouses, each built in 1960. Above, the plaque on the Stanislaus County courthouse. Below right, words carved into stone dedicate the San Francisco Hall of Justice "to the faithful and impartial enforcement of the laws with equal and exact justice to all of whatever state or persuasion."

The Courthouse as Theater or Arena

Trials are often compared to dramas. In both there is a stage (the "well" in the courtroom), actors (judge, lawyers, litigants and witnesses) and an audience. One of our earliest dramas, Aeschylus's *Oresteia* trilogy, concludes with a trial held at the Parthenon (a real Greek temple) presided over by Athena, who convenes the first assembly of citizen-jurors to decide the fate of Orestes, accused of killing his mother in revenge for her murder of his father.

Trials are also akin to athletic contests. Trial by combat was among the direct chronological antecedents of English law courts. The vocabulary that today's trial lawyers use to describe their strategies and accomplishments is full of words drawn from combative sports or just plain combat. An article in a recent issue of *California Lawyer*, for example, contained profiles of aggressive trial lawyers "who combine the qualities of a litigator with those of an alligator." It quotes the managing partner of a Silicon Valley law firm describing trial lawyers as "gladiators in the courtroom" and extolling subtle trial tactics as "judo moves." One featured attorney is described as a "take-no-prisoners employment lawyer," another as "a street fighter," a third as someone who "goes straight for the jugular," and yet another as "a pit bull." Even if we allow for self-glamorizing hyperbole, this terminology reveals an underlying reality. Justice is always depicted as holding a set of scales. Implicit in that image is success for one side, defeat for the other. Trials never end in ties; if the scales were to be evenly balanced by equal weights of evidence on each side, the "burden of proof," imposed by law on one side or the other, would determine the winner.

The dramas or contests played out in courtrooms are charged with emotion. A painful history has almost always led the parties to the courtroom: neighbors feuding over fences, pets or noisy parties; former business partners now bitter antagonists; splintered families struggling for control over money or children. The confrontations in the courtroom themselves evoke powerful emotions. And the decision brings joy to one side, sorrow to the other.

One architect has been quoted as saying that the function of

Two men wait in the hallway of Riverside County's elegant courthouse.

courthouse architecture is "to anesthetize the trauma of legal confrontation."

The Courthouse as Locus of State Power

Justice holds not only a scale, but a sword. Punishment of the guilty is as much a part of the courts' function as is vindication of the innocent. Courthouses are thus the portals to the California prison system, which now incarcerates 160,000 prisoners, with another 75,000 held in custody in county jails. For the first four decades of statehood, executions were also carried out in or near county courthouses. (Marin County's first courthouse had an indoor gallows. After executions were moved to San Quentin Prison, an elevator to the second floor of the courthouse was installed where the gallows had been.)

The potential for violence hovers around courthouses. Often it is the aftermath of violence that is the occasion for a trial. Sometimes violence erupts at the courthouse itself, as the terrible photographs of Marin County's Civic Center in 1971 recall (p. 154) and as signs at courthouses remind us daily.

The Task Force on Court Facilities established by the state legislature in 1997 issued "Trial Court Facilities Guidelines" in October 1999. The guidelines recommend measures that courthouse designers should consider to protect the people who occupy the courthouse and to prevent escape by those in custody. An excerpt:

Exterior glazing that encloses [judges'] chambers, key staff offices or courtroom space should be planned to shield occupants from gunfire or other physical threat. Building exterior details and landscaping should minimize the potential for placement of explosive devices by avoiding creation of hidden or blind areas that could impede security surveillance and monitoring....

Building access points should be in sight of a surveillance source and configured with unobtrusive barriers to prevent violent entry by persons or vehicles. The exterior courthouse grounds should inhibit access of unauthorized vehicles by such means as fencing and landscape design without hindering emergency access for fire, paramedic and law enforcement vehicles and personnel. The courthouse building perimeter should be set back from any public street by the greatest possible distance to avoid public vehicles parking adjacent to the structure.

At least one courtroom should be designed to accommodate trials that involve a high degree of risk to participants. Such a courtroom should have

Below: Judge R. J. Reynolds presides at a hearing in the 1979 trial of former San Francisco Supervisor Dan White, who killed Mayor George Moscone and another supervisor in City Hall.
Bottom: The 1974 trial of Angela Davis. Defense attorney Howard Moore holds the sawed-off shotgun that killed Marin County Superior Court Judge Howard Haley three years earlier. (See p. 154).

electronic screening for all persons attending trial…. Ballistic-resistant glass should be considered between the spectator seating area and the litigation area.

Despite the matter-of-fact language, occupants of courthouses obviously face higher risks of violence than those of any other generally accessible public buildings.

The use of force implicit in sentences of death or imprisonment is an unpleasant but inescapable reality, apparent to anyone who observes the shackled prisoners in orange jumpsuits awaiting arraignment in one of our criminal courts. But the confidence that courts will in fact punish the lawless is the foundation on which society has outlawed private revenge. Lack of that confidence contributed to the rise of extra-legal tribunals in the early mining camps and to the Committees of Vigilance in San Francisco and elsewhere in the 1850s. The "vigilantes" are long gone; the rule of law is well established in California. But we should not imagine that we are immune to the vigilante impulse. The photo-

Some harsh realities of administering justice: signs on a Los Angeles County courthouse entrance; advertisement on bus stop bench near the courthouse in Modesto.

graph at left was taken in 1933, in San Jose. The men are battering down the doors to the Santa Clara County jail. When the doors gave way, these men in suits and fedora hats seized two inmates awaiting trial for the brutal kidnap/murder of the son of a prominent local family. The two were dragged across the street to St. James Park—the elegant centerpiece of downtown San Jose—where they were lynched, within a few hundred feet of the columned entrance to Santa Clara's classical courthouse. Are we really so far removed from the men shown in the picture?

The Courthouse as Workplace

For tens of thousands of Californians, courthouses are familiar places, visited five days a week, fifty weeks a year. Judges (over 2,000 in California) work at the courthouse, as do their direct support

Middle-class citizens of San Jose took the law into their own hands in 1933, when they forced their way into the county jail, then lynched two prisoners in St. James Park.

staff: bailiffs, court reporters, court clerks, and research attorneys. Most of the state's trial courts are housed in mixed-use buildings where courts and court-related agencies (such as the public defender, district attorney, law library and probation department) are the predominant users. Others share space with an array of county functions, ranging from the board of supervisors to the county jail, just as courts did in the earliest days of statehood. And trial court facilities, whether stand-alone courthouses or components of multiple-use government centers, require the presence of other workers who keep the buildings functioning: janitors, plumbers, stationary engineers, gardeners, even cooks, if there is a cafeteria. For many, perhaps most, of these workers, the courthouse is simply a place to work—no different from any other building. But for others, particularly those whose duties require their presence in the courtroom, the courthouse is a special place, one that profoundly engages their emotions.

Andrew Schottky served for many years as superior court judge in Mariposa County in the southern Sierra Nevada. He presided over trials held in a white wooden Greek Revival–style building, constructed in 1854—the oldest functioning courthouse in California. In 1953, he was appointed as an associate justice on the Third District Court of Appeal in Sacramento. The Third District Court of Appeal sits in a grandly scaled, elegantly appointed neoclassical building adjacent to the state capitol. (It is pictured on pages 324–5.) The California Supreme Court hears oral arguments there three times a year. Judge Schottky's appointment prompted him to compose a nostalgic poem bidding farewell to his former workplace. It was published in *Mariposa County Courthouse* and is reprinted here with the kind permission of the authors of that fine book.

Upkeep is an endless task. Painter at work on door of Santa Barbara's courthouse.

Kern County Sheriff's Deputies Brenda Waidelich and Sandy Welch share a table outside the courthouse cafeteria in Bakersfield with court clerk Georgia Morgan.

The Courthouse as the Center of Community

In California's early decades there was often fierce competition among towns to be designated as the county seat. This was in part a manifestation of local pride, but more pragmatic motives were also at work. The presence of the courts and county government made a huge contribution to a town's economic vitality. The judges and county officials were likely to become town residents. Even more important, lawyers, surveyors, printers and others would require office space near the courthouse. And there would be demand for hotels, restaurants and taverns to accommodate the

THE MARIPOSA COURTHOUSE

There's a little white Courthouse, I'm leaving it soon,
  And somehow it seems hard to go.
For this Courthouse has found a place in my heart,
  I shall miss it always, I know.
For there I have studied and labored and dreamed,
  And hoped for advancement, too.
But, oh, in my triumph I'm dreary just now,
  Goodbye, little Courthouse, to you!

And though I may sit in a courtroom ornate,
  With appointments so modern and fine;
Yet well do I know as now I depart
  I shall miss that old courtroom of mine;
I'll think of its white boarded ceiling and walls,
  The long bench and the clean, polished floor,
And I know that in fancy I'll come back
  To sit in that courtroom once more.

I look from my chambers up into the hills,
  In the distance Mt. Bullion I see;
Through the warm winter sunshine so clear and so bright,
  It seems to beckon me.
The hills seem so cheery and peaceful and green,
  With a charm one can never forget.
It's the thrill and romance of the old Mother Lode,
  Where the pioneer spirit lives yet.

How stately you stand there amid the green hills,
  A last wistful look and I go.
A century long you've stood there in the sun
  Above the fog in the valley below;
Your famous old clock is just striking twelve,
  Its tall tower points toward the sky.
And the time has come for me to depart,
  So, little white Courthouse, goodbye!

Judge Andrew Schottky, 1953

I ask you: How many other buildings in California could evoke sentiments of that kind from someone leaving to accept a promotion?

lawyers and their clients who traveled to town for court-related business.

A band plays standards for an enthusiastic audience on a warm Friday afternoon outside the San Joaquin County courthouse in Stockton.

The courthouse, typically situated at the center of town—often in or across the street from a park or square—was the scene of community gatherings of all kinds. John Burns's essay recounts the array of social events held at courthouses in the early days: dances, band concerts, weddings, funerals, religious ceremonies, fraternal society meetings. While most of these activities now occur elsewhere, the courthouse grounds in many counties are still the site of community activities, like the farmer's market held in Stockton, at which a local band entertained in the summer of 2000.

A monument placed by Madera County's Board of Supervisors on the lawn outside the old courthouse celebrates the county's centennial. The text reads:

"This monument is dedicated to the enterprise and vision of the people of the 1800's from the granite cutters, loggers and miners in the mountains to the cattle, sheep and grain growers ranging the rolling foothills, to the entrepreneurs and day laborers, winemakers and homemakers who sought their dreams in the valley. All contributed to the vigorous present of Madera County."

The tradition of political rallies centered on the courthouse continues. And the courthouse grounds are still the place where monuments are raised to honor a county's local heroes—those who died in war or in law enforcement service—and its founding fathers.

Regrettably, not all early Californians would have had reason to see the courthouse as a center of their community. African Americans were barred by law from giving testimony in California courts until 1863; Asians and Native Americans were excluded until 1872. While Californians of Mexican ancestry were permitted to testify as witnesses, their opinion of California courts can be inferred from the reflections of General Mariano Guadalupe Vallejo—a native Californian who welcomed a connection with the United States, and who served in both the 1849 Constitutional Convention and the State Senate. Even sympathetic General Vallejo was bitter:

> All these evils became insignificant in comparison with the swollen torrent of shysters, who came from Missouri and other states of the Union. No sooner had they arrived here than they assumed the title of attorney, and began to seek means of depriving the Californians of their farms and other properties. The escaped bandits from Australia stole our cattle and our horses, but these legal thieves, clothed in the robes of the law, took from us our lands and our houses.… For them existed no law but their own will and caprice, they recognized no right but that of force. It was our misfortune that these adventurers of evil law were so numerous that it was impossible for us to defend our rights in the courts since the majority of judges were squatters and the same could be said of the sheriffs and the juries.… [T]o all these, justice was only a word used to sanction robbery.

These shameful events from California's formative years do not diminish the great contributions to the liberty and equality of all Californians that the courts have made over the past 100 years. But they do help explain why some Californians may still feel ambivalent about the notion of the courthouse as the center of community.

CALIFORNIA AND ITS COURTHOUSES: AT A CROSSROADS

Counties are political subdivisions of the state, through which statewide functions—elections, public health, and criminal justice, for example—are carried out. At the same time, they are instruments of localized democratic government, through which local preferences in such matters as land use control and local budgetary priorities (better roads versus more parks, for example) are implemented by locally elected officials.

The trial courts have had something of a dual nature as well. They are part of the third branch of state government; judges are appointed by the governor and paid by the state. But judges must stand for election locally and, until very recently, the trial

THIS IS _NOT_ THE JURY TRAILER. THE JURY TRAILER IS LOCATED BEHIND THE MAIN COUNTY BUILDING.

courts depended on each county's board of supervisors for their operating costs, including the salaries of court staff, as well as for the physical facilities—courthouses—in which they operate. The Task Force on Court Facilities summarized the historical relationship: "The trial courts evolved as county-level institutions and each developed in its own way based on the needs of the local judiciary and the culture of the local county government." The dual nature of the trial courts is expressed in the caption that traditionally appears on the top of the first page of pleadings filed in Superior Court:

"In the Superior Court *of* California
In and *for* the County of _____"

The three highlighted prepositions nicely describe the complex interrelationship among trial courts, the state and the counties.

Within the past few years, the state has assumed a much greater role in the financing of trial courts. In 1997, the state legislature transferred responsibility for funding trial court operations from the counties to the state. A second change came the following year. Prior to 1998, California's trial courts consisted of superior and municipal courts, each with its own jurisdiction (that of the municipal courts was more limited), judges, staff, and often, facilities. In June 1998, California voters approved a constitutional amendment permitting the judges in each county to unify their separate trial court systems into a single superior court. The expectation of greater efficiencies, better service to the public and access to greater state subsidies overcame initial opposition. By March 2001, judges in all 58 counties had voted to unify.

Legislation enacted in 2000 further diminished trial courts' financial dependence on counties. Previously, people working in the trial courts were county employees. The new law created a trial court employee system that transferred responsibility for personnel matters to the local courts, with funding provided by the state legislature and allocated among the counties by the state judicial council—the policy-making body of the judicial branch.

As of this writing, counties remain subject to a statutory obligation (Government Code Section 68073) to provide trial courts with "necessary and suitable facilities." But this may soon change. As a part of the 1997 legislation assuming fiscal responsibility for trial court operations, the state legislature established a Task Force on Court Facilities. The task force was charged with surveying the condition of existing court facilities, documenting the need for new or modified court facilities, and submitting recommendations for the division of responsibility for funding the court facilities between the counties and the state.

The task force staff and consultants visited every courthouse in the state. Key findings of this first comprehensive statewide inventory of trial court facilities include

- Trial court facilities in the 58 counties statewide consist of 451 buildings, containing 2,136 courtrooms, and comprising over 10 million square feet of usable area.
- The court facilities are mostly county-owned. Counties own nearly three-quarters of the buildings used for courts, comprising nearly 90% of the usable area. The balance of the space is leased.
- Seventy percent of the buildings were constructed after 1960, with the greatest percentage (42%) dating from the 20-year period between 1960 and 1980. A significant need for physical improvements was identified:
- Many of courthouses and courtrooms are not secure. Movement of in-custody defendants through public areas of courthouses presents a real risk to public safety.
- Many courtrooms are undersized and staff/administration areas are overcrowded.
- Courthouses are not freely accessible and many buildings do not meet the requirements of the Americans with Disabilities Act.
- Major improvements are needed in fire protection, life safety, plumbing, electrical, communications and HVAC systems. Moreover, 40% of the courthouse buildings were identified as potentially requiring seismic upgrades.

In addition to rehabilitating the existing inventory, the task force found that existing courthouses were overtaxed as a result of continuing, seemingly inexorable growth in California's population. Moreover, it forecast a need for between 2.5 million and 4 million additional square feet to keep pace with projected population growth between today and 2020. This would entail construction of between 56 and 96 new buildings and renovation of most existing buildings, at a cost of between $2.8 and $3.4 billion. The sheer scale of the estimated need is daunting. If the population

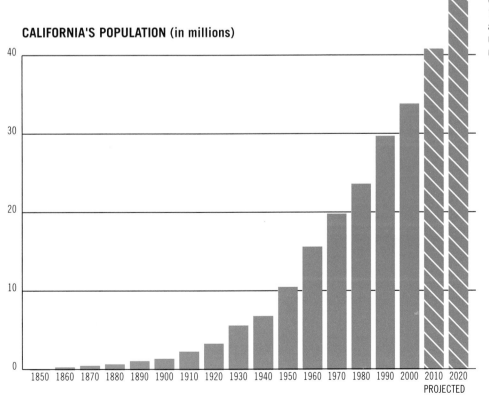

CALIFORNIA'S POPULATION (in millions)

California's population 1850 to 2020. Projections are those used by California Task Force on Court Facilities.

projections for 2020 come to pass, California will have added over 20 million residents since 1980 and will by then have eclipsed most European nations in size.

The task force expectations are straightforward: "A courthouse must be accessible, efficient, convenient and safe." To achieve these modest-sounding but essential goals uniformly across all 58 counties, the task force has recommended that the state assume full responsibility for funding the construction of trial court facilities. This may very well be the only way to insure that all courthouses statewide meet the four basic criteria of accessibility, efficiency, convenience and safety, as they all should. To these ambitious goals, allow me to propose two others:

- Deploy state funding to renovate and restore our remaining older courthouses so that they are neither demolished nor relegated to merely decorative status. They can and should be our "gift to the future" in the words of Richard Moe, president of the National Trust for Historic Preservation.
- Ask that centralized state funding respect and foster the individuality and variety that has been the hallmark of county courthouses for 150 years.

Safety, security and efficiency need not be purchased at the price of mediocrity or bland bureaucratic uniformity. The essays by Judge Victor Miceli and Jay Turnbull/Chris VerPlanck illustrate how venerable court buildings—old by California standards—can be retained in service for another century at least through skillful application of modern engineering and restoration technology. The essay by Charles Drulis demonstrates that courthouses that make full use of emerging electronic tech-

nologies and employ a contemporary architectural idiom can nevertheless fit harmoniously within traditional civic center settings.

There is no reason why California cannot have courthouses that are not only safe, efficient and secure, but as architecturally excellent as the best of those built by earlier generations of Californians. It may be unrealistic to imagine that courthouses designed and built in the 21st century will evoke the same sentimental attachment that Mariposa County's 1854 Greek Revival jewel did for Judge Schottky. But it is not too much to expect that such courthouses will continue to express their connection to the history and traditions of the communities they serve, as, for example, the bas relief on the 1933 annex to Riverside County's courthouse does. Nor is it too much to hope that 21st-century architects will be able to create buildings with the same powerful resonance as civic symbols that so many older courthouses possessed.

Bas-relief below window on Riverside County courthouse annex. Cartouche with county's initial is surrounded with emblems of the county's agricultural economy and heritage.

The Task Force on Court Facilities put it well:

The courthouse is at once a center of the community, a symbol of justice and a reflection of our history and culture. It should function equally well as a setting for the delivery of justice, as a public services center, as a community landmark and as a statement of a community's heritage.

If those principles inform the design of the next generation of courthouses, whatever the source of their funding, Californians a century from now will be able to cherish those future courthouses just as we today cherish the splendid courthouses built a century or more ago.

Perspectives

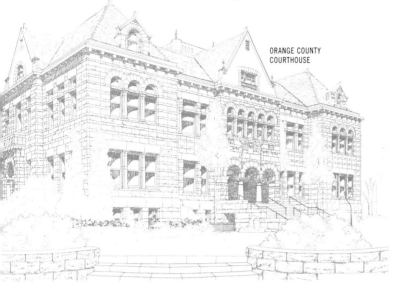

ORANGE COUNTY
COURTHOUSE

TRINITY COUNTY
COURTHOUSE

LAW

HISTORY

ARCHITECTURE

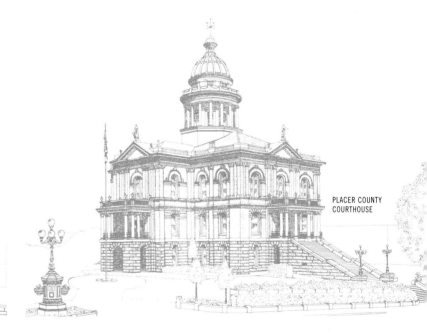

PLACER COUNTY
COURTHOUSE

MONO COUNTY
COURTHOUSE

MODOC COUNTY
COURTHOUSE

MARIPOSA COUNTY
COURTHOUSE

Law

HOW RIVERSIDE COUNTY'S COURTHOUSE
WAS RESTORED AND WHY IT MATTERS
By Judge Victor Miceli

The story of the design and construction of the 1903 Riverside County courthouse is well told elsewhere in this book (Ed. Note—see pages 272–277). My topic is the recent reconstruction and renewal of this wonderful public building.

When new, the courthouse was home to all the functions of county government, except for the jail. As the population of the county grew and more judgeships were created, various county departments moved out of the building and the vacated space

was converted into additional courtrooms. During one of these many remodelings, the ceremonial courtroom, which was then the largest in the state, was divided into two rooms. A false ceiling was installed that concealed both the domed skylight fashioned of leaded art glass and the original coffered ceiling. By the end of the 1980s the building was overcrowded, run down and worn out.

In April 1992, a fortuitous (at least for the building) event occurred—the Landers earthquake. The building sustained little apparent damage, but a structural engineer's survey concluded that the building "would most likely not survive another earthquake of similar magnitude." State Senator Robert Presley sponsored and worked for the passage of a bill authorizing Riverside County to increase its civil filing fees, the additional revenue to be used "to cover the costs of seismic stabilization, construction and rehabilitation of the Riverside County Courthouse" (Government Code Section 26826.1).

Discussions were held between the judges and the county regarding the scope of the remodeling. Providence (or was it otherwise?) struck again—the Northridge earthquake. This time, the building was declared unsafe and was evacuated on April 1, 1994. A chain-link fence completely enclosed the building and the grounds.

Comments were made to the board of supervisors that the old courthouse should be demolished and a "new and modern" structure be erected in its place. Although they heard, the board never gave serious consideration to these suggestions. Instead, the board authorized a comprehensive structural, historical and architectural survey. Based on these studies, and mindful of the historic and symbolic stature of the build-

The Riverside County Philharmonic Orchestra presents a concert on courthouse lawn, July 4, 2000.

ing, the board ordered it restored to its original elegance and reinstated to its position as the crown jewel of the county's structures.

The first task was to remove all the hazardous materials. Seismic stabilization of the building followed. Finally, the main task began: a complete restoration of the building from the foundation to the roof. Historically significant features such as the main courtroom and great hall were faithfully restored, through months of meticulous work. On September 5, 1998, the building was reopened. The project was expensive, costing approximately $24.7 million. But the results were well worth it.

There is no doubt that the physical setting has made a great difference in the courthouse as a place to work. There is a real sense of pride shared by all who work in the beautifully restored building. This pride is evident in the court staff's dedication to their work and their service to the public. Workers do things above and beyond what they are required to do. For example, one member of the custodial staff who was supposed to buff the floor twice a week, did it every day. When chided by his supervisor, the man replied, "On the other days I do it on my lunch hour." The comment is heard every day from lawyers that "I can't wait to try a case in this courthouse." Visitors sing the praises of the building, comparing it to beautiful buildings they have seen in Europe and in other countries. Litigants, witnesses and jurors as well seem to appreciate the importance of their roles in the administration of justice when trials are conducted in the dignified environment of the restored courthouse.

The building is also seeing a return to the days when it was the historic center of community activity. The ceremonial courtroom, used daily as a regularly functioning trial courtroom, has also hosted activities such as swearing in newly admitted attorneys, new judges, and elected officials; presentation of plays; mock trial finals and movie/television productions. The great hall has been the venue for banquets, concerts and lectures, favored because of its unique classic architecture and excellent acoustics. It has been used to accommodate over three hundred people for a sit-down dinner. The exterior main staircase has been the site for patriotic events such as a Fourth of July celebration featuring the Riverside Philharmonic Orchestra using the courthouse as a backdrop. Candidates for the presidency and other elective offices have addressed huge gatherings from the main entrance. (One sad note is that today's social climate has resulted in the installation of security devices that discourage the public's access to and use of the building. Society needs to evaluate the effects of this heightened concern for security and how it is fostering a policy of exclusion from vs. inclusion in public buildings. People need to feel welcomed.)

Overall, the restoration project has exceeded all expectations. In fact, the board of supervisors was so pleased by the results that it directed the original Riverside County seal to be replaced with a rendering of the historic county courthouse. Considering what could have been had there not been a commitment from the board, a source of funds, and the outstanding dedication shown by all the talented workers in the rebuilding effort, we can only count our blessings and pray that the courthouse will retain its grace and serve the legal and civic community for at least another hundred years.

If you haven't seen the beautiful historic Riverside County courthouse, please make it a point to do so. You will not be disappointed!

A carpenter at work on the $25-million renovation carried out from 1994 to 1998. The project not only brought the venerable courthouse into compliance with modern seismic stabilization requirements, it also restored the building to its original grandeur.

History

CORNERSTONE OF AUTHORITY AND COMMUNITY:
COURTHOUSES IN CALIFORNIA'S FRONTIER HISTORY
By John F. Burns

California's principal political and governmental institutions were created during the state's "constitutional era"—the three decades between the first constitutional convention in 1849 and the second (and so far, last) such convention in 1879. The documents crafted at these conventions became the fundamental law establishing the civic rights and responsibilities of Californians. Provisions in the constitution have been modified by subsequent amendments, and the constitutional principles have been elaborated, interpreted and implemented over time through statutes enacted by the legislature and decisions rendered by the courts. But the basic framework of government (including the subdivision of the state into counties and the structure of the judicial branch) was established during the tumultuous frontier period, with lasting impact on California life.

Immense changes took place during the first three decades of California's statehood. The population increased dramatically from about 100,000 people in 1849 to approximately 850,000 by 1879. The number of counties in the state almost doubled, from 27 to 53. Large-scale transportation in 1849 was primarily confined to waterways, but by 1879 railroads connected many California communities and linked California with the rest of the country. In 1849, the economy consisted largely of gold mining, carried out by individual miners or small partnerships. By 1879, mining had become a capital-intensive extractive industry conducted by corporations; large-scale agriculture had replaced the pastoral, ranching tradition of the Spanish-Mexican era; and a diversified manufacturing/commercial sector had developed. California, in 1849, was populated principally by young men; a more balanced mix of men, women and families had settled here thirty years later.

The predominant political issues of 1849 were slavery, the state's boundary, the establishment of law and order, land ownership, and governmental infrastructure. By 1879, these had been supplanted by questions about control over railroads and banks, elimination of legislative corruption, restrictions on Chinese immigration, and improvements in government organization and the court system. Creating governmental institutions that could satisfy the needs of a rapidly evolving, very large political entity was central to the thirty-year effort to meet the challenges of the new state. State government was at the forefront in that effort, but most governmental activity in the nineteenth century was actually carried out closer to people's lives—at the county level. And the focal point of the quest for civic stability and order was the local courthouse, the centerpiece in the development of American-style communities.

Delegates from across California gathered in Monterey in September 1849 to draft a constitution for California. The three years immediately preceding their assembly were, from the perspective of law and government, confused at best. Though the Mexican Californians won some battles, dissension, powder shortages and distance from Mexican support resulted in decisive American victories by the winter of 1846. The surrender of the Mexican Californian military was formalized by the signing of the Articles of Capitulation at a ranch house near Cahuenga Pass, in what is now Los Angeles County, in January 1847. At that point, California was technically still Mexican territory, under the military rule of an occupying army. Commodore Stockton, the military governor, declared that the relations of the territory's inhabitants with one another were to be governed by "former laws and usage"—in other words, by Mexican law.

While the Mexican legal/governmental system ostensibly remained in place, it had neither sufficient facilities nor necessary authority. It had been superceded by the conquest and was ill equipped to deal with the human onslaught soon to be brought by the gold rush. Moreover, the precepts of Mexican governance were unfamiliar to the mostly American newcomers; indeed, it proved almost impossible to discover just what the "former laws and usage" had been.

Mexican local government employed the Spanish practice of having an *alcalde*, a blended judicial/administrative official, serve as a kind of beneficent "village elder." In the small towns of Mexican California, access to that official had been easy and his judgments were rendered based on an investigatory process and a keen knowledge of the community and its people. While the office of the alcalde survived the American military's victory, historian Josiah Royce, writing in 1886, observed that the "Mexican laws could not be said to survive with him.... The known functions of the alcaldes had long been recognized by mere tradition. Beyond those known functions, the alcaldes had possessed very great practical freedom of individual judgment. Their offices were not well supplied by law books.... The alcaldes elected or appointed after the conquest followed the devices of their own hearts. Not only were they commonly judges both of the law and of the evidence, but their position was often practically that of legislators." Even though many of the alcaldes after 1846 were themselves Americans, according to historian David Langhum, "The entire procedure was deeply resented by Anglo-American expatriates. It deprived them of three features they thought essential—prompt trial, a jury trial with confrontation of accusers, and a separation of executive and judicial functions."

The treaty of Guadalupe Hidalgo, signed in February 1848, formally ended the Mexican-American War and transferred what is now the southwestern portion of the United States, including California, into the jurisdiction of the American government. This did not, however, resolve the anomalous legal status of California. It was now a part of the United States, but was neither state nor territory. Moreover, the end of hostilities coincided with the discovery of gold which, fueled by the 19th-century version of media hype, launched a rush of mostly young men, and a few women, from all corners of the globe. Flooding into the foothills of Northern California, these "argonauts" came for the gold, though many drifted into other occupations as the erratic results of "prospecting" became apparent. These were not a general cross section of people. Mark Twain described them as "a driving, vigorous, restless population... not simpering, dainty weaklings, but stalwart, muscular, dauntless young braves, brimful of push and energy... a splendid population." Others took a dimmer view. Bayard Taylor, for example, writing in 1849, commented on the "readiness with which the worthless and depraved class of our own country [i.e., the United States] came to the Pacific Coast."

The impact of this sudden wave of migration into a thinly populated region was overwhelming. In the mining regions, the culture and numbers of native California Indians essentially disintegrated. Californians of Spanish-Mexican descent soon comprised less than five percent of the population and lost much of their land to squatters and most of their political control. Military government, nominally in charge while the United States decided what to do with its new territorial acquisitions, had no capability to enforce much of anything beyond sovereignty. Its ability was further compromised by the desertion of many of the soldiers to the gold fields. Moreover, with the end of hostilities, the legitimacy of the military's continued control over civil affairs came into question. General Bennett Riley, the last military governor of California, continued to insist, "The laws of California, not inconsistent with the laws, constitution, and treaties of the United States, are still in force and must continue in force till changed by competent authority... that power, by the treaty of peace, as well as from the nature of the case, is vested in Congress.... It is important that citizens should understand this fact, so as not to endanger their property and involve themselves in useless and expensive litigation, by giving countenance to persons claiming authority which is not given them by law, and by putting faith in laws which can never be recognized by legitimate courts."

The response of the Anglo-American miners to this chaotic, postconquest state of affairs, was to informally adjudicate and dispense justice based on their existing knowledge and beliefs about self-government. In over five hundred mining camps in the foothills, the prospectors drew up camp mining codes as a practical means to address a fundamental need. The overland trail experience of many of the migrants set the stage for such developments. Even without a formal process, behavior on the trail tended to be governed by the same principles of property ownership and social decorum that were mandated by law back home. The habits of Anglo-American democracy and common law had become such deeply embedded traits that they, rather than church and home, guided the migrants' actions. As the excerpt from Bayard Taylor's account illustrates, punishment for violations could be harsh.

From all I saw and heard, while at the Mokelumne Diggings, I judged there was as much order and security as could be attained without a civil organization. The inhabitants had elected one of their own number Alcalde, before whom all culprits were tried by a jury selected for the purpose. Several thefts had occurred, and the offending parties been severely punished after a fair trial. Some had been whipped and cropped, or maimed in some other way, and one or two of them hung.... We met near Livermore's Ranch, on the way to Stockton, a man whose head had been shaved and his ears cut off, after receiving one hundred lashes, for stealing ninety-eight pounds of gold. It may conflict with popular ideas of morality, but, nevertheless, this extreme course appeared to have produced good results. In fact, in a country without not only bolts and bars, but any effective system of law and government, this Spartan severity of discipline seemed the only security against the most frightful disorder.

Bayard Taylor, *El Dorado: Adventures in the Path of Empire,* 1850

While mining camp codes satisfied the most basic need for order, many pioneers did not view them as sufficient, since they lacked the authority of institutionalized government. As the population continued to escalate, the new arrivals began to accumulate more personal property, open commercial enterprises and acquire real estate. Thus, the requirements of regular government became more urgent. By 1849 in San Francisco, the frenetic and increasingly lawless situation spawned the gathering of the first informal "vigilance" group and an early movement toward local self-government. An assemblage of citizens in Sacramento enacted their own code of laws and elected a city council, all without any authorization or direction from the military government. The U.S. Congress, paralyzed on the disposition of California by the issue of slavery, continued to dither, adjourning in 1849 without making any provision for California's government.

As the pressure for formal, civilian government grew, General Riley announced that, since Congress had adjourned without providing a new government "to replace that which existed on the annexation of California," it had become his "imperative duty to take some active measures to provide for the existing wants of the country." He called upon the people to elect delegates who would then assemble to draft a constitution.

Early in September 1849, 48 delegates elected from across California gathered in Monterey. They met at Colton Hall, which had been the site of California's first jury trial and which was to become the first courthouse for Monterey County. Robert Semple, president of the convention, optimistically forecast in his opening remarks that the "knowledge, enterprise and genius of the old world will reappear in the new, to guide it to its desired position among the nations of the earth." Semple's comments reflected the makeup and predisposition of the convention delegates. They were young—half were under 35—aspiring, forward-looking men. Most had been in California for three years or more and many had already held significant local positions. Three-quarters were from eastern states; seven were Californians of Spanish-Mexican nativity. Fourteen were lawyers, the type of men that historian Gordon Bakken described as "schooled in experience and the American cultural tradition." These men, nearly a third of them with some legal background, brought with them and assiduously applied beliefs in a system of government derived from two hundred years or more of American and English experience. Those beliefs provided the foundation for California's constitution, and later, for county government and its principal locus—the courthouse.

The tenets of the initial California Constitution were mainstream and reassuring to those who fashioned it. Modeled on elements of other state constitutions, the California document promised the American order that most of the new residents desired. Only a few provisions reflected Mexican influence, such as that permitting married women to own separate property and the requirement that all laws be published in both English and Spanish. The design of the constitution was so familiar that it generated little opposition and it was overwhelmingly ratified in November 1849.

Article XI, Section 4 of the Constitution required the legislature to establish "a system of county and town government which shall be as nearly uniform as practicable throughout the state," but left all the details to the legislature.

The first legislature met in San Jose, in a building that would later be used as Santa Clara County's courthouse. Men from northeastern and southern states dominated the legislature, as they had the convention.

Everything had to be started from scratch. There were no state agencies or local governments, no supplies, no procedures, no budget and no revenues. Proceedings were rather informal. Judson Grenier's study of the early legislature found that "during debate, smoking, chewing and whittling were the norm and, everyone being armed, occasionally horseplay with bullets would elicit howls of laughter."

Evaluations of the abilities and the competence of these first legislators have differed. They were vilified as "The Legislature of 1,000 Drinks," due to the social generosity of the head of the Senate Finance Committee, Thomas Jefferson Green. However, one of his colleagues, Elisha Crosby, asserted "there was very little dissipation among the members in general compared to some legislatures of later days." And many years later, historian William Henry Ellison claimed that "it is doubtful whether… any legislature has ever done more work… or more important, or better work, than that done by the first…. The adaptation of the governmental structure of the state to changing conditions is a perennial tribute to the devotion and political wisdom of the builders of California's first legislative session."

Irrespective of their drinking habits or individual abilities, the first legislators did implement the Constitution and launch the government. They provided for government finance, assembled the state's governmental machinery and essential documents, organized a court system, and authorized courthouse construction. They also established 27 counties. Most were in the north, particularly in the mining regions, because that is where the population was concentrated when the state was formed. Many coastal counties followed districts initially laid out by the Spanish and Mexican governments and they retained their Spanish names. But most of the institutional structure of local government came from the reservoir of long-standing Anglo-American practice.

The model was the English system of counties that had been imported to the Americas by the early colonists, which California's founders knew well and with which they felt quite comfortable. Although all eastern counties had roots in the system of English "shires" or counties, there were important differences. In New England and the mid-Atlantic states, where settlement was town centered and more dense, local government powers were shared with cities. But in the southern and border states, more rural and with a lower population density, county government was generally the most powerful and visible. This was the model most often emulated in the West, including California, where the county was both the agent primarily responsible for implementing state policy and the principal vehicle for local self-government outside the major cities.

Expectations of county government centered around maintenance of law and order, protection of property and recordation of property-related documents. Providing even these basic services in California's frontier environment was far from easy. Travel was difficult and dangerous; geographic features such as mountains and rivers, which are barely noticed by an automobile driver on a paved highway, were formidable obstacles to a traveler on foot or horseback. The need for proximity to the judge, recorder, etc. led to demands for new counties with more accessible county seats. Eighteen more counties had been created by 1860, six were established during the period 1861 to 1870 and three more during the 1870s, essentially doubling the complement of county authorities within 30 years.

The early courts faced daunting challenges, almost immediately. First, they confronted a violent society. As noted above, the early population was largely male and young. It was also racially and ethnically diverse, as Europeans, Mexicans, African Americans, Australians, Chileans, and Chinese joined the rush for wealth. And it was essentially homeless, a vast band of "adventuring strangers" in Kevin Starr's neat phrase, though discriminatory laws soon gave "adventurers" of white nativity considerable advantage. Early settlements had been notably law-abiding. But by 1850 and 1851, as the population surged, criminals appeared and the mining camp codes of conduct broke down. Historian J. S. Holliday observed that "for some, chicanery, thievery, even violence offered the best promise to get the few thousands that could make possible a triumphant homecoming…. So many temptations, so many disappointments, so many men desperate to win."

William Brewer, a professor at Yale who spent four years in the early 1860s on a scientific survey of California, recorded in his journal a visit to a ranch near Los Angeles in the winter of 1860:

> We were received with the greatest cordiality and were entertained with the greatest hospitality. A touch of the country and time was indicated by our rig— I was dressed in colored woolen shirt, with heavy navy revolver (loaded) and huge eight-inch bowie knife at my belt; my friend the same; and the clergyman who took us out in his carriage carried along his rifle, he said for game, yet owned that it was "best to have arms after dark." Here let me digress. This southern California is still unsettled. We all continually wear arms—each wears both bowie knife and pistol (navy revolver), while we have always for game or otherwise, a Sharp's rifle, Sharp's carbine, and two double-barrel shotguns. Fifty to sixty murders per year have been common here in Los Angeles and some think it odd that there has been no violent death during the two weeks that we have been here.

The vigilante impulse that arose in reaction to this epidemic of violence presented another challenge to the legitimate court system. William Coleman, leader of the San Francisco Committee of Vigilance in both 1851 and 1856, reflected years later on the conditions he argued justified the "vigilantes":

> The rapid and continued increase of crime in San Francisco impressed on every thinking man the conviction that some more vigorous action of the legal authorities was imperative, and must be stimulated and insisted upon, or self-preservation would make it necessary for the people to take the matter into their own hands, and assert the law and establish order in their own way. The police

Stephen J. Field, the first Californian to serve on the United States Supreme Court, arrived in California in 1849. He was elected alcalde of Marysville, where he practiced law, and was elected to the state legislature in 1851. Writing in 1877, he recalled violent incidents involving California judges, in the early days of statehood.

In 1850, District Judge William Turner ordered Field imprisoned for contempt of court—his offense being, apparently, that he cited a new statute to the judge while appearing in court. Field sought a writ of habeas corpus from County Judge Henry Haun, which was granted and Field set free. Judge Turner, enraged, ordered that Judge Haun be imprisoned and directed the sheriff to arrest him—and, if necessary, put him irons. The sheriff, with a posse, entered the courtroom of the Court of Sessions and was proceeding to seize Judge Haun on the bench. The judge, however, "stepped to a closet and drew from it a Navy revolver, cocked it and, pointing it towards the Sheriff, informed him in a stern manner that he was violating the law; that whilst on the bench he, the Judge, could not be arrested and that if the Sheriff attempted to do so he would kill him." The Sheriff retreated.

The following year, District Judge William Barbour challenged Field to a duel and then refused to proceed on the grounds that he might forfeit his office. The next day, however, he crept up behind Field, then gathering kindling wood for his office fireplace, placed a cocked revolver against Field's head, and cried out, "Draw and defend yourself." Field whirled around, confronted Judge Barbour and dared him to shoot. Barbour backed down.

Field concluded: "I do not give these details as having any importance in themselves; but they illustrate the semi-barbarous condition of things in those early days, and by comparison show out of what our existing condition has been evolved, and how far we have advanced."

Stephen J. Field, *Early Days in California*, 1880

were notoriously inadequate and inefficient; the courts had been accused of corruption; the prisons were small and insecure, and it was boldly proclaimed through the streets that with packed juries and venal judges, false witnesses and dishonest officials, our criminal courts had become a failure and a reproach.

The early counties did not have the luxury, in such an environment, of postponing activities, including trials, until suitably impressive courthouses were built. Courts had to be "open for business" from the very outset. As a result, the earliest courthouses were rented or adapted structures, of basic, sometimes primitive, construction. A description of early Butte County courthouses is illustrative. In 1850, the county used "an old shake house, belonging to Mother Nichols, a widow, who lived in one corner of it." By 1853, that house had been replaced by "an old storehouse, which had been imported from Australia… a poor apology for a barn." Hotels, storehouses and fraternal halls were all pressed into service. Decorum in these provisional courthouses was uneven. One writer noted in San Diego, "It was common practise to throw inkwells in court and gunfire was always imminent." And proceedings were quick. Gold rush historian John Caughey related that "courts would listen to testimony, but had little patience for argument. And lacking jails and reformatories and personnel to stand guard indefinitely, they specialized in quick punishment: whipping, hanging, ear-cropping, branding or banishment."

Such makeshift courthouses were replaced by more permanent facilities as soon as the counties had the ability to fund their construction. Building a real courthouse was one of the counties' most urgent priorities, for reasons both practical and symbolic. On the practical side, to protect records and safeguard public monies, the county needed a fireproof building and a safe or vault. To prevent prisoners from escaping, it needed a secure brick or stone jail. In general, it needed a place where it could perform the basic functions expected of it efficiently and reliably, so as to earn the confidence of its people and establish its legitimacy.

On the symbolic side, county leaders, as the front line of the newly sovereign state of California, no doubt wanted to conduct affairs within a building that was a tangible symbol of American authority. Such symbolism was especially germane in an area recently acquired from another nation, as a means of cementing the new sovereignty. Drawing on their experience, county leaders created structures along the American lines they knew. According to architectural historian Sally Woodbridge, "The first civic buildings constructed after California obtained statehood are a good example of the Americanization of the state's architecture." In practice this most often meant a Greek Revival–style building, such as the courthouses in Benecia and Mariposa, both built in the early 1850s. As Harold Kirker concluded, the Greek and Roman derivative styles, drawing from the "long classic tradition in American public building… absolutely dominated civic architecture on the California frontier."

Another aim was to support and reflect community stature. The report that was commissioned for the recent restoration of the 1894 Placer County courthouse recalled that "the courthouse, often the most prominent public building in the county, was built with great pride and attention to detail for its builders intended it to represent the county's stature, prosperity and confidence in the future." While Californians were often thrifty about public expenditures, they were generally ready to take on substantial financial burdens to assure that the courthouse made the appropriate kind of statement about the county's character and prestige. The legislature authorized local bond funding to construct courthouses, and many counties imposed a courthouse construction tax assessment. In most counties, no civic expenditure was as important as that to finance and maintain the courthouse.

As in other parts of America, county functions in the mid-19th-century courthouse revolved around two basic activities: the administration of justice and the systematic storage, preservation and retrieval of records. Both activities are essential to the maintenance of order in a civil society based on law.

The significance of the courts is widely recognized; most people understand that courts interpret and enforce the law and are central to society's effort to see that disputes among its citizens are resolved peacefully. The record-keeping function, while less universally appreciated, is hardly less significant. The law that created the recorder's office in 1850 stipulated that "the Recorder shall have the custody of and shall safely keep and preserve all the books, records, deeds, maps, and papers deposited and kept in his office, and it shall be his duty to record or cause to be recorded correctly… deeds, mortgages… documents received from the Mexican authority… marriage contracts… commissions and official bonds." The county recorder was also the officer required to keep naturalization records and "a set of books for the registration of the separate property of the wife," as well as all manner of other records such as those related to Spanish-Mexican land grants, patents, mining claims, water rights, wills, homesteads, tax sales, marks and brands for horses and livestock, liens and attachments, vital statistics, partnerships, and "sole traders," a provision in law that permitted women to transact business in their own name. As a result of these record-keeping functions, county courthouses became the archives and repositories of the county's history.

Additional functions were in the hands of other officers, those of the auditor, treasurer, assessor, tax collector, sheriff and jailer, coroner, and superintendent of schools. Also normally located in the courthouse, each of these activities generated records and required space, as did the elections function, a local responsibility of substantial state and national importance. In some cases the crowding was severe enough to mandate the creation of separate structures for certain activities, most frequently a hall of records for archives and long-term storage of documents, and a sheriff's office/jail for the handling of law enforcement and the confinement of prisoners. As the state matured, the range of county functions expanded and both county and court processes became more refined. By the 1870s, frontier patterns of violence and the efforts to control it, and steps to establish basic property ownership, had gradually given way to more systematized law enforcement efforts and to more sophisticated systems of filing and recording the information deemed essential to the conduct of community affairs. In turn, such progress required the building of larger courthouses, which also tended to be grander, more elegant structures.

The county courthouse was typically also the place where the county board of supervisors held their meetings throughout the first three decades of statehood. Thus, the courthouse was home to all three branches of local government—the legislative and executive, as well as the judicial. The presence of the democratically elected local legislature may explain the appearance of domes on the larger courthouses of the 1870s, since the domes were adaptations of those on the United States and state capitol buildings—each of which is occupied by the legislature.

As the most significant and sometimes the only public building in town, the county courthouse became the focus of important civic and community activities, as well as the site of governmental functions. A description of Tennessee courthouses applies as well to those of California: "Because of its central administrative and judicial focus, the courthouse quickly became an integral part of the community. Often it was the only central meeting place, apart from churches, and it frequently became the focus of celebrations, emergencies, sometimes religious services, dances, and Masonic gatherings… the courthouse was frequently the most interesting and important building in the county… the most typical location was in the public square in the middle of the downtown area."

Happenings at the courthouse were attended with great interest. In a treatise on everyday life in early America, historian David Freeman Hawke noted that on court days "the neighborhood gathered to watch and judge friends and acquaintances accused of crimes. They studied the lists of marriage licenses posted on the county clerk's door, they paid off and collected debts, they drank, they gossiped and generally socialized." In California, various sources describe courthouses hosting weddings, funerals, parties, meetings, community festivities, lectures, musical and dance events, exhibits, dramatic presentations, and religious services. They became a locale for historical commemorations, a gathering place for the retired, and a park site for the community, all in addition to the recognized, customary governmental functions. And, until well after the second Constitutional Convention in 1879, they were also the site where condemned criminals were executed.

Santa Rosa, Cal., May 4, 1882.

Mr. *J. S. Taylor*

You are invited to be present at the execution of H. E. BROWN, to take place at the Jail Yard, Santa Rosa, Sonoma county, Cal., at 1 O'clock, P. M.. on **THURSDAY, MAY 18, 1882.**

J. L. DINWIDDIE, Sheriff.

By W. H. BOND, Under Sheriff.

[BRING THIS CARD.]

An invitation to a hanging in Santa Rosa.

Accounts of activities in county courthouses provide a litany of the highlights of local life. In Los Angeles, when the courthouse opened in 1858, festivities "were climaxed by a gala ball where everyone danced all night in the soft glow of tallow candles." Mariposa County's courthouse with its surrounding square "has played host to most of the large gatherings of note during our county history…. The separation of church and state was brushed aside when a traveling minister would use the courtroom for services. Fraternal organizations used the facilities until more suitable quarters could be found (and) Christmas parties, including a tree with lighted candles (were held) on more than one occasion. The area in front of the building proved to be a favorite place to congregate for group pictures." Amador County in 1854 celebrated a Christmas Day ball in the new courthouse, which "lasted until daylight." In Napa County in the 1850s, the courthouse "lower room was occasionally occupied on Sundays as a place of worship, or at other times for lectures or shows." In Colusa County "the courthouse not only served as a seat of justice, but also served as a community center where activities ranging from dances to political rallies were held."

The grounds surrounding the courthouse were enjoyed by early Californians for picnics, concerts, civic celebrations and as spots for summer evening strolls. Plumas County commemorated the 1876 national centennial on the Fourth of July with a great parade ending at the courthouse where "a fine, shady arbor had been erected." In Butte County, "the courthouse square is a lovely spot. No pains have been spared to handsomely enclose and cultivate the grounds. The green grass sward, the shade and ornamental trees, the shrub, and the vine, all grown to maturity, and ever wearing their spring-like garb, and blooming fresh and bright, delight the eye, whilst the courthouse building, with its nicely graveled approaches from all directions, constitutes a magnificent spectacle, and a pleasing picture."

Nineteenth-century Californians were emotionally invested in their courthouses.

Mono County's courthouse built in 1880, one year after the state's second Constitutional Convention.

Their pride and optimism are evident in the words used at their groundbreakings and dedications. In 1876, Fresno County's district attorney called the new courthouse "the grandest and noblest edifice that has ever been contemplated in this county [and] when completed, is expected to stand the heats of summer and the storms of winter for the period of 1,000 years, or more." For Merced County "the wonderful progress of the county during its life of twenty-five years may be readily comprehended [through its] new and beautiful courthouse," which was built in 1875 in a spacious new courthouse square in downtown Merced. The words of Judge J. E. Prewett at the dedication of Placer County's courthouse in 1894, while spoken a few years after the second Constitutional Convention, express perfectly the aspirations of the early Californians for their chief public building.

> We today lay the cornerstone of a grand structure that is expected to endure until our children's children shall have turned old and gray and passed into the great beyond… an adornment of the whole of Placer County.

The judge's expectations have been met, thanks to the hard work of his children's children's children, who saw to the restoration of the courthouse in the 1990s. The Placer County courthouse still stands, its dome still gleams—a proud and prominent landmark on the hilltop in Auburn where it was built over a century ago—still an adornment of Placer County.

California society and life have certainly grown more complex since the "constitutional era" of the mid-nineteenth century. The expansion of the state and national governments, the pervasive influence of the media, and the advent of a global economy have all made the county courthouse a less prominent centerpiece for community and citizenship than it was in earlier times. Yet even today the county government and county courthouse maintain daily contact with a diversity of people in a way that no other California institution of government does. Chief Justice Ronald M. George

Frederic Hall, a Santa Clara County attorney, chronicled events in San Jose from the 1850s through the 1860s. He saw the "splendid" and "magnificent" courthouse built in 1868 as tangible evidence of the city's having outgrown the disorderly, lawless days of the early 1850s. The new courthouse embodied the arrival of harmony and civilization:

> From whatever direction chance brings the visitor to San Jose, the first object that greets his eye is the strong-ribbed and gracefully-curved dome which surmounts this grand and spacious structure.
>
> The earliest light which comes streaming through the pearly gates of Morn smiles upon its noble façade, fashioned after the forms modeled by the artistic hand of Pericles, to adorn the Athenian city, to attract the Athenian gaze; and the last rays of the setting sun linger and play in rose and purple tints on its glassy dome.
>
> ...This noble and massive pile is a lasting monument of the wealth, the generosity, the taste, the pride, and the advancement of its contributors. From its lofty dome, what beauty, what grandeur present themselves! You may behold the city of San Jose sitting like a queen surrounded by her regal estate, in the fairest valley of the land, bathed in all the glory of the morning sun.

A far cry from gunfights in the streets.

Frederic Hall, *History of San Jose and Surroundings,* 1871

made this point in his recent State of the Judiciary address, delivered to a joint session of the California legislature in March 2001:

> We are well aware that, for many individuals, their dealings with the courts—whether through paying a parking fine, serving as a juror or obtaining a divorce—are their only direct contact with government. We take very seriously the fact that our branch's ability to meet their needs can affect their view of state government as a whole.

The Chief Justice's remark echoes the observation made many years ago by historian John Brinckerhoff Jackson: "The importance of the nineteenth century courthouse was that it served as a political institution for making citizens."

Architecture

CONTINUITY AND CHANGE IN CALIFORNIA COURTHOUSE DESIGN, 1850–2000
By Michael R. Corbett

When Ray McDevitt first mentioned Courthouses of California *to me, several thoughts came immediately to mind. Long before I was an architectural historian, I knew something about courthouses from childhood drives in Texas that often included a stop to look at a courthouse. Even as a child I knew that the county courthouse was a point of local pride, that it occupied a prominent location in the center of town, and that it was a grand and solid-looking building. Since I became an architectural historian, I have often been in courthouses, but it did not take long to realize that Ray's associations with courthouses and mine were different. As a lawyer, Ray thinks about courtrooms, jury deliberation rooms, judges' chambers, law libraries, and jails, about the terrible traumas that bring people to courtrooms and the life-changing decisions rendered in them. As a historian, I think of the offices of the assessor, recorder, clerk, and engineer with dusty books and microfilm readers that provide information about property ownership, probate inventories, land surveys, tax assessments, births, marriages, and deaths. Courthouses have still other meanings for other visitors. Victims of crime, criminal defendants and jurors, for example, all experience the courtroom in quite different ways. This essay explores some of the ways that the architecture of California courthouses has represented, and sometimes failed to represent, the diverse meanings of these buildings to the people who use them.*

County courthouses are rich and complex symbols of California history. The name we give to these buildings—courthouse—reflects the essential and dominant purpose they serve as the place where trials and other legal proceedings are held before judges and juries. In most California counties since the first courthouses were built in the 1850s, they have accommodated not just the courts but county government as a whole. For many people who rarely enter a courtroom, the courthouse is nonetheless a familiar place. Until the 1950s, the government that people most regularly encountered, besides the post office, was the county government. The county courthouse, then, has been designed to accommodate local government and to represent that government to its citizens.

There are many ways to look at courthouses. We can look at their physical attributes—at the methods and materials of construction and at the mechanical, electrical, and heating systems that make them more or less safe and comfortable. We can look at their architectural designs and decorative embellishments. We can look at the functions they house and how these are accommodated by the plan of the building. And we can look at their settings—whether they are built in squares at the center of town, on Main Street, or at the periphery of town—and at the features of their settings, such as lawns, fountains, park benches, statuary, war memorials, secondary buildings like jails or libraries, and parking lots. Courthouses can reveal local attitudes about government and about the nature of society and justice. They are measures of a community's sophistication, wealth and power. Some are embodiments of corruption and extravagance; others of caution and conservatism. Some are innocent expressions of local pride; others are products of competitive local boosterism aimed at "one-upping" the neighboring counties.

Courthouses can be looked at over time. Underlying the changes in the 150 years since the first counties were established is the very simple fact of enormous population growth. Apart from any other considerations, courthouses have changed because they have had to serve far more people and accommodate more functions. Courthouses can be looked at in any and all of these ways.

The following essay is organized around changes in the physical plan and functional arrangement of courthouses from 1850 to the present. By looking at examples of courthouses from several distinctive periods within this time, we can see the changing character of the courthouse and its evolving meaning in California history.

ARCHITECTURAL ANTECEDENTS

California's counties have been renting, buying, building, remodeling and tearing down courthouses for 150 years. But the story of California's courthouse architecture begins long before the first county courthouses were built here. California's population in 1850 had come predominantly from other parts of the United States. These newcomers brought with them a long-established tradition of American county courthouse building, which was adapted to new conditions in California.

In the 1820s to 1840s, designers of American county courthouses developed a repertoire of features, including classical imagery and buildings in the form of temples. These features conveyed the authority of the government, analogies with the longevity and forms of government of ancient Greek democracy and Roman republicanism, and a position of government in society comparable in importance to that of the church. Early American courthouses were provided with domes and towers that symbolically represented the power of government to look out over its territory. They were typically set in the center of a courthouse square or high parklike ground surrounded by subsidiary buildings, monuments, and landscaping. The locations and settings of these complexes expressed their importance as institutions in each town as well as aspects of social hierarchy within the town.

The United States Capitol, the Virginia State Capitol designed by Thomas Jefferson and other government buildings inspired these features. These highly self-conscious models expressed ideas about the new country, its government and its society. Builders of county courthouses relied on these models in developing the earliest county courthouses. While county courthouses changed with changing times, conditions and regions, these original models long remained as powerful references. California's courthouses were built in full awareness of this American tradition.

Colton Hall, Monterey (1849). Built as the town hall before California's counties were created, Colton Hall was the first government building in the state designed with the traditional imagery of American government. Its symmetrical design and central portico were familiar symbols of governmental authority.

THE FIRST COURTHOUSES

About six months before California was admitted as a state in September 1850, the legislature created the first 27 counties. The most immediate needs of those early counties were for law and order on the one hand and for the recording of property transactions on the other. Law and order appears to have been the highest priority. Meeting that need required sheriffs and jails, judges and courts—in other words, courthouses.

Some of the first courthouses were tents and temporary sheds. These did not last long and many counties rented space or bought existing buildings originally constructed for other purposes. Before any permanent courthouses were constructed, counties occupied houses, hotels, commercial buildings, fraternal halls and old mission buildings. San Joaquin County used an abandoned ship run aground in Stockton's harbor. Little attention was given to the appearance of these temporary courthouses, most of which were occupied only while permanent courthouses were under construction.

The history of permanent courthouses in California actually began with two buildings that were designed for other purposes, but that were used as courthouses and that established the familiar American repertoire of images and features for government buildings. These were Colton Hall in Monterey and the Jenny Lind Theater in San Francisco. Colton Hall, site of the state constitutional convention and the first jury trial in California, was described as the best-built building in California when it was completed in 1849. It was situated like a New England courthouse, set back in a public open space. Its principal room, originally a meeting hall and later a courtroom, was

upstairs, reflecting its greater importance. The pedimented portico provided the classical image of governmental authority.

The Jenny Lind Theater was built in 1851. Its façade was designed with the ground-floor entrance arcade beneath a giant pedimented temple front that reflected the size and importance of the second-level public space inside, thus projecting an image suitable for governmental purposes as well. The board of supervisors, concluding that it would make an ideal city hall and courthouse after interior remodeling and construction of a rooftop bell tower, purchased it later that same year.

Among the first buildings occupied as permanent courthouses in California were three others built not strictly as courthouses, but as multipurpose public buildings. One of these in Benicia, county seat of Solano County, and two in Sacramento were built to attract the state capitol as well as to house various local functions. Each of these buildings differed from other early courthouses that required one large space for a courtroom, in providing two large spaces to accommodate the senate and the assembly, as well as courtrooms. They were of more expensive construction than other courthouses of the period—they were built of brick at a time when the brick industry was new. They were architecturally more impressive than other California courthouses that had been built by that time. The two Sacramento buildings were larger than other courthouses. And among all courthouses built before the 1860s, the Sacramento buildings were among the few designed by architects.

The Sacramento County courthouse of 1851 was designed by A. P. Petit. He was

Sacramento County Courthouse (1854), designed by Farquharson & Knox. Among the early buildings in California designed specifically as courthouses, some of the most ambitious architecturally were intended to attract and accommodate the state capitol as well. The impressive courthouse with its relatively complete evocation of a Greek temple, served as the state capitol from 1855 to 1869.

the architect and builder who would later participate in the design and construction of courthouses in San Mateo, Napa, Mendocino, and Lake Counties. The 1851 courthouse was impressive for its size, brick construction, domed tower and portico, but it was awkwardly proportioned and detailed and its roof leaked. In the first half of 1854, this courthouse also housed the state government. After this courthouse burned in 1854, it was replaced by a larger building designed by the firm of Farquharson & Knox. David Farquharson, the designer, was trained in Scotland and was one of the most prominent architects in California from the 1850s to the 1870s. He designed banks, business buildings, a stock exchange and the first permanent buildings at the University of California. Later, he was among the first architects in California to attempt to design buildings that would resist earthquake forces. His Sacramento County courthouse of 1854 was the most ambitious work of architecture among buildings occupied as courthouses in the 1850s. It was a three-story structure with its walls articulated by a Greek Ionic order, and with a prominent portico, designed as if it were the front of an Ionic temple. This courthouse also served as the state capitol from 1855 to 1869.

The third of these early, multipurpose buildings was built in Benicia in 1852 to 1853 by San Francisco contractors J. Franklin Houghton and L. A. Rider. This was designed as the city hall and served as the California State Capitol in 1853 and 1854, as well as the Solano County courthouse from 1853 to 1858. The distinctive façade of this building, with its pair of Doric columns set in the plane of the wall within a recessed porch, may have been derived from a published plan for a chapel by Peter Nicholson in several editions of the *New Practical Builder* in the 1820s. In addition to the Benicia building, Alameda County's courthouse of 1856 followed much the same model. The plans of these buildings, which are associated with a more significant aspect of California courthouse design than their façades, are discussed below.

Apart from these substantial buildings in urban counties, from 1851 to the 1860s, several small counties with limited budgets built courthouses. These were modest structures, most of which were demolished or burned down long ago—few images and little information survives about most of them. One remarkable example has survived—the Merced County courthouse at Snelling. It was built in 1857 and served as the courthouse until the county seat moved to Merced in 1872. Thereafter, it was a justice court and today it still serves occasionally as a branch court. This is a two-story rectangular structure with a gable roof trimmed with characteristic details of the Greek Revival style. There is a jail in the stone ground floor and a courtroom and clerk's office in the wood frame second floor. The building is no wider than the distance that can be spanned by wood joists—less than 25 feet.

As small and unpretentious as this building is, it possesses a combination of features that link it to American courthouses in the eastern states and to California courthouses that follow. It occupies a special position in town, distinct from all other local buildings—set back from the street in the center of a public open space. Its courtroom

Benicia Capitol (1853). Built as the city hall, this building also served as the California State Capitol and the Solano County courthouse. Its façade was derived from a church design in an English pattern book. Its floor plan was the first example of the most common California courthouse plan in the 19th century.

Merced County Courthouse, Snelling (1857). This is a rare surviving example of the simplest type of early California courthouse—one room wide and two stories high, with its courtroom above the jail. Despite its simplicity, it contains the essential symbols of hierarchy and authority that are present in most courthouses.

is located in a place of honor on the second floor. Its ornamentation speaks of the authority of government and the courts.

At the same time that it is part of an American courthouse tradition, the Snelling courthouse belongs to its time and place. The combination of jail and courtroom in the same building and the dominance of the law-and-order component of county government reflect social conditions in newly settled land. The use of Greek Revival stylistic details here and throughout California in this period can be seen as a way of manifesting Americans' claims to land so recently annexed as part of the United States. The Greek Revival was the first architectural style adopted throughout the United States and was strongly associated with the nation. In California, which had long been under the control of the Spanish-speaking countries of Spain and Mexico, the Greek Revival style asserted the presence of a government of white, English-speaking and largely Protestant Americans.

STANDARD PLAN COURTHOUSES

In the same period that the Merced County courthouse at Snelling was built, other more prosperous counties with larger populations—many with mining wealth—erected a more substantial kind of courthouse. In shape, these were two-story, rectangular, gable-roofed boxes. They had three bays of windows on the front end and four to six bays on the sides. Inside, they had a central corridor on the ground floor with offices for the assessor, recorder, clerk, tax collector, and sometimes others on either side, and a courtroom upstairs. In some, a jail and sheriff's office were located in the basement. These courthouses were built from the mid-1850s to the 1880s in a series of styles, typically by builders without the participation of an architect.

Throughout the 19th and early 20th centuries, building plans were commonly published in newspapers, journals, architects' plan books, carpenters' and builders' handbooks and manufacturers' catalogs. While the private house was the most common building type represented in these sources, several others were included in lesser numbers, including a few courthouses. Published plans could be purchased and used without modification to replicate a design. Much more often, however, architects and builders used published plans as a starting point and made changes freely to suit local conditions, tastes and needs.

Asher Benjamin's widely circulated *American Builder's Companion* (issued in several editions from 1806 to 1827) presented a courthouse plan that might have been a

Benicia Capitol, ground-level senate chamber. The columns in this space are masts taken from ships abandoned in Benicia's harbor during the gold rush. They illustrate the structural requirements of the ground floors of all 19th century California courthouses. In contrast, the upper floors of nearly all 19th-century courthouses, including this building, are freed of columns by the use of roof trusses. Thus, the structural systems, spatial organization and symbolism of these buildings are all integrated.

precedent for some of the common three bay courthouses in California. Benjamin was a Boston architect who had an enormous impact on American architecture through this book and six others, several of which were still in print in the 1850s and were used in California. Benjamin's courthouse was roughly rectangular in plan, having three bays across the front and five bays along the sides. The ground floor had a central corridor with three rooms on either side. A courtroom and two jury rooms were located upstairs. The front was designed with a ground-floor arcade surmounted by a two-story pedimented portico. The building was covered by a hip roof with a domed octagonal tower. The California three-bay courthouse box is a simplified version of this widely disseminated plan.

The earliest and best-known example of this type in California, built in 1852, served as the Benicia City Hall, Solano County courthouse, and California State Capitol building. To function as the state capitol, its plan was a modification of the standard type that included a second large room for the senate at the rear of the ground floor. The essential features of the Asher Benjamin design were all present

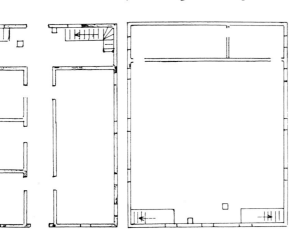

Mariposa County Courthouse, plans as it was built in 1854. Like the Benicia Capitol and most 19th-century courthouses, the ground floor was organized with offices on either side of a central corridor, and the column-free second floor accommodated the courtroom. The division of the ground floor structurally into three sections is reflected on the front in the arrangement of the doors and windows into three bays.

with one significant structural difference. The ground floor was supported by interior columns or walls on either side of the corridor so that the rooms on either side could be spanned by wood joists. The much larger space of the second-floor courtroom was spanned without columns by means of roof trusses.

Mariposa County Courthouse. Like most three-bay courthouses in California, this is a simple rectangular box decorated in the Greek Revival style —by means of corner piers, an entablature under the eaves, and a triangular pediment. Some pre–Civil War Greek Revival courthouses had intentional associations with the political ideology of the Southern states.

Greek Revival Style

Most of the three-bay courthouses were decorated in the Greek Revival style or some approximation of that style. Stylistic purity was rarely a concern of the carpenters and builders who constructed most of these buildings. Greek or Roman orders or simplified, cartoonlike versions of orders were applied to buildings that have been referred to as Greek Revival.

A representative example is the Mariposa County courthouse built in 1854, a two-story rectangular wood structure with a gable roof and a clock tower above the entrance. It is decorated with a few details—corner pilasters, a frieze under the eaves, the gable treated as a pediment, and a framed doorway—that give it the character of the Greek Revival style.

The Mariposa County courthouse is also interesting for its setting in a courthouse square—a full block set aside for a courthouse. Like many California courthouse

squares, this is located in a residential neighborhood on the wealthier side of town, slightly removed from the main business district. Just as the design and setting of a courthouse can reflect the relationship between citizens and their government, they may also reveal elements of social hierarchy. Locating the courthouse on high ground in a pleasant residential neighborhood where the homes and churches built during the same period as the courthouse were built in the same style, implied a harmony of interests between the county government and its more affluent citizens.

San Joaquin County Courthouse (1854). This Federal-style building was among a minority of pre–Civil War courthouses whose imagery was associated with buildings in the northeastern United States —the antislavery states.

Other Styles—Federal, Romanesque, Gothic

Whereas the Greek Revival style was initially associated with the United States as a nation, by the end of the 1850s it came to be identified with the South in the tensions leading up to the Civil War. In Colusa County, for example, whose early population was dominated by pro-Confederate Southerners, the three-bay courthouse built in 1861 with its projecting portico was designed to express local support of the Southern cause.

Several three-bay courthouses were built in distinctly non-Greek Revival styles. While the specific reasons for these choices are not known, it can be inferred that at least some of them were made to express allegiance to the North, if for no other reason than that they rejected an image that was strongly associated with the South while adopting imagery from buildings in the pro-Union Northeast.

Several three-bay courthouses, none of which has survived, were built in a manner that recalled Federal style public buildings from the late 18th and early 19th centuries in the northeastern United States. The designers of these buildings worked with a somewhat different repertoire of features including classical orders and other details, exposed brick walls, hip roofs, and lantern towers based on 18th-century English models. Although different in style from the Greek Revival, these buildings evoked some of the same associations. The Federal style may also reflect the regional origins and political sympathies of the county's dominant populations. The most impressive of these Federal style three-bay boxes was the 1854 San Joaquin County courthouse, whose design recalled Faneuil Hall in Boston with its rectangular form, brick orders and octagonal lantern with a cupola. Nevada, Mendocino, Solano and Tehama counties all built three-bay courthouses in variations of the Federal style from 1857 through 1860.

When a new three-bay courthouse was built in Amador County in 1863 to replace a Greek Revival style courthouse that burned in 1862, a simplified Romanesque design was adopted. It seems likely that Civil War tensions were a factor in choosing this style in a county where in response to the burning of a Methodist church by Southerners, pro-Unionists in Boston donated a new church bell, Thomas Starr King delivered a widely reported pro-Union speech, and the local pro-Union militia set up a cannon to intimidate Southern sympathizers. While it is hard to say what, if any, particular associations the Romanesque Revival style had, it was clearly not associated with the South.

Still other stylistic variations of the same three-bay type include the Gothic Revival (Yuba County, 1855), the Italianate (San Diego County, 1872), and the Colonial Revival (Inyo County, 1887) styles. This variety of styles executed over a period of more than thirty years on the same building type illustrates the practical usefulness of the three-bay type.

United States Capitol. The high dome of the capitol, designed by Thomas U. Walter in 1855, was under construction during the Civil War and served as a powerful symbol of the federal government that ultimately prevailed in the war.

POST–CIVIL WAR COURTHOUSES

Events during the 1860s reshaped California's society and economy, establishing an altered context for the development of new courthouses. The Civil War was accompanied by a booming population, especially in San Francisco, by substantial foreign immigration, and by industrialization. The transcontinental telegraph (completed in 1861) and the railroad (completed in 1869) created both technological and psychological connections to the rest of the United States.

At the same time, two buildings established a new architectural frame of reference for designers of courthouses. The United States Capitol was enlarged and remodeled with a new high dome replacing the original low dome in the center of the building; it was under construction during the Civil War, and it was completed in 1865. The remodeled Capitol with its round dome on a high drum encircled by 36 columns (representing the states of the Union) powerfully symbolized the Union cause and the strong federal government that won the war. In roughly the same period, the California State Capitol in Sacramento was designed and built in the image of the newly remodeled United States Capitol.

After the Civil War, new courthouses were increasingly built of fire-resistant materials to protect essential county records, many of which had been lost in the fires that often destroyed early courthouses. The same materials and structural systems that produced fire-resistant buildings also made larger buildings possible. Because California's population grew substantially in every decade between 1860 and 1900, larger courthouses were necessary in most counties. Even without a growing population or the addition of new county functions, the accumulation of records over time required more space.

To handle the complexity of the design and construction of these larger buildings, counties turned increasingly to architects. Whereas the first courthouses in California were built mostly by people who called themselves builders or contractors, beginning in the late 1860s, courthouses were increasingly built by people who called themselves architects.

At that time there were no licenses or other standards to clearly distinguish a builder from an architect. The first architecture school in the United States, at the Massachusettes Institute of Technology, opened in 1868. Most architects acquired the title after an apprenticeship with another architect. Many others were builders—

California State Capitol. Designed in 1860 by Minor F. Butler, based on an earlier design by Reuben Clark and later modified, the California State Capitol was built in the image of the newly remodeled United States Capitol. The California design expressed the loyalty of the state to the Union during the Civil War.

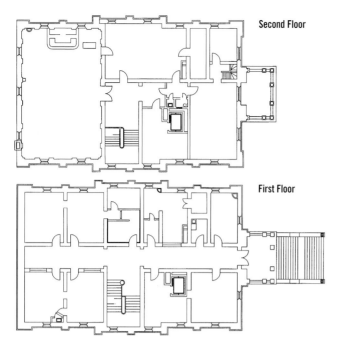

Second Floor

First Floor

people who know the practical business of construction and who may have had experience designing buildings as well—who called themselves architects. Some who were unqualified simply announced that they were architects as a way of promoting business. Among the mix of people who had come to California in the 20 years of its existence were representatives of each of these types.

Two post-war courthouses designed by trained and accomplished architects were those in Santa Clara and San Francisco.

The Santa Clara County courthouse of 1868 was larger and more expensive than earlier courthouses. Designed by Levi Goodrich with a monumental temple front and a high dome, this structure was more like a state capitol than like other California courthouses of the period.

San Francisco City Hall was an enormous, sprawling, four-story structure on a triangular multiblock site. The ornamental scheme was derived from major churches, palaces, and other buildings of Renaissance Europe, but the composition of the building was irregular, picturesque and characteristic of the Victorian era. The Larkin Street entrance pavilion, housing the courts, was the only portion of the design treated as a temple front—with a pediment above its giant order. In the same spirit, the entrance to the courts wing was the only pedimented doorway into the building.

PERSISTENCE OF THE THREE-BAY PLAN AND NEW APPROACHES TO DECORATION

The Santa Clara and San Francisco courthouses stand out as special cases. The majority of new courthouses between 1865 and 1902 would continue to be built in variations of the standard three-bay plan. Variations of the plan consisted primarily of side entrances and perpendicular wings that provided more space for ground-floor offices and second-floor courtrooms. These perpendicular wings sometimes resulted in buildings that appeared very different from the earlier three-bay courthouses. However, the interior arrangements were essentially the same—ground floors with central corridors and offices on either side, and second floors with courtrooms, jury rooms, judges' chambers and law libraries. Whatever the plan and overall organization of the courthouse, these buildings were generally far more elaborately decorated than those before the Civil War. While the courthouses of this period generally maintained references to classical architecture and associations with the imagery of authority and government, this imagery was different—much of it derived from the state capitol or from the idea of a capitol.

The dominant new type of courthouse was one that can be represented by the work of two architects, A. A. Bennett and J. M. Curtis who, alone or in partnership, designed ten courthouses and remodeled others. These were two of the leading architects in the state, whose experience provided a direct link between the state capitol and San Francisco City Hall and the state's courthouses. Bennett was one of the supervising architects of the state capitol and Curtis was one of the supervising architects of San Francisco City Hall. Between 1863 and 1898, Bennett designed six courthouses, Curtis designed two courthouses, and the partnership of Bennett and Curtis designed two courthouses. The first of these was an ornate example of a three-bay courthouse built in Yolo County in 1863. Between 1873 and 1876, five very similar courthouses were built in the San Joaquin Valley counties of Stanislaus, Merced, Fresno, Tulare and Kern. These were followed by four more between 1884 and 1898 that were more elaborate versions of the middle five. These ten courthouses represent the evolution of courthouse design evident in virtually all California courthouses in that period.

The Yolo County courthouse of 1863 was a larger, more substantial version of the pre–Civil War three-bay courthouse. This was a brick building with numerous chimneys and exhaust stacks for a comprehensive system to heat (by fireplace) and ventilate (by passive air flow) each room in the courthouse.

Bennett's next five courthouses—Stanislaus (1873), Merced (1874), Fresno (1875), Tulare (1876) and Kern (1876)—were so similar in appearance that they have been referred to, incorrectly, as "patternbook" designs. These were larger buildings than in Yolo County—three stories instead of two. The additional story was a ground level that housed the jail, sheriff and space for offices that could not be accommodated on the second floor. The second floor was the main public floor and was entered from large outside staircases. The first and second floors had central corridors with rooms on either side. The third floor housed one or two courtrooms and ancillary spaces for judges, juries, the district attorney and law library.

These buildings were Italianate in style, but in addition to Italian Renaissance sources, there were echoes of current French fashions. The second-level pilasters were paired and a segmented pediment at the center of the front recalled details of the Paris Opera, which was completed in 1875 and was then perhaps the most famous building in the world. The parapets were lined with balustrades, pedestals, pediments, chimneys, exhaust stacks and statuary. The statuary—like many statues of saints in contemporary Roman Catholic churches—was not sculpted for the individual buildings, but was manufactured elsewhere and sold in catalogs. The most common images in these and other courthouses were drawn from Roman mythology, such as Justice holding her scales and sword.

Each of these courthouses except Stanislaus was built with a domed tower in the center of the roof. The towers were similar, each consisting of a lower drum defined by a ring of columns, an upper drum and a dome surmounted by a statue. While the design of these tower domes was loosely based on those of the United States and the California State Capitols, the proportional relationship between the tower domes and the buildings was quite different. The domes of these courthouses were much smaller in relation to their buildings than the traditional domes of the Renaissance.

Towers were popular, although they cost more money and were generally of no practical value, because they helped express the significance of the building and the activities inside. They were requested by the public because they provided popular observation points. Unlike the state capitol and other traditional domed buildings where the dome enclosed the upper part of a central ceremonial interior space, these courthouse domes were simply attached to the roofs and did not involve any ceremonial interiors. With or without a dome, these courthouses looked the same inside.

Curtis' last courthouse, for Placer County, was both a continuation and the culmination of the Bennett and Curtis courthouse type. With its cruciform shape, tower dome attached to the courthouse building without an interior spatial connection and its large outside staircases to the main second floor, it was similar to several others. At the same time, it introduced a cruciform interior-corridor plan. This cruciform plan established a centralized space that, in the 20th century, would be a basic feature of most courthouses.

Placer County Courthouse (1898), designed by John M. Curtis. This was similar in many respects to the previous nine courthouses by Bennett and Curtis. At the same time, the whole building was like a state capitol—not the capitol of the Civil War era, but a regional capitol in a period of economic development.

The most distinctive aspects of the Placer County courthouse were visible on the outside. Unlike the earlier domed courthouses, the proportions of the dome were related to those of the rest of the building so the dome looked less like an optional attachment; here the whole building was analogous to the state capitol. Situated on a hill visible to passengers on the transcontinental railroad, this reference to the state capitol in 1898 was no longer primarily a statement about support for the Union, but rather an assertion of the importance and prosperity of Placer County in a commercial age. The image of this courthouse was that of a capitol of its region.

At a time when many other mining counties were in economic decline, Placer County's economy had entered a new era. The railroad that connected the county to San Francisco and the rest of the United States made possible the development of several local industries, many of which were showcased in the courthouse.

Except for the steel structural frame and the slate roof, virtually all the building's materials came from Placer County. Granite for the ground floor, the stairs, and the monolithic porch columns came from Rocklin. The upper walls were clad in plain and molded brick with terra-cotta trim, all manufactured by Gladding, McBean and Company in Lincoln. Gladding McBean also made the hollow clay tile blocks used in the flat arch floor structures. Local lime was used for mortar to lay up these various masonry elements and for interior plaster wall surfaces. Timber from Alta was used in the framing of the roof and the tower dome and marble from Colfax was used for interior finishes.

This was a technologically sophisticated building. It was fire-resistant—called "fireproof"—with its steel frame encased in masonry, its masonry walls and its hollow clay tile floors. It had electric lights, flush plumbing and a heating and ventilating system. Unlike several counties that were beholden to the railroad for the county seat and support for the courthouse, Placer County financed its courthouse in large part with tax money gained in a settlement of a lawsuit against Southern Pacific. In that way it truly represented the power of local interests, as reflected in the materials provided by the county's major employers.

Bennett's and Curtis's courthouses were so similar in facilities, design, materials and cost that they were almost interchangeable. A few courthouses by other designers, including some of California's best-known architects, shared many of the same features. Among these were courthouses for Santa Barbara County in 1872 by Peter J. Barber, leading architect of Santa Barbara and author of a patternbook; Marin County in 1873 by Kenitzer & Raun, commercial architects in San Francisco; Monterey County in 1878 by Levi Goodrich, the New York–trained architect of the Santa Clara County Courthouse; Napa County in 1878 by Joseph and Samuel Cather Newsom, prolific architects with a statewide practice, best known for the Carson House in Eureka; San Mateo County in 1882 by Augustus Laver, architect of the monumental San Francisco City Hall (and county courthouse); San Benito County in 1887 by John Gash, architect of the central dome of the Conservatory of Flowers in Golden Gate

Park and author of *A Catechism of Architecture* for architects preparing to practice in California; and Shasta County in 1890 by A. A. Cook, a Sacramento architect with a regional practice.

THE END OF THE CENTURY AND THE SEARCH FOR NEW MODELS

In the 1890s and early 1900s, the old patterns began to give way to a variety of approaches to courthouse design without any dominant new pattern emerging. The new courthouses were larger buildings serving larger, and in several cases, more urban populations. While the plans and images of these building differed from earlier courthouses and from each other, they shared several characteristics—they were fireproof structures, they were monumental in appearance, and for the first time they accommodated sizeable public ceremonial interiors.

San Joaquin County Courthouse (1891). To express local aspirations for status as a regional economic capital, San Joaquin County hired Elijah E. Myers, a Detroit architect who had already designed four state capitols and many county courthouses outside of California.

Like Placer County, several counties built new courthouses more convincingly modeled after the California and United States capitols than earlier domed efforts. In 1891, two of the most impressive of these capitol-type courthouses were completed, for Fresno and San Joaquin Counties, at a time when they were emerging as among the richest agricultural counties in the United States. For an appropriate image as a regional capital, San Joaquin hired Elijah E. Myers, a Detroit architect who had already designed four state capitols—for Michigan, Idaho, Texas and Colorado, and who designed a total of 100 county courthouses scattered throughout the United States. Myers's design for San Joaquin County blended elements of massing and exterior detail from his Michigan and Texas state capitols. Inside, perpendicular corridors met on each floor in a central skylit space under the dome, with stairs and balconies leading up to a public viewing area in the dome.

Later in the same year, Fresno completed a more modest but still monumental expansion and remodeling of its 1875 A. A. Bennett courthouse. Bennett's courthouse constituted the central structure of a much bigger building with a new central pedimented portico and a round copper-clad dome on a drum encircled by columns. This remodeling and expansion was designed by William Curlett, an Irish immigrant trained as an architect at the Art Institute of Manchester. After a fire in 1895 that destroyed the dome, the courthouse was rebuilt with a new, slightly larger dome and other changes designed by J. M. Curtis.

Apart from capitol-type courthouses, this period produced one-of-a-kind designs, such as an exotic fantasy for Kern County in 1896 by C. C. McDougall; an eclectic design for Tuolumne County in 1900 by William Mooser; and an Italianate courthouse for Napa County in 1878 designed by Samuel and Joseph Cather Newsom with a Moorish tower dome in three stages.

RICHARDSONIAN ROMANESQUE

Among the most interesting of the various experiments in courthouse design in this period were several in the Richardson Romanesque style, most of which were clustered in Southern California. The first and by far the largest and most impressive of these was the Los Angeles County courthouse completed in 1891 and designed under the direction of Theodore Eisen while he was working for the firm of Curlett and Cuthbertson. Eisen, the son of a Swedish immigrant architect, was an innovator. As early as 1882, in a speech to the San Francisco chapter of the American Institute of Architects (A.I.A.), he advocated a return to a simpler expression of structure and

San Bernardino County Courthouse (1898). This courthouse was one of a cluster in Southern California in the Richardsonian Romanesque style, expressing a regional identity with Los Angeles as its capital. Despite the distinctive appearance, adopted in an effort to develop an architecture particularly suited to California, the interior arrangement was no different from other courthouses of its time.

materials in architecture, while criticizing the routinely overdecorated buildings and use of classical imagery of the time.

Among California architects, Eisen was unusually receptive to the architecture of H. H. Richardson, which spoke to some of the same issues in a larger American context. Richardson's recently completed 1888 Allegheny County courthouse in Pittsburgh, Pennsylvania, served as a starting point in the design of the Los Angeles County courthouse. The composition of the façade with its hip roof, projecting end pavilions, and tall central tower, was the same. The large, rough, red sandstone blocks that formed the exterior surfaces of the building were comparable to the gray granite walls of Allegheny County. The round arched opening and other details that referred to the pre-Renaissance architecture of southern France conveyed a similar impression, but in a different context.

The Los Angeles County courthouse was an effort to establish an image more suitable for California than the typical imagery of classicism could convey. The allusions to the French Romanesque period were intended to create an image whose principal association was to its indefinite age rather than its relationship to other cultures. The rough western sandstone reflected the hands of anonymous workers, like those who built the California missions. The naturalistic stone and the image of antiquity were ways of suggesting that the courthouse and the people who built it were part of this place: Like the Indians who built the missions, the new Anglo population of Los Angeles belonged here. Considering that Los Angeles had been little more than a small village 20 years earlier, these were bold assertions to make.

In the next ten years, three more California courthouses, in Santa Cruz, San Bernardino and Orange Counties, were built in the Richardsonian Romanesque style. The clustering of three Richardsonian Romanesque courthouses in Southern California suggests the emergence of a regional identity, following the lead of Los Angeles. It also reflects the greater self-consciousness in Southern California about a distinctive architectural expression of the life and culture of the state. Much of the energy, enthusiasm and skill that produced the architecture most specifically associated with California came from this region. Those architects receptive to the Richardsonian Romanesque were interested in the same set of ideas that later produced bungalows, Mission Revival and Spanish Colonial Revival.

A NEW CONSENSUS: PROGRESSIVISM, IMPERIALISM AND THE BEAUX ARTS

In the first decade of the 20th century, the design of California courthouses underwent a major shift at the hands of a new group of architects. After a period of experimentation in the 1890s and early 1900s, most courthouse architects came to share a common architectural philosophy that resulted in a group of buildings built from 1904 to 1932 that, despite a superficial variety, possessed a strong common character. These were not virtually identical buildings like those represented by the three-bay Greek Revival courthouses of the 1850s or the Bennett and Curtis courthouses of the 1870s to the 1890s, but they also formed a readily identifiable group.

Unlike the courthouses of earlier periods, many of these are still standing. Most were designed with the participation of professional engineers and to the standards of building codes that were based increasingly on scientific knowledge and decreasingly on old rules of thumb and political considerations. These were generally steel frame structures whose fire-resistant construction extended to the roof and tower structures, unlike earlier "fireproof" courthouses. These structures were substantially larger than their predecessors, to accommodate the needs of larger populations and larger county governments.

Apart from their size, the most obvious new quality in these buildings was their imagery. After the period of experimentation in the 1890s, courthouse designers returned universally to large-scale classicism, comparable to that of ancient Rome.

This imagery was first presented to the American public at the World's Columbian Exposition in Chicago in 1893. The centerpiece of the Chicago exposition was a lagoon surrounded by monumental neoclassical buildings all painted white, referred to as the "White City." It offered to Americans a vision of an orderly city and society. At a time of tremendous immigration and social turmoil based on race, ethnicity and class, it obscured deep differences by suggesting a unified society with common cultural roots. At a time when American cities were considered visually chaotic and dirty, it presented an image of order, harmony and cleanliness. The juxtapositions of buildings in different styles and sizes; the proximity of dirty factories and crowded tenement houses; the noises and smells of streetcars, horses, and people; the unregulated proliferation of lights and signs; and the mere presence of people who spoke, looked, and dressed differently—all of these were jarring to the old elites. While these conditions were most pronounced in the largest cities, they were also felt—or feared—in small cities as well.

The image of the White City was a principal inspiration for the City Beautiful movement. Proponents of the City Beautiful movement advocated the construction of monumental classical buildings as a first step toward solving America's urban problems. If these buildings were erected at key locations in the city or in a primary cluster such as a civic center—by the government or by enlightened private citizens—others would be inspired to build similar buildings. The ultimate result would be the reconstruction of American cities in the image of the White City. Like Paris with its boulevards, American cities would consist of streets lined with grand neoclassical buildings. In place of the social and visual chaos of the time, there would be social and visual order.

The creators of the White City, most advocates of the City Beautiful movement, and most of the architects of new buildings in the spirit of the City Beautiful movement were influenced by the teachings of the Ecole des Beaux Arts in Paris. The Ecole des Beaux Arts was the leading architectural school in the world at that time. Promising students came from many other countries, especially the United States, to study there. Graduates of the Ecole returned to the United States where they trained young architects through apprenticeships in their offices and in separate organizations like the San Francisco Architectural Club. Most of the early architectural schools in the United States were organized to teach in a manner derived from the Ecole des Beaux Arts. Among these was the first architectural school in California, the School of Architecture at the University of California at Berkeley, established in 1903.

The Ecole des Beaux Arts taught principles of architecture and a process of design, rather than particular architectural styles. The most successful students in this system were skillful draftsmen (and a few women) who could quickly conceive the outlines of a solution to an architectural problem and render it persuasively in ink and water.

California architects embraced the approach of the Ecole des Beaux Arts more enthusiastically than those in other regions of the United States. More architects trained at the Ecole were practicing in San Francisco than in any other city in the country outside of New York. While the Ecole did not teach any particular style, a readily identifiable style of public buildings quickly emerged in the United States, often called Beaux Arts classicism. Most Beaux Arts buildings in the United States built between the 1890s and 1930 were designed as monumental structures based directly on Roman models or on Renaissance and baroque descendants of the Roman originals. These buildings were designed following principles of symmetry, hierarchy, axiality and unity. They were characterized by giant classical orders and by rich decorative detail, often in expensive materials such as marble and bronze. Beaux Arts classical buildings were embellished inside and outside by the work of artists and craftspeople in sculpture, decorative metalwork, decorative plaster, and murals.

Conditions outside the world of architecture also influenced the adoption of Beaux Arts classicism for courthouses. In California, Beaux Arts classicism was an emblem of the Progressive reform movement after the turn of the century that rejected the corrupt machine politics of the late 19th century. For the United States, it was an assertion of the nation's new stature as an imperial power. This had a special appeal in California, where San Francisco aspired to control trade around the Pacific Ocean. The 1898 victory of the United States in the Spanish-American War resulted in the annexation of the Philippines and produced an occasion for the annexation of Hawaii. The victory was gained in part with soldiers and supplies sent from the San Francisco Presidio, and it resulted in building up the United States Navy with its Pacific headquarters in San Francisco Bay.

After the turn of the century, then, California's county courthouses were a vehicle for expressing a complex package of ideas, including political reform, the new world stature of the United States, and aspirations for urban, architectural, and social order. In many county seats, the county courthouse, together with the Carnegie Library and the United States Post Office, boldly reflected a set of related ideas about the place of the local community in the larger society. When these three buildings were built near one another, as was often the case, they formed a small civic center and an outpost of the City Beautiful movement.

The first county courthouse that unambiguously represented the new era was the Riverside County courthouse of 1904, designed by the firm of Burnham & Bliesner. The designer, Franklin P. Burnham, had moved to Los Angeles from Chicago where he had practiced in the firm of Edbrooke and Burnham from 1877 to 1891. While Burnham's design for the Riverside County courthouse has been described as modeled on the Grand Palais at the Paris Exposition of 1900, the basic composition of its façade also recalls that of Edbrooke's United States Government Building at the Chicago Exposition of 1893. In either case, inside and outside, it was modeled after an exposition building.

The choice of this imagery was related to the particular history of Riverside County, which had been created only ten years earlier. The separation from San Bernardino County was acrimonious, following the construction of a Richardsonian Romanesque–style hall of records in the city of San Bernardino in 1891 that was strongly opposed by residents of the city of Riverside. If Riverside County wanted to express its regional identity through the design of its courthouse, as San Bernardino and Orange Counties had done by following the lead of Los Angeles County, it could hardly have chosen a style that resembled San Bernardino County's courthouse. Instead, it selected a design that represented the agricultural bounty of the region, which was on display in international expositions every few years. Inside, its principal corridor was lit by skylights, as in exposition buildings.

The Riverside County courthouse is unusual for the exuberance of its design and for its allusion to the architecture of expositions. It is also unusual as one of the few courthouses built on one floor. Because of this, its courtroom was not on a higher floor than the entrance and other spaces. The symbolic importance of the courtroom, easily achieved by a second-floor location, was obtained here by the entry sequence: through a triumphal arch and under a dome to the courtroom.

From 1913 to 1922, thirteen courthouses were built in California. Most of these were designed by architects who had studied at the Ecole des Beaux Arts or in the Beaux Arts system in the United States. All of these courthouses reflected the influence of the Ecole des Beaux Arts, mixing to varying degrees references to ancient Rome and to the Renaissance. The façades of most had symmetrical compositions

Riverside County Courthouse (1904), designed by Burnham & Bliesner. This was the first county courthouse in California in a new style associated both with exposition architecture and the Ecole des Beaux Arts in Paris. The exuberant classicism of the buildings of this era expressed the new international stature of the United States as an imperial power following the Spanish-American War.

with projecting pavilions at the center and ends, like Riverside, and giant orders. In contrast to most 19th-century courthouses, which were oriented with a short end of the building facing the principal approach, these were oriented with a long side facing the view. This orientation made large buildings appear even larger. In plan, these courthouses were elongated versions of their predecessors with long central corridors on two or three floors and a circulation and ceremonial space at the center. Jails were still incorporated in the basements of some of these courthouses. Courtrooms were on the upper floors. While the central corridors provided a clear organization of functions to the public, the spaces off these corridors were no longer simple rooms, but suites of rooms often with their own internal corridors.

Among these buildings, the Kern County courthouse, designed by Frederick H. Meyer of San Francisco in 1910, had special requirements. Meyer was an advocate of the City Beautiful movement for two of its principal objectives: beautification and modernization through the use of engineering. When the Kern County courthouse was under construction in July 1910, the *Architect and Engineer* wrote that Meyer's design "successfully combined beauty and utility, at the same time keeping in mind the unusual climactic conditions of Bakersfield—summer heat at 115 degrees in the shade." The courthouses of this period were typically praised for solving the twin problems of beauty and utility—problems that were ideally solved simultaneously. In this case, the central pavilion, designed as a pantheon in the manner of Thomas Jefferson's library at the University of Virginia, also functioned as the principal air intake of the mechanical ventilating system.

By far the largest and most expensive of the courthouses was San Francisco City Hall, completed in 1916, designed by the firm of Bakewell and Brown, both graduates of the Ecole des Beaux Arts. Despite its size and grandeur, the city hall represented an evolution of the typical pattern for courthouses rather than a departure from it. Like the others, it consisted of a rectangular base housing offices and a central circulation and ceremonial space. The great central space and the tall dome were exaggerated versions of the central space found in smaller courthouses. Although the courtrooms were included on a temporary basis, with a separate hall of justice projected, they were housed on upper floors in the traditional manner. Larger than many state capitols and built in the image of a capitol, it symbolized San Francisco as the unofficial capital of a vast region. This building possessed "utility"—it was admired for its good planning and accommodation of its many functions. It also possessed "beauty" when beauty is understood to mean not simply high aesthetic values, but also appropriate political and social meaning.

In the spirit of the City Beautiful movement, several courthouses were designed in the context of larger civic center plans. The most completely realized civic center plan was that of San Francisco, adopted in 1912, of which the city hall was the focal point. A civic center was proposed for Fresno by Charles Henry Cheney, a leading figure in the new field of city planning in California, in 1918. In each of these cases as part of ensembles including city, state and federal buildings, the presence and position of the county courthouse represented a different role than it held in the past when it was the undisputed main architectural attraction in town.

Fresno Civic Center proposed (1918) by Charles Henry Cheney, city planner. With the existing courthouse at the focal point of a group of new public buildings, *Architect and Engineer* described this as "one of the finest vistas in America." In the early 20th century, courthouses were often conceived as part of monumental ensembles, expressions of the national good government of the Progressive era. Cheney's ambitious plan was never built.

These civic centers were only proposed for a few of the largest cities in the state. In most counties, no such civic centers were planned. At the same time, clusters of public buildings that were sometimes referred to as "civic centers" often grew up in the early 20th century in small county seats. These were ensembles that increased in size as new buildings were needed. In contrast to the formal civic centers, when new buildings were added, their design and placement followed different criteria of pragmatism, utility, hierarchy, and imagery. New buildings were added to courthouse grounds where there was room or where functional linkages could be made, for example, between a courthouse and jail or a courthouse and hall of records. Secondary buildings like jails and halls of records were placed behind the courthouse. Rather than seeking a harmonious architectural character, counties continued to commission buildings in the appropriate image for their use—gothic for a jail, perhaps Renaissance for a hall of records. Occasionally groups of county buildings were augmented by other public buildings such as a post office, city hall, public library, and veteran's memorial building, the design and placement of which might be developed according to familiar aesthetic criteria. These groups might be further enhanced by the presence of churches and fraternal halls. As a result of this informal process, a number of counties developed diverse collections of public buildings around the county courthouse in the early 20th century.

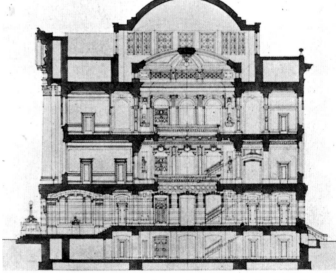

Kern County Courthouse (1910), section through entry and central domed space. Designed by Frederick H. Meyer. The ever increasing size of courthouses and more ambitious symbolic programs required increasingly complex interiors. This view shows the richly decorated intersection of the primary corridor plan on each floor with the central ceremonial rotunda and the air intake for the mechanical ventilation system.

During the first three decades of the 20th century, one courthouse, built for Santa Barbara County in 1929, stands out for its distinctive plan and appearance. In an article in the July 1929 *Architect and Engineer*, M. MacLean Finney contrasted the Santa Barbara County courthouse with other courthouses: "Who can muster any enthusiasm about just another public office building?... But I had not then seen the Courthouse at Santa Barbara. How refreshingly different!" This was the only courthouse in the Spanish Colonial Revival style. Its style, its asymmetrical composition, its lack of regular fenestration, its rich and varied furnishings and decorative features, the variety of its spaces and decoration—all these were unlike any other courthouse. Yet even this courthouse shared many characteristics with other courthouses of its era that were produced in the context of the City Beautiful movement by architects trained at the Ecole des Beaux Arts. While it looked more like a palace or a museum than a courthouse, the building housed the same functions as other courthouses of its era. Like many 19th-century courthouses, it had a tower for public viewing. Its principal offices were on the ground level and its courtrooms were upstairs. Although not classical in style like most City Beautiful–era courthouses, its style and design were generated with the intention of enhancing the Spanish Colonial character of the city. The integration of the work of artists and craftspeople with the architectural design was characteristic of the highest aspirations of the Beaux Arts.

DEPRESSION—FEDERALLY FUNDED MODERNE

Few new courthouses were built during the Great Depression of the 1930s, although several counties built annexes or additions to existing courthouses. Almost all of these courthouses and additions of the 1930s adopted a different imagery from that which prevailed during the 1920s and earlier. David Gebhard has called this the "PWA Moderne" style. "PWA" stands for the Public Works Administration, a New Deal program of the federal government, which partially funded many of these buildings. "Moderne" was a style that drew on the imagery of modern transportation and from the exhibits of the 1925 Paris Exposition des Arts Decoratif, among other sources. The PWA Moderne blended the classicism traditionally associated with government buildings and the Moderne, with its simpler and more future-oriented character.

Although superficially different in style from their Beaux Arts predecessors, most of these were similar buildings in organization and composition. The San Luis Obispo County courthouse of 1936 to 1941, for example, with its abstract classical orders and red tile roof, would have been indistinguishable from courthouses of the 1920s if it had been ornamented in Beaux Arts classical details.

The Alameda County courthouse of 1935 foreshadowed future courthouse design in a more fundamental way. This was an eleven story PWA Moderne style building designed by a board of locally prominent architects. While Los Angeles County had built tall buildings—the 12 story hall of records of 1909 and the 14 story hall of justice of 1925—and Oakland and Los Angeles had built skyscraper city halls, this was the first general-purpose county courthouse in a tall building. Despite its height, this was a traditionally organized courthouse with the assessor, recorder, auditor, and tax collector on the ground floor, other offices in the second floor of its two-story base, courtrooms in the shaft, and a public observation area at the top.

Alameda County Courthouse (1935), designed by a temporary association of leading local architects. This was the first all-purpose courthouse in a skyscraper and one of many PWA Moderne style courthouses of the 1930s funded in part by the federal government. Although distinctive in appearance, its interior was organized according to traditional principles for courthouses.

MID-CENTURY GROWTH, TECHNOLOGY, MANAGEMENT, AND MODERNISM

By the middle of the 20th century, the conditions and attitudes that had produced a unified body of courthouses between 1910 and 1930 and a related body of courthouses in the 1930s were under severe stress. The state's population was continuing to grow rapidly but its distribution was changing, with many counties becoming increasingly suburban. Inner cities were deteriorating. In response to the poverty associated with the depression of the 1930s, the federal and state governments established new government functions with a local presence. These functions changed the size, structure, and public expectations of local government. There were more county functions, larger county functions, and more county employees. To manage these changes, county governments became more centralized, adopting an organizational model borrowed from big business. Under this model, in many cases the diffused structure of separate and independent departments was placed under a professional manager with a title like "county administrator."

Counties met their new space requirements in two distinct ways. Most built one or more courthouse annexes, by various names, to handle the overflow from different departments. Some built a new building for most or all of their functions, sometimes called a "courthouse" and other times given a new kind of name like "government center." To accommodate the transformation of county governments into organizations more like businesses, county courthouses were designed to be more like office buildings. Like other office buildings of the time, these housed uniform spaces for interchangeable units of the bureaucracy. Like other buildings of the time, their functioning was more dependent on improved electrical and mechanical technologies. Better and more efficient lighting, heating and ventilating systems and the first generation of commercial air-conditioning systems made it possible to eliminate light wells, light courts and skylights and to have larger floors. With these changes, every desk did not rely on proximity to a window for light and air. With larger floors, buildings became bulkier.

The architects who designed these buildings belonged to a profession that had changed in the 1930s. The old Beaux Arts model of the design process, beginning with a quick drawing of the finished building based on an ideal floor plan and followed by a protracted period of providing details for that initial design, gave way to a very different, more scientifically based process. In the new process, information was gathered about practical needs long before an image of the final building was produced. From the information came a floor plan and a structural solution. The image of the building reflected this design process and therefore it expressed the interior organization and structure of the building. The most influential source of the new design process was the Bauhaus, a German school of architecture and related design fields in the 1920s and 1930s. When the leading figures at the Bauhaus, including Walter Gropius and Mies Van der Rohe, fled to the United States from the Nazis in the 1930s, they taught methods of European modernism in American architecture schools. These methods spread to most architecture schools throughout the country. In 1959, for example, the College of Environmental Design was established at the University of California at Berkeley on the Bauhaus model, incorporating the old departments of Architecture, Landscape Architecture, City Planning, and Decorative Arts.

The first county building in California designed according to the new method in the modern image of the International Style was an annex to the old Stanislaus County courthouse built in 1940. In an article titled "Functional Design in Modesto County Building" in the *Architect and Engineer*, Russell Guerne De Lappe, the architect, described the building and his approach to its design. The first step in the design process was the circulation of a questionnaire to department heads. This questionnaire "provided explicit data on the floor areas required and the nature of their use, furniture and equipment to be installed, storage needs and expansion possibilities." This information was used to develop a building program that recognized, for example, a need for flexibility in the allocation of space. This need generated the window design that could accommodate the repartitioning of floors "without loss of natural lighting or disturbing the balance of walls to voids within rooms."

The architect, a graduate of the University of California, wrote with the self-confident cockiness typical of many early modernists in proclaiming the superiority of an undecorated building: "In the new county building at Modesto, California, a dearth of Goths, Athenians, Romans, et al, in the community, precluded the adoption of any traditional architectural style. Mild evidences of economic forces resulted in restraint serving as the better part of design." In the design process, the architect emphasized the practical and functional needs of the county. He considered that the

Merced County Courts Building (1950) by Walter Wagner, architect. Like other post–World War II modern courthouses, the principle decorative features of this building were exposed elements of its structural frame, the screened concrete panels that enclosed its windowless courtrooms, and its prominent ceremonial entryway. The clarity of these features reflected new confidence in rationality and technology as tools for solving problems.

expression of those needs in the composition of the volumes of the building and in the undisguised use of materials—concrete, glass, and glass block—would produce an inherently strong design.

After this self-conscious first example of a modernist county building, only seven courthouses or annexes were built in California in the next 15 years because of shortages of materials during and after World War II and the Korean War. Most new county buildings in this period were small, low-budget structures that departed from traditional patterns of plan, massing, and imagery. The various features of these buildings reflected confidence in rationality and technology as means of solving problems. The designs incorporated new values of clarity, honesty, and openness in exposed structure, undisguised use of materials, and correspondence of size and appearance to function. Functional design, mechanization, efficient and rational organization had served the United States well in World War II. In the aftermath of the war, these same values were widely accepted in architecture.

With the end of the Korean War and the renewed availability of building materials, many large and amply funded courthouses were built around the state. Between 1956 and 1970, the majority of new courthouses were International-style buildings. These were characterized by an office wing and a courts wing joined by a ceremonial and circulation space. Between 1958 and 1968, seven courthouses and related county buildings of this type were completed. Perhaps the purest example was the Humboldt County courthouse of 1958, designed by Mitchell Van Bourg and Gerald D. Matson. Van Bourg studied architecture with Walter Gropius at Harvard. He was Russell G. De Lappe's last partner and continued the practice after De Lappe died. The Humboldt County courthouse was distinguished by its exposed reinforced concrete frame. Between the vertical members of this frame were walls of precast panels, steel sash office windows, glass block jail floor windows, and adjustable louvers in the top-floor jail exercise yard and mechanical area. Above the entrances on each side were large exterior mosaics, designed by Sophie Van Bourg, the architect's wife, depicting the resources of Humboldt County. Altogether this was a striking design, despite the constraints of a low budget. At the opposite end of the spectrum from the minimalist courthouse in Humboldt County was the Kern County courthouse complex of 1959. Utilizing similar design principles and a much larger budget, the architects produced a functional composition ornamented by a rich variety of materials.

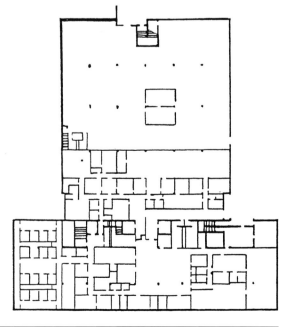

Humboldt County Courthouse (1958), designed by Mitchell Van Bourg. Second floor plan. This diagram shows the square courts wing at the top, the rectangular office and jail wing at the bottom, and a narrow connecting area between them where the principal entrances to the building are located at either end of lower floors. This illustrates the radically different approach to planning courthouses by modernist architects.

The best-known county buildings of this type are the Los Angeles County Hall of Records and the Orange County courthouse, both designed by teams headed by Richard J. Neutra. According to his biographer, Thomas S. Hines

Few architects were as zealously messianic about the practical and aesthetic values of modernism as Richard Joseph Neutra (1892–1970). He championed the architectural implications of such machine age phenomena as assembly line production and the interchangeability of prefabricated parts. His artistic temperament and his sure eye for form and proportion gave a fine aesthetic balance to his commitment to practicality and replicability of design.

Neutra had a profound influence on American modern architecture through his buildings, his writing and speaking, and his employment of others who later established separate practices. More than other early modernists, Neutra drew on research in the social sciences, physical sciences, and biology as a basis for design decisions. Like Frank Lloyd Wright, whom he admired, he sought to respond to the natural environment in his buildings. He believed in Louis Sullivan's idea that "form follows function" but he argued that function included emotional as well as practical requirements. In a later edition of Neutra's 1954 book *Survival through Design*, the rationale for the design of the Orange County courthouse, identified as the "Palace of Justice," was described as follows: "Neutra and his colleagues endeavored to instill psychosomatic principles of design from applied climatology to sensitive acoustics, so as to have building design aid jurisprudence and interindividual fairness."

Neutra's influence in the world of California architecture was such that several courthouses designed by others, and built before his own, display the impact of his ideas. The Kern, Stanislaus and San Diego courthouses all exhibit features and characteristics that reflect the example of Neutra's ideas and architecture.

While many of the most notable courthouses of the post-war era reflected an approach to modernism embodied in the work of Richard Neutra, other influences were also at work in the same period. Among the most important factors in the design of any courthouse were economy and utility.

Orange County Courthouse (1968), designed by Richard J. Neutra with Ramberg and Lowrey. Neutra was the most influential modernist for the designers of California courthouses. The sunshades and louvers shown in this photograph were characteristic details that played an important role in his architectural response to the natural environment. These details were widely imitated.

These were primary considerations for one of the architects of the joint Oakland and Alameda County Hall of Justice, designs for which were published in the *Architect and Engineer* in 1958. Ray Willis of Confer and Willis, architects of the building with Donald W. Anderson, wrote of the design without ever mentioning its appearance:

There are three basic and outstanding elements in the plan of the Oakland Hall of Justice which make for economy and efficiency. These three things are: a. Expandability b. Flexibility c. Utility. This building will provide comfortable, efficient, flexible space for housing the activities of the employees and will satisfy the demands of the future without penalizing the present. The foregoing all being accomplished within a container which can be maintained at a minimum cost.

In the same years that many courthouses were designed as complexes of wings of

Alameda County Hall of Justice (1958), designed by Confer and Willis with Donald W. Anderson. Presentation drawing. *Architect and Engineer* praised this design for its expandability, flexibility, utility and low maintenance costs.

different sizes, several were designed as single blocks, like corporate office buildings. These ranged from modest annexes in Nevada County (1963) and San Luis Obispo County (1964), to major buildings like the Sacramento County courthouse of 1965 and the Los Angeles County Criminal Courts Building of 1972. Like most office buildings, these were rectangular structures with a uniform exterior design. Such designs reflected the business model that county governments had increasingly followed. At the same time, they did not reflect the variety of functions and spaces inside, which included courts, halls for boards of supervisors, jails and record storage. In urban settings, the regular forms and façades of these buildings are more orderly and do not call attention to themselves. They are less special and more ordinary, reflecting the receding prominence of county government in relation to other institutions of society.

The earlier functional model had a second life in a number of county buildings of the 1960s and 1970s. The designs of several of these were based on a design philosophy that stressed the undisguised expression of structure, usually in reinforced concrete, known as Brutalism. One of these, designed for Santa Cruz County by Rockwell and Banwell, was described in a 1968 article in *Architectural Record:*

> The unusual architectural statement results in a lively and highly articulated exterior whose directness and honesty is further expressed in the interior. There, mechanical and electrical systems are treated as elements in the design and are forthrightly left exposed throughout virtually the entire complex. What might have been an uncompromising principle of ruggedness is turned, by precise and elegant detail, into a clear statement of strong conviction.

The language used in the architectural press to describe this building and others like it typically stopped short of stating an explicit connection between "the directness and honesty" of the building and the purposes for which it was built. The writer might have asserted the appropriateness of this design for a courthouse. Instead, whereas earlier architects spoke of the suitability of their designs to the important public institution of the courts, where justice, fairness, and honesty are striven for—in this case it was not the institution but the building that was considered honest. The relationship between the building and its users had changed.

Santa Cruz County Governmental Center (1968), designed by a team headed by architects Rockwell and Banwell. While the planning and organization of this complex is similar to that of post-war International-style courthouses, its Brutalist style is different. The variation of modern styles on the same building type parallels a similar development on 19th- and early 20th-century courthouse types.

SUBURBAN COURTHOUSES AND GOVERNMENT CENTERS

The majority of new post-war courthouses of the 1950s and 1960s were built on traditional courthouse sites—adjacent to old courthouse squares or in other central locations. For most of these, the pull of tradition, the availability of a site and the presence of long-established support services like bail bonds, law offices, title insurance companies, restaurants and bars kept new courthouses in old locations. However, several counties moved to new locations in the suburbs. This happened for several related reasons. Old central locations were crowded. The expanded needs of traditional county functions and the expansion of county responsibilities simply required more space. With the general decline of public transportation, parking was needed for an ever increasing number of automobiles belonging to employees and visitors. Just as courthouses were first located in elite residential neighborhoods or surrounded by prosperous downtown merchants, now they moved to the suburbs along with elite residential neighborhoods and downtown stores that had moved to the mall.

The first of these new suburban county centers was occupied in 1957 in Tulare County, followed by Marin County in 1962. Both were characterized by their suburban locations, strikingly modern architectural images, and by their development as complexes of buildings, parking lots and landscape features on large sites. The main buildings in each complex were horizontal structures with central corridors, designed with sensitivity to their natural settings. As has usually been the case with radical changes in the architecture of courthouses, both reflected political upheavals in their respective counties.

The Tulare County courthouse complex was designed by Horn, Mortland & Clark in the spirit of Richard Neutra's buildings. The main building of the complex consists of two principal wings in a T-plan—a three-story office wing and a one-story courtroom wing. Responding to its hot Central Valley location, its continuous glass walls are shaded by cantilevered planes at the roof and floor levels. Unlike most buildings by Neutra and his followers, its predominant colors are earth tones—to harmonize with its landscaped grounds. These colors are inherent in the materials—stained concrete, precast panels with exposed aggregate and Roman brick, a material made popular by Frank Lloyd Wright.

The Marin County Civic Center, designed by Frank Lloyd Wright, who died before construction began, was developed and built under the direction of his successor, Taliesin Associated Architects, in association with Aaron Green. The wings of the main building were built in two phases, the administration building completed in 1962 and the hall of justice completed in 1970. The civic center consists of the main building, a post office designed by Wright, extensive landscaped grounds designed by

Wright and Green, and the Marin Veterans' Memorial Theater designed by Taliesin Associated Architects.

The Marin County Civic Center is the most famous of California's courthouses—it has an international reputation as an innovative design and the last major work of one of America's most important architects. In many respects, it is unique among American courthouses. In its appearance and organization it has no obvious predecessors. At the same time, it has links to traditional features and symbols in the history of architecture and in the history of courthouses.

The Marin County Civic Center has been widely written about as a work of architecture, but less frequently as a courthouse. As a work of architecture, it is an embodiment of Wright's notion of "organic architecture," which has to do with its relationship to its natural setting. This relationship is developed in many ways. Its colors, textures and forms are intended to harmonize with and enhance its setting. Its design allows the outside in. The interior is lit, like an early-20th-century office building, by a central skylight in each wing that brings light to the ground floor level and by partitions that bring outside light to the central corridors with ample use of glass. The building is open to the outside by views from the center, it opens into the natural hillside at the south end, it is penetrated by roadways under ground-level arches, it is lined by balconies on each level, and it opens onto a landscaped terrace at the center. In general terms, its curved forms and details and the juxtaposition of these curves with the angular spine of the central radio and television tower recall the streamlined Moderne style of the 1930s, and the allusions of that style to the technology and spirit of transportation. In turn, these evoke an optimism about the future.

As a courthouse, the most important aspect of the Marin County Civic Center, an embodiment of Wright's "architecture for democracy," was its inverted organization. While courtrooms have traditionally been located in an elevated or separated place of honor, here they are at the bottom of the lower wing of the building, beneath the jail, for security and efficiency. In the higher wing, the school department and the library were on the top level, with the library in the place of honor under the dome.

In addition to the parallels with the Tulare County courthouse, the Marin County Civic Center is related to traditions of courthouse design in several ways. Although there are no classical orders or pediments here to represent the authority of the government, a similar association is made through reference to Roman engineering. The linear wings with arcaded sides that stretch between the hills suggest the aqueducts of the Romans—an image of power and permanence. In another way, while the forms of the building are futuristic, the "organic" aspects of the design are simultaneously associated with the Arts and Crafts tradition and with the contemporary expressions of that tradition in the Del Norte and Kings County courthouses. Like the many 19th- and 20th-century courthouses with towers that both enhanced their visibility and symbolized the relationship of the county government to the population of the county as one of surveillance, this complex is sited along the county's major transportation artery and provides a multiplicity of views of the surrounding region.

Marin County Civic Center (1962 and 1970), designed by Frank Lloyd Wright with Taliesen Associated Architects in association with Aaron Green. The Marin County Civic Center was one of the first courthouses to move out of the central city to the suburbs. Among all other courthouses, its unique appearance was matched by the functional and symbolic inversion of the normal pattern. Here, the courts are on the lowest level under the jail for security and efficiency, and the school department and library are at the top, embodying Wright's notion of "architecture for democracy."

TRADITION-BASED MODERNISM

Despite the great diversity of organization, form and character among post-war courthouses, the architects of all but a few shared some important common assumptions. Whether International style or Brutalist, whether in a traditional location or the suburbs, whether a courthouse or a government center, whether low-budget and utilitarian or expensive and architecturally ambitious, they adhered to the maxim that "form follows function" and that structure and materials should be frankly expressed. When form follows function, then courtrooms or groups of courtrooms should stand apart from other types of spaces. Whereas in the 19th and early 20th centuries, courtrooms were almost always located above the ground floor in a place of honor, these post-war courts were usually in a separate building or a separate wing of a larger building. The courts wing was usually smaller than adjacent office, records or jail wings, but this was also a place of honor. Like the Bank of America World Headquarters Building and numerous other California banks of the 1950s and 1960s, where the banking hall was in a separate, much smaller building than the adjoining office tower, the courts were in a place of honor precisely because they were housed separately. To build a separate building for the user with the smallest space requirements was in itself a statement of value—otherwise the courts could have been included in the office tower like the assessor, recorder and other traditional county functions. In the change from the old pattern to the new, the form was changed but the principle was the same—to signify the importance of the courts by architectural means.

In contrast to the architectural main stream, in the 1960s and 1970s several counties built courthouses on different models. In some of these, all of the functions typically included in a courthouse were accommodated in a single structure occupying a single volume and provided with a unified image. Sometimes referred to by terms like "the New Formalism," these were designed with references to historic buildings or styles. These references were not literal but were abstractions of historic buildings or elements of historic buildings executed in modern materials.

The designs of the Lake and Glenn County courthouses of 1968 were small, low-budget versions of Lincoln Center, especially the Metropolitan Opera House just completed in New York. These were rectangular boxes screened on four sides by round-arched arcades that looked like two-dimensional cutouts. More ambitious was the Fresno County courthouse of 1966, an eight-story block designed like an early-20th-century skyscraper, with a base, a shaft, and a cornice. The exterior walls are screens of concrete blocks. This design was influenced by the work of Edward D. Stone and Minoru Yamasaki, two unorthodox architects who rejected mainstream design principles. The designers of these buildings were attempting to restore to courthouses the formality and dignity they felt was lost in the irregularity of most modern architecture, through symmetry and visual connections to the history of architecture.

Others reacted to the modern architecture mainstream in a different way. Like the New Formalists, they looked to other sources for design inspiration. Instead of Greek temples and other monumental historical building types, their sources were vernacular. Rather than a reassertion of central authority, these buildings drew on images that were informal and suggested a loosening or diffusion of authority.

The most ambitious of these was the Kings County Government Center (1977) designed by Kaiser Engineers. The model for this suburban complex was Foothill College (1962) in Los Altos Hills, designed by a team headed by Ernest Kump. David Gebhard and his coauthors of *The Guide to Architecture in San Francisco and Northern California* called Foothill College "the perfect California design of its era." Like Foothill, the Kings County Government Center is a campus composed of a number of similar square and rectangular buildings placed on an undisturbed natural site. The informal arrangement of the buildings creates landscaped interior courtyards and an automobile-free center.

HIGH TECH, HIGH SECURITY, AND BACKWARD-LOOKING DESIGNS

In the 1970s and the 1980s, most new county facilities were either additions to existing building or annexes on nearby sites, or they were new suburban government centers. The need for courtrooms was filled in large part by the establishment of branch courts in new and rented facilities. Among county functions, courts in particular were inadequately provided for both in numbers and in the character of facilities. The design of new county facilities generally responded to familiar programs and followed models of one of several stylistic varieties of modernism—corporate modernism (Sacramento), Brutalism (Santa Cruz), New Formalism (Fresno) or Bay Area Tradition (Del Norte).

In the 1990s, a new generation of courthouses was built to updated standards. Architects of these buildings made full use of computers in developing designs. These buildings gave new emphasis to security concerns—not just controlling the movement of prisoners, but protecting judges, attorneys and parties to court cases from the general public. New technologies of all types, especially communications technologies, were provided. Disabled accessibility requirements were incorporated in the program from the beginning. In addition, an evolving judicial system and expanded support and social services were principal new factors in the design of courthouses.

By this time, the term "courthouse" referred only to a building for courts and directly related functions. The needs of other county functions were so large and so specialized that they required entirely separate facilities. Even the visually cohesive suburban government center of the 1950s and 1960s was anachronistic. Now, like a chain of shopping malls, counties built separate complexes for administration, the courts, social services, prisons and other purposes. In Stanislaus County, for example, in addition to the administration and courthouse facilities in the old courthouse square, new suburban complexes have been completed in the 1990s for social services, a prison and agriculture programs.

Ironically, as courthouses became increasingly complex and technologically sophisticated, their architects began to look backward. Whereas the Moderne-style of the 1930s was inspired by visions of the future, and the modernist architecture of the 1950s and 1960s purported to have cut its ties with the past, in the 1990s architects looked to the past not only for inspiration but often for specific forms and details. Stylistically, the incorporation of historic character in modern buildings is called postmodernism.

The architects of this period have been motivated by several considerations. In part, post-modernists have reacted to the frequently bland or antiurban quality of much modern architecture and have sought to design buildings that reinforced the qualities of existing urban and architectural contexts. Designers of government buildings and especially of courthouses have sought to reaffirm the authority of the government and of the courts through familiar symbols—especially through the use of classicism. At the same time, in contrast to the mainstream of modernism up to this time, when frank expression of function, structure and materials was a virtue, the exterior appearances of these buildings no longer have much relation to structural systems or interior arrangements.

CONCLUSION

The history of California courthouse architecture is in one sense simply an aspect of the general history of the architecture of the state. At the same time it represents an important special case because for most of California's history the county courthouse has been the most prominent and widely experienced example of public architecture. Courthouse architecture reflects the changing social, architectural and political life of the state. Just as the character of courthouse architecture has changed continually over the past 150 years, it will continue to change in the future.

The Courthouses

·FRONT·ELEVATION·

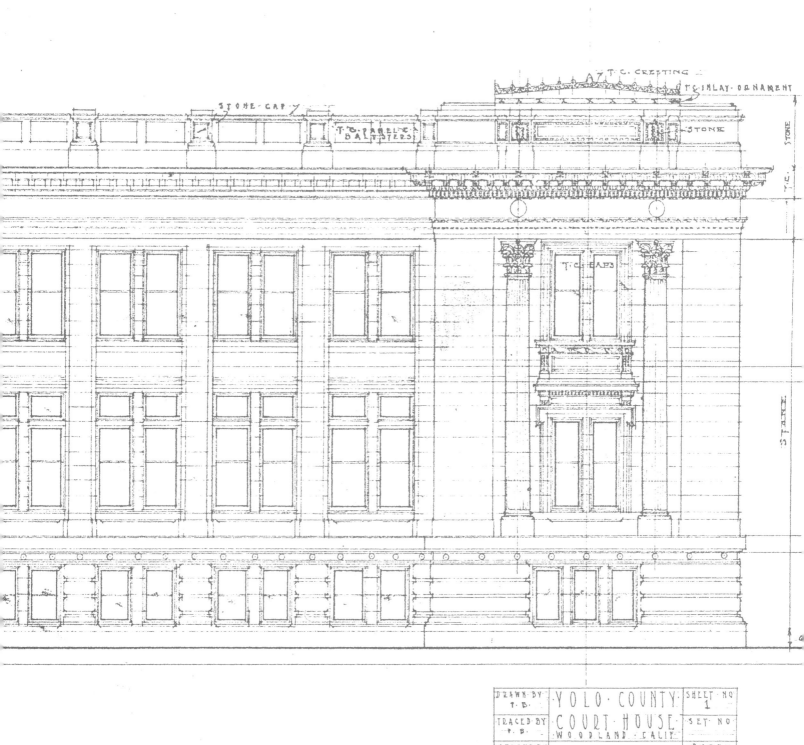

STONE·CAP·

T.C.·CRESTING

T·C·INLAY·ORNAMENT

T.C.·PANEL·&
BALUSTERS

STONE

STONE

T.C. CAPS

T.C.

STONE

DRAWN BY T. B.	YOLO·COUNTY·	SHEET·NO 1
TRACED BY P. B.	COURT·HOUSE· WOODLAND·CALIF	SET·NO
CHECKED	W H WEEKS·	DATE 7/12
APPROVED	ARCHITECT· 75·POST·ST·SF·CAL·	SCALE 1/8·1'-0"

California Counties

. Crescent City
DEL
NORTE

Yreka .

MODOC

SISKIYOU

Alturas .

. Eureka

Weaverville

SHASTA

LASSEN

TRINITY

Redding ·

Susanville

HUMBOLDT

Red Bluff ·

PLUMAS

TEHAMA

. Quincy

MENDOCINO

GLENN

BUTTE

Downieville

Willows ·

Oroville ·

SIERRA

NEVADA

Colusa ·

YUBA

Nevada City

Ukiah ·

Lakeport

Yuba City . Marysville

PLACER

COLUSA

LAKE

SUTTER

Auburn

Woodland

EL DORADO

SONOMA

YOLO SACRAMENTO

· Placerville

· Markleeville

NAPA

★

ALPINE

Santa Rosa ·

Sacramento

AMADOR

Napa SOLANO

Jackson ·

· Fairfield

San Andreas

· Bridgeport

MARIN

Martinez

Stockton

CALAVERAS TUOLUMNE

San Rafael ·

CONTRA
COSTA

SAN
JOAQUIN

Sonora

San Francisco ·

Oakland

MONO

· Modesto

MARIPOSA

ALAMEDA

STANISLAUS

Redwood City ·

Mariposa

SAN MATEO

San Jose

Merced

MADERA

SANTA
CLARA

MERCED

Madera

SANTA CRUZ

Santa Cruz

Hollister

· Fresno

· Independence

Salinas

SAN
BENITO

FRESNO

INYO

Hanford

· Visalia

MONTEREY

TULARE

KINGS

SAN LUIS
OBISPO

· San Luis Obispo

· Bakersfield

KERN

SANTA
BARBARA

SAN BERNARDINO

VENTURA

LOS ANGELES

Santa Barbara

· Ventura

Los Angeles

· San Bernardino

· Riverside

ORANGE

RIVERSIDE

Santa Ana

SAN DIEGO

IMPERIAL

· San Diego

· El Centro

The North Coast

DEL NORTE
HUMBOLDT
LAKE
MENDOCINO

County of Del Norte

The aptly named Del Norte County is the northernmost coastal county in the state. It was created in 1857 from the now-vanished Klamath County, which was disestablished in 1876. Crescent City has been the county seat from the beginning. The town was laid out in 1853 to serve as a port of entry and supply center for the miners who had been drawn by gold found near the Klamath and Trinity Rivers. Logging replaced mining as the principal industry but Crescent City remained the port, the largest town and the county seat.

Judge Cutler holds court, circa 1900.

Preceding page: Humboldt County courthouse dedication, Eureka 1889.

Construction of the first county-owned courthouse was completed in 1884. It was a two-story structure built entirely of wood on a stone and brick foundation, well proportioned, with elegant, restrained Victorian decoration. A wide hallway ran through the building on the first floor and a stairway on either side led upstairs. On the first floor were the board of supervisors chambers, the assessor's office, the sheriff and tax collector, the school superintendent, the county clerk, auditor and recorder, surveyor and coroner's rooms. The second floor housed the judge's chambers, jury room, district attorney, the law library and a spacious courtroom.

The Victorian courthouse served the county for over 60 years and might well be still in use had it not been destroyed by fire in January 1948.

District Attorney John Childs was reflective when interviewed the night of the fire. "It was 56 years ago that I entered the courthouse as County Clerk and have served there in some capacity continuously ever since. Yes, it is a great loss—but we'll have to get started to build again and we can't look back…."

It took a decade to rebuild. In 1958, a new courthouse opened for business. This courthouse served its purpose well for 30 years, until Pelican Bay State Prison was located in Del Norte County. Because of the dramatic increase in population (both prison employees and inmates), a larger and more secure courthouse was needed. The courthouse was substantially enlarged and remodeled in 1990.

The stylish 1884 courthouse. A group of gentlemen regard the photographer from the porch while another gazes at him and leans against the balustrade—a later embellishment.

Top: The town of Crescent City, circa 1920. The prominent two-story white building in the left distance is the courthouse.

Above: The 1884 courthouse ablaze during the January 1948 fire that destroyed it.

Right: The 1958 courthouse prior to its 1990 remodeling to accomodate the opening of Pelican Bay State Prison.

Left: The courthouse as expanded in 1990.

DEL NORTE COUNTY

County of Humboldt

The early residents of the western portion of Trinity County, primarily loggers and fishermen, had little affinity for the miners whose camps were scattered on the eastern, inland slope of the Coast Range. Indeed, they refused to attend court proceedings held in Weaverville, the mining camp that had become the Trinity County seat. By 1853, the coastal towns had prevailed on the legislature to partition Trinity County, with everything west of the Coast Range crest being designated as the new Humboldt County, named for Baron Alexander von Humboldt, a famous German geographer and explorer.

The court spent three years in rented quarters in Uniontown (now Arcata), the first county seat. In 1856, the county seat was moved south to Eureka, which had both access to a port and proximity to the U.S. Army's Fort Humboldt.

In 1860, the board of supervisors purchased a building in Eureka that had previously served as the boarding house for the crew of Hinckle and Co.'s sawmill. The county renovated it for use as county offices, courthouse and jail.

Klamath County was dissolved in 1874 and its southern portion added to Humboldt County. While the old "Hinckle House" had been substantially expanded in 1872, the sudden increase in the county's size and the steady growth of the timber industry led the supervisors to consider a new courthouse. In 1883, they sponsored a design competition and selected the plans submitted by the San Francisco firm of Curtis & Bennett. (A. A. Bennett had by then designed courthouses for at least six other counties and Bennett and Curtis had collaborated on Sonoma County's new courthouse completed a few years earlier.)

The architects' plans envisioned a symmetrical Italianate structure, with two grand entries on opposite sites, each reached by monumental staircases. One departure from the standard Bennett model was the tall, four-sided tower, which rose in a sequence of styles to 176 feet at its pinnacle.

Also unique were the "baker's dozen" of statues of classical figures that adorned the courthouse, 12 placed around the perimeter of the roof and one, Minerva, atop the central tower. All were made of zinc, coated with a heavy gray paint and then sprayed with gray-colored sand to give them the appearance of stone.

The pride of the community in its grand new courthouse is evident in a newspaper account of its dedication in February 1889:

"At last, through the enterprise and liberality of new citizens and the zeal and public spirit of those who have in the past shaped her legislation, the County has one of the finest buildings of its class to be found in the State, fully equipped from basement to cellar with all the latest appliances in the way of office furniture."

Humboldt County's first courthouse, the old Hinckle House, served from 1861 to 1889. Partially destroyed by fire in 1897, it was turned over to the Eureka Fire Department and deliberately burned to the ground in the department's annual Washington's Birthday drill in February 1898.

The April 1906 earthquake that devastated San Francisco shook Eureka so forcefully that, according to a witness, "Minerva on the courthouse was tipped nearly 45 degrees so she looks as if she were just ready for a high dive." Minerva was restored but the other 12 statues were removed because of fear that future earthquakes might topple them to the grounds below.

By 1924, winter storms rolling in from the Pacific had taken their toll; Minerva was deteriorating and cracked. One day her spear broke loose and fell through the roof into the courtroom. Shortly thereafter, in July 1924, she was removed "to be

supplanted by a rude ball ostentatiously besmeared with lowly light bulbs" in the disapproving rhetoric of a contemporary reporter.

The tower survived a fire later that year but was dismantled for safety reasons in 1950. In December 1954, another powerful earthquake jolted the city. Huge cracks appeared in the courthouse's walls and ceilings; the courthouse was soon vacated and then demolished in 1956.

The new courthouse was constructed on the same site: a large (193,000-square-foot) four-story concrete building designed by Mitchell Van Bourg that incorporated the county jail and other county offices. It was dedicated in April 1960 and remains in use, as expanded and remodeled in the 1990s.

A full courtroom on a rainy day in Eureka, circa 1950.

On September 7, 1924, a painter's blowtorch set the courthouse tower afire. The blaze was extinguished and the tower saved.

Fire—
Humboldt Co. Court House
Eureka, Calif. Sept 6th 1924

The 1960 courthouse. The tall flagpole in the foreground is all that remains of the grand 1889 courthouse.

Below: The main entrance of the current courthouse. The mosaic mural is 20 feet wide by 36 feet high, made of multicolored ceramic tiles and depicts the history and industry of Humboldt County.

County of Lake

Lake County was established in 1861 out of territory that had been northern Napa County. Lake County encompasses the watershed of its dominant feature—Clear Lake—the largest natural freshwater lake in California.

The first courthouse was quickly built at Lakeport, a two-story wooden structure, 20 feet by 50 feet, described as "neither pretentious nor showy," but entirely serviceable.

In 1866 residents of the southern part of the county persuaded the legislature to authorize another election to choose the county seat. Lakeport supporters argued, in effect, "We already have a courthouse, why spend the money to built another?" When the courthouse mysteriously burned to the ground in the middle of a cold February night in 1867, Lakeport residents suspected that partisans of its rival, the town of Lower Lake, had been responsible. Whether culpable or not, Lower Lake narrowly won the election later that year. County offices moved to temporary quarters in Lower Lake, but Lakeport refused to concede defeat. It challenged the election, claiming fraud, and prevailed. The judge, however, referred the matter back to the legislature, which set a final, decisive election for 1870.

When Lakeport regained the crown in 1870, the supervisors were ready. They had already had plans drawn for a new courthouse on the same site in Lakeport and advertised for bids. Once the election results were announced, the Supervisors

A view of Lakeport in 1895 shows the town, the lake and Mount Konocti in the distance. The courthouse, seen from the rear, can be identified by the round water tank on its roof.

COURTHOUSES OF CALIFORNIA

The courthouse and hall of records (right) depicted on a postcard, circa 1900. The cannon on the lawn was donated for scrap during World War II.

awarded the contract to A.P. Petit, who had earlier prepared the plans. A contemporary account describes the courthouse as "being of the modern style of architecture; not at all showy, it is plain and tasty… and if a good fence were put around it, the place would compare favorably with any in the state." It was subsequently denominated "Chippendale-Georgian." The basic facts are that it was a two-story structure, 66 by 44 feet, built of bricks from a local kiln, with a gently peaked tin roof. A wrought iron balcony on the second floor, above the main entrance, provided the bailiff with a prominent place from which to announce that court was in session.

The celebrated British actress Lillie Langtry lived briefly on a large ranch in Lake County, staying only long enough to secure a divorce from her unfortunate husband, Edward, in the Lake County courthouse in 1897.

In 1968, the county built a new courthouse in Lakeport and the supervisors considered auctioning off the old courthouse site. Some Lake County residents were determined to save the venerable building. After successfully nominating the courthouse to the National Register of Historic Places, they raised $500,000 to restore the building so that 10 years later (January 1978) it could be rededicated in its new role as the Lake County Museum.

We made a passing visit to the Lake County courthouse at noon [on December 20]. It showed evident signs of there once having been some inhabitants…. But at the time we speak of there was no sign of any person having been there for who knows how long…. Everything around the old shanty reminds one of some old waste barn that has been deserted and given up for the abode of owls and bats.

After making some inquiry of the citizens of the town of Lakeport as to the cause of all this dearth in legal business, I was informed that owing to the good behavior of their citizens and general willingness to pay their just debts, there had not been a lawsuit either civil or criminal during the last twelve months and their County officers have been compelled to revert to other occupations in order to procure a livelihood, as follows: County Judge, clerking in store; Sheriff, dealing in cordwood and swapping horses; District Attorney, hunting quail…

Clear Lake Courier, December 29, 1866

The courthouse, now stucco covered, as it appears in its current role as Lake County Museum.

A new courthouse was built adjacent to the old in 1968. The elongated arches may have been influenced by the design of the Metropolitan Opera at Lincoln Center in New York, which opened in 1966.

County of Mendocino

Above: Workers installing lights to illuminate the courthouse dome for a celebration in 1909.

Mendocino County takes its name from Cape Mendocino, named by 16th-century explorers in honor of Don Antonio de Mendoza, viceroy of New Spain. While one of the original counties, it was so sparsely populated that it was administered by Sonoma County officials until 1859. In that year Ukiah was chosen as the county seat. Within months, the newly elected Board of Supervisors had acquired a square block fronting on State Street and awarded a contract for a courthouse and jail. The building, in the middle of what became Courthouse Plaza, was constructed in four months and accepted in January 1860.

Little more than 10 years later, the board of supervisors awarded a contract for a much larger courthouse. Growth in county business required more space. Frequent escapes by prisoners led the grand jury to complain that "the jail is not a jail at all." And the mysterious fire that destroyed neighboring Lake County's courthouse in 1867 heightened the desire for a fireproof repository for county records.

The "old" courthouse was demolished and replaced by a much larger structure, completed in 1873. Its builder was A. P. Petit, who had designed and built Lake County's new courthouse a few years before. But the new courthouse in Ukiah left

The 1860 courthouse was a plain version of a standard plan courthouse, common in California and elsewhere in the 19th century, characterized by a rectangular form and a hipped roof. Note the pigs in the street, which later was to become U.S. Highway 101.

Above: Workers installing lights to illuminate the courthouse dome for a celebration in 1909.

no doubt as to which county was more prosperous. The courthouse was larger (111 feet by 70 feet), taller (two stories, rising 71 feet to the top of the dome), and more modern—with gas lighting and heat and indoor plumbing.

In 1892 a pair of small classical revival buildings were added to the western side of the plaza, one a jail and the other a hall of records. And in 1928 a graceful French Renaissance annex was built between them, also facing onto School Street.

In 1951 the old courthouse, the jail and hall of records were all demolished, replaced by a three-story steel frame and reinforced concrete structure, 142 feet wide and 115 deep, in the International style. Devoid of ornament, the building is distinguished by a monumental front staircase leading to large plate glass panels in steel framing, which rise two stories over the front entrance.

A Fourth of July parade along State Street in 1903 passes by the courthouse on its way to the cemetery. State Street wasn't paved until 1911.

The front elevation of the 1873 courthouse, flanked by the Hall of Records, left and jail, right, each added in 1892. The ungainly columns and the peculiar windows projecting from the polygonal dome were design features unique to this courthouse.

A view of Courthouse Plaza in Ukiah looking westward, in the 1890s. The buggy parked on State Street (left foreground) belonged to the Redemeyer girls.

The view of Courthouse Plaza from School Street in the 1940s. The jail and hall of records are gone but the 1928 courthouse annex, with its elegant sandstone façade, remains.

The current courthouse circa 1955.

Shasta Cascade

LASSEN
MODOC
SHASTA
SISKIYOU
TRINITY

County *of* Lassen

Lassen County's first courthouse completed in 1867 and, to the right, a partial view of the stone hall of records.

Lassen County was created in 1864 in the aftermath of the "Sagebrush War," during which the Plumas County sheriff led a 90-man posse into what rebellious settlers claimed was a separate county and part of the Nevada Territory. After a daylong siege, in which four men were shot, a truce was declared with both camps agreeing to abide by a survey conducted by the governors of California and the Nevada Territory. The survey confirmed that the rebels were indeed in California, but the state legislature thought it prudent to emancipate them from Plumas County.

The present courthouse, like its predecessor, sits on a block of land donated by Isaac Roop, one of the leaders of the secession movement, after whose daughter the county seat, Susanville, is named. Built in 1917, it is the earliest of six California courthouses designed by George Sellon, a prominent Sacramento architect. The others, all still in use, are Plumas (1920), Tehama (1920), Nevada (1931), Amador (1939), and Sierra (1954). The Lassen County courthouse is a handsome but restrained Classical Revival building, dominated by a tall colonnaded entry pavilion with Doric Order portico, flanked by symmetrical wings. The building is faced in native stone and embellished with architectural terra-cotta.

In a 1915 editorial, the *Lassen Advocate* called upon the "truly loyal and progressive citizen" to vote for bonds to build a courthouse that "presents a substantial and attractive appearance and one that any citizen may well feel proud of." The sturdy stone courthouse in Susanville, now on the National Register of Historic Places, is just such a building.

Preceding page: Modoc County courthouse nears completion, Alturas, 1914.

Left: The courtroom is one of the most richly detailed historic courtrooms in California. Among the notable architectural features visible in this photograph are the pilasters along the wall, decorated cornice, chandelier, and elaborate brackets and frieze above the doorways.

Above: The second courthouse was designed by George Sellon, previously California's state architect, and built in 1917. The building to the left is the jail built in 1911, designed by Frederick DeLongchamps, one of the early buildings in his remarkable career.

WELL SAID, MR. PARDEE:

"Let justice here her court maintain
Each suitor's cause with fairness hear
Here hold her scale in equal poise
Sans prejudice, sans fear"

Inscription displayed in Lassen County courtroom, attributed to Julian E. Pardee, an early and respected member of the Lassen County Bar.

County of Modoc

Prospectors arrived in the far northeastern corner of California in the early 1860s, followed by cattle ranchers and farmers. The early history of the region is marked by recurrent, violent confrontations between the original inhabitants—the Modoc, Paiute and Pit River tribes—and the settlers, eventually aided by the U.S. Army. The Modoc War of 1872–73 was the bloodiest encounter between the army and Modoc warriors, who were determined to resist the tribes' forced relocation to an Oregon reservation shared by their ancient enemies, the Klamath peoples.

With the end of the Indian Wars, the move to secede from Siskiyou County gained force. The impetus was the region's distance from Yreka, the county seat, and the indifference of Siskiyou County supervisors to the concerns of their lightly populated eastern frontier. Legislation was introduced to create the new county, to be called Canby, in honor of General Edward Canby, killed during the Modoc War. Opponents amended the bill to change the name of the new county from Canby to Modoc, thinking that residents of the area would abandon their desire for a separate county if it were to be named for their feared and hated enemies. But the change was accepted and the bill signed into law in 1874. (The county seat has always been Alturas.)

For the first 10 years, court was held in the community hall, which also accommodated church services, dances, and community dinners. The first real courthouse was built in 1883 to 1884. Practicing law in Alturas in the 19th century was not for the timid. For example, after serving as superior court judge, G. F. Harris returned to private practice in 1890. Shortly thereafter Harris became so enraged at opposing counsel in a hotly contested trial, John Raker, that he stabbed him in the chest and neck. Raker survived, and was subsequently elected to the superior court himself.

The county's second courthouse, completed in 1915, was an astonishing accomplishment for a remote community with such a small population (only 6,000 in 1910).

The first courthouse was a plain, two-story frame building, Its only decorative touches were the modest porch with a railed balcony and the small lantern (or tower) on its hipped roof.

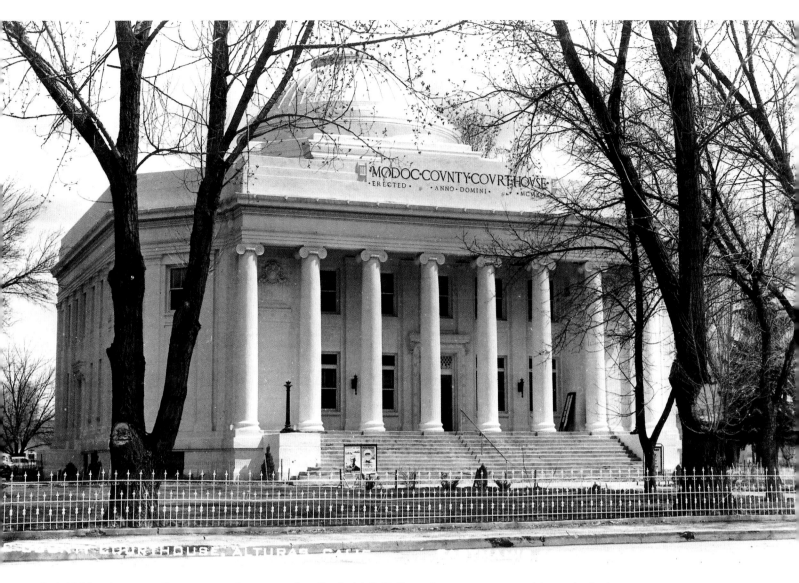

County supervisors turned to Frederick J. DeLongchamps, a young architect who had already designed courthouses for two counties in Nevada and was at work on plans for a third. The recently completed courthouse in Reno, which DeLongchamps had designed for neighboring Washoe County, was just what Modoc County leaders must have had in mind. Like the Reno courthouse, the building DeLongchamps designed for Modoc County is monumental neoclassical architecture with a pronounced Beaux Arts influence. Both buildings have massive copper-clad domes with ribs, and a row of heavy columns that support a two-story portico sheltering a grand entry. The interiors have similarities as well; in each, a central marble stairway ascends to the second floor and multicolored tiles decorate the floors. The goal in both cases was achieved: a decisive break with the 19th century and a public building of the first rank. There are differences as well. The large racks beneath the spectator's seats in the Modoc courtroom are unique. They were designed to accommodate the cowboy hats favored by Modoc County ranchers.

The *Alturas New Era* reported in July 1914 that the courthouse construction "is the center of attraction for sidewalk superintendents. The star of the show is a cement mixer that is run by a gas engine. Nothing like it has ever been seen here before.…"

The marble stairway in the second courthouse lobby is brightened by light that pours through the glass ceiling of the shallow dome.

County of Shasta

As originally laid out by the 1850 legislature, Shasta County stretched from Butte County north to the Oregon border and from the crest of the Coast Range east to what was then the Utah Territory.

The legislature specified that the county seat was to be at "Reading's Ranch." This was Rancho Buenaventura, the home of Major Pierson Reading, one of the first settlers in the area and the recipient of one of the last and the most northerly of the Mexican land grants. The court of sessions dutifully convened at Major Reading's isolated adobe in February 1851, and then immediately adjourned to Shasta, a thriving mining camp that was already functioning as the de facto county seat.

The first county-owned courthouse was this two-story log structure, built in 1854 in Shasta.

The first courthouse was commissioned in 1854 after three years spent in rented quarters. This was a Spartan affair—a 20-foot by 28-foot, two-story log building with a courtroom on the first floor and an office and two iron jail cells on the second.

By 1861, the log courthouse had been outgrown. The county purchased and remodeled an existing brick building that had housed several stores. County officers moved into these more spacious quarters (five offices, in addition to a courtroom and larger jail) in December 1861.

Detailed view of 1854 courthouse and jail.

Shasta's fortunes were tied to mining. Its economic importance as a center for transshipment of goods to the mines waned in the 1860s as mining activity decreased. In the early 1870s, the Central Pacific Railway, then extending its track north, couldn't justify running the line through Shasta. Instead, it chose a more direct and level route through the valley and established its depot and station near a bend in the Sacramento River, which it named "Redding" after B. B. Redding, its land agent who had laid out the town. By the 1880s, Redding had eclipsed Shasta and, while it took two elections and a California Supreme Court decision, the county seat was moved to Redding in 1888.

The new courthouse in Redding, completed the following year, was far larger and more impressive than its utilitarian predecessors in Shasta. It was the first to have been designed by an architect—A. A. Cook of Sacramento whose plan called for a brick, three-story Victorian complete with clock tower and dome crowned with a statute of Justice, set on a hill overlooking landscaped grounds. An adjacent hall of records was built in 1910.

When the first Redding courthouse was built, there was only one superior court judge in Shasta County. So the courthouse had only one courtroom, though it was large and ornate. By 1951, a second superior court department was created. The new judge, Hon. Richard B. Eaton, had to improvise for courtroom space. His court reporter, Albert Peterson, recalls that when both the large courtroom and the chambers of the board of supervisors were in use, Judge Eaton would hold court in the jury room on the third floor. The room was "cold in winter and hot in summer." And Mr. Peterson recalls, the pigeons would come in through open (or broken) windows during the proceedings and "coo at each other in the back of the room."

A new courthouse was built in 1956 in the International style. The old courthouse continued in use until 1963, when it was demolished to make way for an annex to the 1956 courthouse. Additional criminal courtrooms were added with the construction in 1984 of an adjacent justice center/jail complex.

In 1861, the county purchased a brick building constructed in 1855 by James Loag. The courthouse is the one-story building whose porch is sheltered by a roof supported by six wooden posts. To the left is the two-story Empire Hotel.

The restored courthouse is now a part of the museum at the Shasta State Historical Monument. Much of the original courtroom furniture has been returned and is on display.

After the county seat moved to Redding in 1888, the Shasta courthouse continued to serve as a jail and later for occasional dances and community events. By 1922, it was in ruins—only a shell of brick walls and rusted iron jail cells remained. The building and site were purchased in that year by the McCloud Parlor of the Native Sons of the Golden West in the hopes of somehow preserving it.

The statue of Justice, once perched atop the 19th-century courthouse, now stands at ground level. Her sword is missing, having been taken by vandals. Plans call for the statue to be restored and relocated within the courthouse.

Below: The Victorian courthouse built in Redding in 1888 and, to the left, the 1909 hall of records.

Above: The courthouse dome, a landmark for 75 years, is unceremoniously demolished in 1963.

The Shasta County courthouse constructed in 1956.

County of Siskiyou

Within a few weeks after Abraham Thompson's discovery of gold at Yreka Flat in March 1851, over 2,000 miners had arrived, their tents and makeshift cabins stretching for miles along Yreka Creek. The following year the legislature created Siskiyou County; Yreka has been the county seat from the earliest days.

As was typical for most counties established in the 1850s, Siskiyou's county offices and courtroom were initially lodged in rented quarters in the commercial center of Yreka. By 1856, the county had put aside sufficient funds for the board of supervisors to have a two-story brick courthouse built in the center of Yreka's only public square. While frequently remodeled and greatly expanded over the following years, the courthouse remains in the same square—though little of the square itself remains.

The *Yreka Journal* applauded the supervisors' decision in 1883 to build new outhouses, replacing "the old dilapidated shanties now disfiguring the… courthouse park." Improvements undertaken a few years later (in 1885) drew a more mixed response: "The old courthouse, with a new iron roof and cornice, looks like a man in seedy clothes with a new stovepipe hat—hence neat porticos and cornices for doors and windows are now needed to make everything correspond."

The unifying ornamentation was incorporated into a large-scale expansion undertaken in 1896 and 1897 when wings were added to the north and south sides of the original courthouse, a cupola provided and electric wiring installed.

The arrival of electricity was welcomed by the *Journal* for its contribution to both beauty and utility. "When the electric lights in all the offices and dome are burning at

The first courthouse was a two-story brick building completed in 1857 and placed in the center of Yreka's public square.

In 1896 and 1897, two wings, a tower and a cupola were added, along with Italianate embellishments such as the cornice, balustrade and pedimented windows.

night the extensive building looks like a state capitol illuminated." The newspaper observed that the new electric bells and gongs "make the court work expeditious and a great savings of expense… the old style of yelling 'Court' from the courthouse door or window and hunting down the lawyers and witnesses is done away with by ringing the gong, which gives notice that the next witness is needed…."

In 1954, a massive concrete wing replaced the front lawn, obscured the front façade of the old courthouse and swallowed up the hall of records. But the older buildings were not demolished and the courtroom built in 1856 remains in existence and in use.

On August 25, 1895, four men awaiting trial on charges of murder were dragged from the county jail and lynched in front of the courthouse. According to the account in the extra edition of the *Siskiyou Daily News* printed the next day, "The men were taken to the corner of the Court House Yard nearest the jail where a steel rail from the railroad track had been placed between locust trees about ten feet from the ground and quickly and quietly swung into eternity." The youngest, Garland Stemler, was only 19 years old.

Above Left: The main courtroom (still in use today) seen here in 1903, Judge John Samuel Beard seated at the bench.

Above Right: Grace Johnson, seated at her desk in the county clerk's office. The photograph was taken in 1903.

Right: The hall of records added in 1910 featured a classic temple portico.

THE COURTHOUSE ELK

In April 1876 an elk was brought to Yreka to be sold to the town butcher. Instead, the elk became a celebrity—being "interviewed by nearly all the little (and old) folks in the city" as the *Yreka Union* reported. Kindhearted citizens took up a collection and purchased the elk, which was then pastured in the courthouse square. The next month the cynical editor of the competing paper, the *Yreka Journal*, opined, "The elk at the courthouse yard has made a well-worn trail around the Court House Park, along the line of the fence, and travels a good many miles every day in making the circuit. We think the damage to the clover is greater than would be the loss of the elk."

In early July the tame elk wandered out of the courthouse square and headed for home. It was retrieved, however, and the hard-hearted *Journal* editor was pleased to relate, "We hear it is to be used for the barbecue so that all who want roast elk as well as beef, mutton, etc., can be accommodated." The elk's fate was, indeed, to be barbecued at the picnic held on July 4, 1876, as part of the Centennial celebrations.

In 1954, a monolithic concrete wing swallowed up the front façade of the old courthouse, the 1910 hall of justice and most of the remaining lawn.

A statue of the late state senator and one-time judge Randolph Collier (the "Silver Fox of the Siskiyous") seated in front of the courthouse.

This sign in the courthouse parking lot mysteriously appeared in 1996, as a "gift" to then Presiding Judge Robert F. Kaster.

County of Trinity

May Day celebration (1911) in front of the Weaverville courthouse. The Union Hotel, to the right, burned in 1939 and the site was acquired by the county as a parking lot for the courthouse.

Trinity County was one of the original 27 counties. The county seat has always been Weaverville, named for a Mr. Weaver, a prospector who found gold in the area in 1849. Weaverville has been the commercial as well as political center of the county. The first courthouse was built in 1852 to 1853 by J. F. Chellis, who later become lieutenant governor. The wooden, 20-by-60 foot, three-story structure, built on a ridge overlooking the town was not widely admired. The 1860 grand jury reported, "We have examined the public buildings and find them in deplorable condition." Their report disclosed that "bedbugs had invaded the office of the Sheriff and County Clerk, had defiled the records, and in several instances had even attacked the Judge on the bench." When fire destroyed the building in September 1866, the *Trinity Journal* observed, "That model of architecture, the Old Courthouse, is in ruins. Were it not for the adjacent property destroyed and the loss to the Masonic Fraternity [which had purchased the top floor from the county] the void which exists on Court House Hill would not be considered generally an aching one" (*Trinity Journal*, Sept. 15, 1866). By then the county board of supervisors had acted on the grand jury's recommendation. In 1865, they purchased a three-story building from Henry Hocker who had constructed it in 1856. It was one of many brick buildings constructed in Weaverville in the mid- to late 1850s after a series of disastrous fires had destroyed the wooden buildings that had preceded them. The Hocker Building was made of locally fashioned bricks, its flat roof of tin sheets seamed and soldered together. Iron shutters flanked the French doors and windows giving protection against fire. Additions to the back of the building have not altered its overall appearance. It is one of approximately 25 buildings in downtown Weaverville that were included in the National Register of Historic Places in 1970 as a historic district.

The brick building, which has served as the courthouse since 1865, was originally built in 1856 for use as offices, a store and the Apollo Saloon. Seen here in 1912 are District Attorney Horace Given (fourth from left) and Judge James Bartlett (sixth from the left).

Above: The courtroom and law library after the installation of electric lighting circa 1894. According to county historian Patricia Hicks, the man in the photograph is most likely Superior Court Judge Theodore E. Jones.

Left: The courthouse in 1998. The iron balcony, first added in 1873, has been replaced by more substantial ironwork and the cornice, pediments and other decorative features have been given emphasis through contrasting paint. But the building retains the original evenly placed upper and lower sets of French doors with iron shutters.

The Sierra Nevada

AMADOR   MARIPOSA   PLUMAS
CALAVERAS NEVADA   SIERRA
EL DORADO PLACER   TUOLUMNE

County of Amador

Jackson Cal.

ll feeling between the northern and southern portions of Calaveras County promoted frequent appeals to the Legislature to change the county seat or divide the county in two. Wearying of the matter, the legislature put the issue to the county voters in June 1854. The upshot was the division of the county, with the territory north of the Mokelumne River becoming Amador County. The new county was named for Jose Maria Amador, an early miner in the region and a prominent Californian.

The first courthouse was a two-story wooden building constructed on a hilltop site. Completed in early 1855, the newly opened courthouse was the scene of a Masonic ball described by the *Sacramento Union* as "the most brilliant party ever gotten up in the mountains." The courthouse was destroyed, along with most of the rest of the town, in the Great Fire of August 1862.

By December 1863, a new courthouse, built of stone and brick, had been completed on the same site as the previous one, now known as "courthouse hill." Within a week of moving into the building, county officers discovered one design oversight, which they quickly remedied by awarding a contract for construction of a "privy."

In 1893, the county constructed a hall of records, similar in size and design to the 1863 courthouse and separated from it by a space about 20 wide feet. A few years later, a second-story bridge had been erected to connect the two buildings. By the early 1920s a plain, tall, thin structure was built, filling in the gap and linking the two older buildings.

In 1939, the county hired George Sellon, a prolific designer of courthouses, as architect for an ambitious remodeling of the tripartite courthouse/hall of records complex. The distinctive tan and green WPA Moderne courthouse Sellon designed presents a coherent and unified façade. As Amador County Archivist Larry Cenotto put it, "What builders had made single, remodelers wed."

Preceding page:
Placer County courthouse,
Auburn, 1955.

The first courthouse, completed in January 1855, was described in the *Sacramento Union* as a "large and commodious courthouse containing rooms for all county officers." It was destroyed by the Great Fire of 1862, which swept through the town, consuming most buildings.

The Hanging Tree of Jackson where 10 men were executed between 1851 and 1855, following trials of varying degrees of legitimacy. The tree was damaged in the fire of 1862 and cut down shortly thereafter. The men hanged were one Native American, one Swede, two Chileans, and six Mexicans.

A new courthouse was built of brick and stone, immediately after the 1862 fire. The ground floor walls, enclosing the jail, were two feet thick.

The "original armchair detectives" sun themselves in front of the courthouse well, circa 1895.
(From left to right, Pat Dwyer, A. Caminetti, August Laverone, Virgilio Podesto.)

The 1863 courthouse, the 1893 hall of justice and the 1920s linking annex, circa 1930. The iron structure in front is the courthouse well, dating from the 1850s. It was removed in 1940 as part of the major courthouse remodeling. The site is marked with a plaque that recounts the well's history and concludes "Gone is the Ancient Equipment But Still the Living Waters Flow."

The courthouse after its extensive remodeling in 1940. The WPA Moderne style, then in vogue, was a dramatic departure from the traditional architecture of "Gold Country" courthouses. The architect was the prolific George Sellon, who designed six courthouses between 1917 and 1954, all of which are still in use.

County of Calaveras

Rivalry among California towns contending for the honor of being the county seat (with the attendant increase in property values) was widespread during the 1850s. Calaveras was not unique in this regard, but the consequences of the struggle were more profound—the death of the county clerk at the hands of the county judge and the division of the county.

Calaveras' first operating county seat was tiny Double Springs, whose single building served as store, saloon and courthouse. It was clear that with the election of 1851

In 1850, Sam Brannan imported prefabricated camphor wood houses from China, one of which was assembled in Double Springs as Calaveras County's first courthouse. It still stands, much renovated, and in private ownership.

the crown would pass to another town, but which of the two contenders (Mokelumne Hill or Jackson) would prevail was uncertain. The election was contentious, the outcome disputed. Colonel Lewis Collier, the county clerk, declared Mokelumne Hill the victor. But County Judge Fowle Smith ordered a recount, at which Jackson prevailed. Colonel Collier was incensed and announced that he was prepared to shoot the judge on site. Alerted to these threats, Judge Smith armed himself and, encountering Colonel Collier in the street, shot and killed him. A coroner's inquest ruled the judge acted in self-defense and he escaped a trial. But public opinion forced him to resign.

Mokelumne Hill persisted in its efforts and, after an election held the following year (1852), claimed the title of county seat. Its victory led to the movement to divide the county, which culminated in creation of Amador County.

For the first three years at Mokelumne Hill, court was held at one end of a "large public drinking and gambling saloon." In 1855, the board of supervisors ordered the construction of the first courthouse owned by the county.

By 1863, San Andreas had surpassed Mokelumne Hill in population and challenged it for the county seat. Despite San Andreas's narrow victory at the election of 1863, county officials refused to concede defeat, or move, until the state supreme court upheld the trial court's writ of mandamus in 1866. While citizens of Mokelumne Hill were distressed at the loss of the courthouse and county offices, they did not regret the departure of the inmates of the county jail. When prisoners were moved to San Andreas, the local newspaper observed, "They were neither profitable, ornamental, nor useful." (*Calaveras Chronicle*, March 14, 1864.)

After the county seat moved to Mokelumne Hill, a courthouse was built, which was subsequently incorporated into the Leger Hotel, seen here circa 1930.

The board of supervisors approved the designs of
D. L. Morrill for a two-story brick courthouse in San
Andreas approximately 50-by-66 feet with an attached
jail, which was built in 1867. This courthouse served until
courts moved to the new county government center in 1966.
The most famous trial in the courthouse's 99-year history was
that of the notorious highwayman Black Bart, whose real name was
Charles Bolton. During the 1870s and early 1880s this legendary figure robbed 28
stagecoaches, without having to fire a shot, occasionally leaving poems behind to
mock the authorities. His 28th holdup, near Copperopolis in Calaveras County, was
to be his last. Tracked down by County Sheriff Ben Thorn and Wells Fargo agents,
arrested in San Francisco and returned to San Andreas for trial, Black Bart was convicted and sentenced by Judge C. V. Gottschalk to six years in San Quentin.

By 1893, the county had grown to the point that the old courthouse could no
longer store the volume of documents the county had amassed nor house all the
county officials. A Richardsonian Romanesque hall of records designed by William
Mooser of San Francisco was constructed of brick and stone from the local quarry.

Through the years the courthouse, as well as the adjacent hall of records, have
undergone various restorations, the latest
being in 1976. Today all is very much as it
was in the early 1900s when the complex
was first combined. Much of the original
furnishings have been restored to the courthouse and placed in their original settings.

While no longer used on a daily basis as
a courtroom, the old building and the hall
of records are frequently used by various
county officials in need of more room, for
various civic functions, weddings, motion
picture and TV settings, tourist groups, etc.

BLACK BART "THE PO8"

After robbing a stage near the Russian
River, in Sonoma County in 1877, Black
Bart left behind a note with the following
lines:

"I've labored long for bread
For honor and for riches
But on my corns too long you've tread
You fine haired sons of bitches"
The note was signed "Black Bart, the Po8."

Both buildings are now part of the Calaveras County Museum, which houses an outstanding display of goldrush artifacts and Indian baskets. A large number of museum
tours take place each year for school children, senior citizens and other groups.

The architect of the Richardsonian Romanesque hall of records built in 1893, was the second of three architects named William Mooser. He subsequently designed Tuolumne County's courthouse and participated in the design of Santa Barbara's famous 1929 Spanish Revival courthouse.

The two-story brick courthouse built in San Andreas in 1867 still stands, now serving as part of the county museum.

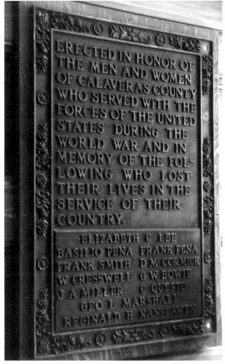

Above: Finely wrought bronze tablet, typical of those found at many county courthouses, honors Calaveras County's veterans of World War I.

Left: The five bays of the Calaveras County courthouse.

Courthouse complex built in 1966 continues the county's tradition of simply designed public buildings, in a mid-20th-century architectural idiom.

County of El Dorado

This is where it all began—ground zero of the gold rush. In January 1848, James Marshall noticed shining particles in the waters of the south fork of the American River, where he was constructing a mill for John Sutter. They were tested and proved to be gold. The event changed the course of history on the Pacific Coast.

Charles Preuss, the cartographer for Captain John Fremont, was in Washington, D.C., just finishing his map of Fremont's second expedition through California when news arrived of Marshall's discovery. Preuss placed the legend "El Dorado or the Gold Region" near the discovery site and the legislature applied the name (connoting "the Gilded One" in Spanish) to the county in 1850.

By 1849, there were 5,000 men camped near Sutter's Mill. It was natural that Coloma, the town that emerged, should be selected as the first county seat.

For the first six years, the courthouse and county offices were located in rented quarters in Coloma. In 1856, the county constructed a two-story, 80-by-45 foot wooden building to house the court and county offices with an adjacent jail, soon enlarged and fortified. The very next year, however, county residents persuaded the legislature to move the county seat to Placerville, a thriving and more centrally located mining town.

The courthouse erected in Placerville was a typical Western vernacular structure, with a wide roofed porch on the second floor and a jail in the basement. It was badly damaged by a fire in 1910 and subsequently demolished.

The county rebuilt on the same site, but on a much grander scale and with more durable materials—steel and concrete. The neoclassical courthouse was completed in 1912. When structural weaknesses were discovered in the 1960s, the board of supervisors determined to restore, rather than demolish, the building. The rehabilitation work was completed and the courthouse rededicated in 1971.

The roofed porch on the second floor had been removed by the time this photograph was taken, circa 1900.

The ruins of the courthouse just after fire swept through it in May 1910. Firefighters kept the safe on the second floor cool by drenching it with water throughout the night. Records in the safe were saved.

Veterans of the Grand Army of the Republic (the Union Army in the Civil War) stand at attention on the courthouse steps joined by local boys and young women, as well as by a black cat with a distinctly military bearing.

The county built a monumental courthouse on the site of the old. Completed in 1912, it was restored and rededicated in 1971.

At the March 5, 1971, dedication ceremony, Court of Appeal Associate Justice Bertram Janes delivered the principal address. Justice Janes's remarks give the flavor of the tumultuous political climate of the early 1970s, as well as the aspirations for civil order implicit in the courthouse as a government building:

This is not only a temple of justice, but a house of government. Judges and lawyers have arranged this occasion, but the courthouse belongs not to them but to all the people, especially those whose tax monies and planning efforts have made its restoration possible. Court and local government decisions affect the taxes we pay, the jobs we hold, the rearing of our children, and after we are dead, their education and distribution of our property. Today when daily courts and lawyers are attacked, law and government defied, expressions of hatred lead to riots and the execution of civil rights gives way to civil wrongs, there is a need for mutual confidence and understanding between the government and the people; this building offers a common ground and meeting place for establishing that bond.

Civil War cannon guards the main entrance to the courthouse.

County of Mariposa

The white clapboard courthouse in Mariposa, built in 1854, is the oldest courthouse in California. It might also be the oldest courthouse in continuous use west of the Mississippi. Without doubt it is the most famous, and most beloved, building in the county.

In 1854, the court of sessions approved plans for a courthouse drawn up by Perrin Fox. Those plans reflected Fox's New England roots: a simple two-story Greek Revival building, with a plain pedimented gable and undecorated frieze. The contract for construction was awarded to Fox and his partner A. F. Shriver.

In 1909, the corner pilasters and front door trim were painted to resemble granite blocks and the tower trimmed in a darker color. The innovation was not popular and a few years later the courthouse was once again all white.

Fox and Shriver used local materials: slate rock for the foundation and lumber from nearby pine forests. The framework has mortised joints secured with wooden pegs. Square handmade iron nails were used to fasten the floor, wall and ceiling boards to the supporting frame. The editor of the *Mariposa Gazette*, writing in 1935 upon the completion of the last major structural changes to the building, praised the craftsmanship of the early builders who "did honest work and used honest materials…. The old courthouse certainly is a monument to the faithfulness, integrity and honor of those pioneers who 'Builded Well'."

The advance of technology can be tracked at the courthouse: a telephone was installed in 1895; gas lights in 1899; electric lights in 1907. Piped water arrived in 1925. The wood-burning pot-bellied stove that heated the courtroom

OSA — THE PRESENT COUNTY SEAT IN 1854
MARIPOSA GRANT

was replaced by an oil stove in the 1930s and then by radiators in 1950. Fire sprinklers were installed in 1974.

There have been a number of relatively small additions to the courthouse. A brick vault, with three-foot-thick walls, was added to the north side of the building in 1861 to store county records and expanded 30 years later. The clock tower (with its bell and clock imported from Sheffield, England) was constructed in 1866. A freestanding annex was constructed to the rear in 1900; a second story was added and the breezeway between the annex and the main building enclosed in 1935.

The first major structural repairs were carried out with county funds in the 1970s. More substantial renovations (strengthening of roof, walls and foundation; updated electrical wiring; etc.) were undertaken in the 1980s, utilizing state bond funds. Great care was taken to see that original materials were replaced intact.

This Carleton Watkins photograph taken in 1854 shows the newly built courthouse on a hillside slightly outside of "downtown" Mariposa.

Above: The courthouse in winter sometime between 1926 (when the metal fence was installed) and 1935 (when a second floor was added to the annex to the rear of the courthouse and the breezeway enclosed). To the left is the brick vault in which county records were stored.

Volunteers restoring wooden window shutters on a sunny weekend in May 1973.

Left: The venerable courthouse (the oldest in California) as is appears today, after extensive, sensitively executed restoration work carried out in the late 1980s. Sacramento architect Robert McCabe, who supervised the restoration work, spoke admiringly of the courthouse: "Our forefathers put that one together very well. It survived the fires and ravages of time and it's in remarkably good shape."

Below: The courtroom in 1933, during the long period (1903–38) in which Superior Court Judge Joseph J. Trabucco presided. The judge's bench is nine feet long to accommodate the three judges of the "court of sessions" who performed legislative, as well as judicial, functions from 1851 to 1855.

County of Nevada

Nevada City, the picturesque county seat of Nevada County, has as legitimate a claim to the phoenix as a symbol as does San Francisco. A late 19th-century history of the county makes the case with characteristically florid prose: "Twice have the destroying fingers of flame seized upon the building [i.e., the courthouse] and in a few moments demolished the work of months. Yet justice must have a temple and criminals must have a secure abiding place and each time that the edifice has met with disaster a better structure has reared itself upon the ruins."

That confident judgment might not have extended to the 1900 remodeling, which added a third floor and removed the graceful columns. It almost certainly would not have withstood the more drastic modernization carried out in 1936 to 1937. The streamlined façade certainly offers a "strong visual contrast to the otherwise Victorian town" as one architectural historian rather neutrally observes. A local resident was less restrained: "That architecture everywhere was at its all-time nadir in the 1930s is evident in the existing Nevada County courthouse. With federal and county funds the lovely traditional building was transformed into a stucco monster with stark, modernistic lines, wildly at odds with the old buildings clustered around it."

From today's perspective, we are more likely to appreciate the stylishness of George Sellon's mid-1930s design while disdaining the glass curtain wall and concrete annex of the mid-1960s.

Nevada County's first "permanent" courthouse, the two-story brick and stone building, was completed in September 1855 and destroyed by fire in July 1856.

Above: The county recon-
structed the courthouse on
the same site by early
1857. This building too was
destroyed in the fire of
November 1863 that swept
through Nevada City. This
time, however, the county's
records, stored in substantial vaults, survived.

Left: The courthouse, once
again rebuilt from 1866 to
1867 on the same site. A
19th-century history of
Nevada County pronounced
it "a great improvement
upon the others in every
respect."

Top Left: In 1868, one year after its completion. Blaze's was a saloon popular with lawyers who would stroll down from the courthouse to celebrate, or seek consolation, from proprietor John Bazley. It also served as a temporary courthouse after the fire of 1863.

Bottom Left: An early-20th-century view, after the remodeling in 1900 had added a floor and enclosed the portico. A planned clock tower never materialized.

**FOUR VIEWS OF THE
NEVADA COUNTY COURTHOUSE**

Top Right: Later in the 19th century, Blaze's is gone and the courthouse is now enclosed by a stone wall and iron fence.

Bottom Right: In the 1960s. The courthouse after its drastic remodeling in the mid-1930s.

Two views of the 1932 WPA Moderne courthouse. The old courthouse once accommodated the board of supervisors and county offices as well as the courts. Now, it and the 1960s annex (seen below) combined are insufficient. The two buildings house courtrooms, judges' chambers and support facilities such as the law library. All other county offices have moved to a new government center just outside the city limits.

County of Placer

uburn, the site of Placer County's courthouse since the county's formation in 1851, is among the oldest of California towns. Gold was discovered in the region in 1848 and by the following year, a mining camp had sprung up. Apparently many of these early miners had come to California in 1846 (to fight in the war against Mexico) with Stevenson's volunteer regiment from Auburn, New York, and named the new town after their old home.

The first courthouse, a crude wood frame and canvas affair, was built in 1851 on a knoll overlooking the town that had been the site of bull and bear fights staged by the miners. The *Placer Herald* applauded the county's decision the following year to replace this "crazy wood and cloth tenement," observing that not only was it too small, a fire would quickly consume it and the "valuable records of the county," by which the editor meant "land titles, miner's titles, etc."

The second courthouse was completed in 1853. A modest but much more substantial wooden building, 60-by-40 feet and two stories, it provided space for county offices, the grand jury and a huge safe in which to deposit the "books and moneys of the county," in addition to a courtroom and jury deliberation room. The adjacent log jail burned in 1857 and was replaced by a two-story brick structure. The second jail and courthouse were considered satisfactory for a generation.

By the early 1890s, however, the county was ready to replace both. The board of supervisors hired prominent San Francisco architect John Curtis, whose firm had designed many government buildings, including courthouses for Humboldt and Sonoma counties. Curtis proposed a far larger (nearly 100,000 square feet, compared to about 5,000) and much grander courthouse, three stories in height, with a tall Renaissance dome. The main (second) floor was reached by monumental staircases on both the north and south faces.

All of the lumber and most of the other materials used were obtained from Placer County: granite for the stairways and first floor exterior (housing the jail) were quarried in Rocklin; the marble came from Colfax; the bricks and terra-cotta ornamentation, as well as the statues, from the famous Gladding, McBean firm in Lincoln. The slate for the roof came from nearby El Dorado County. Only the iron and steel was imported from the East Coast. (The bell, salvaged from the old courthouse, was also exotic, having been cast in Sheffield, England, in 1859.)

The courthouse completed in 1898 served the needs of the county until the 1960s,

The county's second jail and second courthouse stood together, their second stories connected by an iron bridge, for 40 years.

Old Jail 1857. Old County Court House. 1854. Auburn, Calif. #30

COURTHOUSES OF CALIFORNIA

when a gradual shift of offices from the courthouse to a new county administration center and other locations began. By 1980, the historic courthouse had become a shell, unused for county business. It faced an uncertain future. A committee of citizens to "Preserve the Courthouse for the Courts" formed, raised funds and mobilized public opinion against abandoning or demolishing the courthouse. Lardner & Lardner, a local architectural firm, oversaw an ambitious, decade-long restoration project financed with over $3 million in funds from Placer County, the citizens' committee and state and federal grants channeled through the State Office of Historic Preservation. The goal—"to provide modern government facilities for the courts and court-related functions within the framework of the 'Grand Old Courthouse' motif"—was achieved and the restored courthouse rededicated on July 4, 1990.

The courthouse with another local landmark in the foreground—a 15-foot-tall water fountain donated to the City of Auburn in 1908 by Jacob Hart Neff, a wealthy miner prominent in county and state politics.

View of the 1857 jail (left), 1853 courthouse (right) and new courthouse (in background) nearing completion. The old jail and courthouse were demolished once the new courthouse was occupied in 1898.

A view of Auburn in the early 1900s shows the courthouse dominating the skyline, as it still does.

County of Plumas

Plumas County takes its name from the river that runs through it, "Rio de las Plumas"—known in English as the Feather River. The county was formed in 1854 out of the eastern portion of Butte County. H. J. Bradley, a rancher who had lobbied the legislature to create the new county, now offered the county the use, free of charge, of a "rude shake building" in the back of his American Ranch Hotel in Quincy, a town he had laid out and named for his hometown in Illinois. This humble structure served for five years as the county's first courthouse.

When the first election, in November 1854, drew near, Elizabethtown emerged as a rival for the county seat. As an inducement to keep the county seat in Quincy permanently, Bradley and two other public-spirited citizens donated land for a public square and a more substantial courthouse. Quincy won the crown, and over the next two years funds to build the courthouse were raised by subscriptions (or pledges). The new courthouse, an elegantly simple, wooden Greek Revival building, was completed in 1859. The day after the county took possession (May 2, 1859), the board of supervisors passed the following resolution: "Ordered that on payment of the sum of one hundred and fifty dollars subscribed by the County Judge to the courthouse fund he be permitted to occupy the northeast room in the second story of the courthouse for chambers until the expiration of his present term of office." *A History of Plumas County* reports that the judge, E. T. Hogan, "enjoyed the thorough businesslike manner in which the Board was collecting its subscriptions and with a pleasant smile came up; paid his subscription and took possession of his office, which he occupied for many years."

Sixty years later, the county had outgrown the modestly sized white wooden courthouse. The board of supervisors embarked on a tour of courthouses in neighboring counties and selected George Sellon, whose Sacramento firm had designed a new courthouse in nearby Susanville. Sellon's plan for Plumas called for a four-story reinforced concrete building finished in stucco. Much larger than its predecessor, the new courthouse consolidated all county offices, the library, the museum, the jail and the courts in one building. The interior was richly appointed. Blue and gray marble from quarries in Tuolumne County was used for stairways and floors in public areas, accented with pink Tennessee marble. Oak was used for wainscotting, doors and windows throughout. The building also incorporated the most modern engineering: steam radiators, a powerful ventilation system, elevators, fireproof vaults and an internal telephone system.

As the dedication ceremonies drew near, the September 1, 1921, *Plumas National Bulletin* reported mounting enthusiasm and diligent preparations. The paper revealed that "Fred Morrison, commander of the Plumas [American] Legion Post and a former army captain has been reduced in rank for the occasion and will act as mess sergeant. Three tables, each 100 feet long, are to be installed in the courthouse and the guests are to be served 'a la chow line'."

The 1859 courthouse would have looked at home as the town hall of a New England village from which many of the gold rush era Californians had migrated. A birdhouse, a miniature version of the courthouse itself, sits below the semicircular window in the gable.

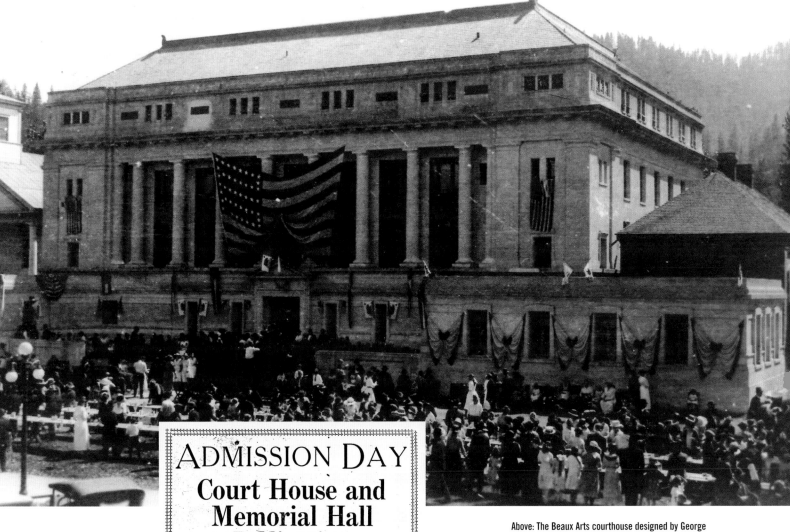

ADMISSION DAY

Court House and Memorial Hall Dedication

Quincy, Cal., September 9th

Under auspices of
PLUMAS POST. No. 252 AMERICAN LEGION
QUINCY PARLOR, No. 131, N. S. G. W.
PLUMAS PIONEER PARLOR, No. 219, N.D.G.W.

W
E
L
C
O
M
E

PROGRAMME

10:30 A. M.

Place—Court House, Quincy, Cal.

Music by Kerak Shrine Band of Reno

Opening Address, A. W. Keddie.....
.... President of the Day

Invocation ..... Rev. C. H. Stephens

Song "Let the Hills and Vales Resound" .... Choir

Dedication Address ....
.... Hon. J. O. Moncur

Song "Our Soldiers Welcome Home," .... Choir

Reading .... Mrs. Phil Blume

Music .... Band

Memorial Hall Address ....
.... Senator W. W. Kellogg

Song "Red, White and Blue," ..Choir

Admission Day Address and introducing Governor William D. Stephens, of California .... M. C. Kerr

Address by His Excellency, the Governor of California,.............
.... William D. Stephens

Chorus "America" ....:... Choir

Barbecue 1 P. M.,

Baseball game, 2:30 P-M., Professionals vs. Old Timers.

Dance, 9 P. M., Music by Hatch's Orchestra of Oroville.

The barbecue will be free, but admission will be charged at the ball game and the grand ball in the evening

Free Barbecue,

2 beeves, 2 porkers and several mutton, to be cooked by Manager Grosse of the Riverside Hotel, Reno, Nev. We expect to serve 1500 people and visitors. Come and help us eat it.

Band Concert

Music will fill the air on this Memorable event. Kerak Temple Shrine Band will be here from Reno, with a large following. Come and hear them.

Ball Game

Professional men vs. the Business men of Quincy. This will produce the merriment of the day. At High School diamond.

Grand Ball

Music for this big event will be furnished by Hatch's Oroville Jazz Orchestra. Good Time, Fine Floor. Pretty Girls.

Good Singers and Talkers Everybody Come!

Above: The Beaux Arts courthouse designed by George Sellon decorated for its dedication on September 9, 1921. The old 1854 courthouse can be seen to the left and the 1895 hall of records to the right of the new courthouse. Both were demolished once the new courthouse was occupied.

A poster announces the program for the dedication of the new courthouse held on Admission Day 1921. Admission Day marked the anniversary of California's admission to the United States on September 9, 1850.

BIRDS EYE VIEW   QUINCY, CALI

Above: A "bird's-eye view"
of Quincy shows how the
1921 classical courthouse
dominates the town and is in
turn overshadowed by a
wooded slope of the Sierra
Nevada.

Above: The second courthouse after a Sierra snowstorm. Directly behind the courthouse is the peaked roof jail built in 1863. Note the figure on the roof of the courthouse surveying the scene.

Left: The grand scale of the monumental 1921 courthouse is evident in this 1930s winter scene.

County of Sierra

Sierra County was created from the eastern part of Yuba County in 1852. Its population (3,500 as of 2000) makes it the second smallest county in the state.

The county seat, Downieville, is named for William Downie, a Scotsman, who arrived in November 1849, leading a diverse band: 10 black sailors, a Native American, an Irish boy and a native Hawaiian.

The court of sessions met above the famous Craycroft Saloon until a courthouse was completed on Durgan Flat, across the river from the business district in December 1854. The iron doors and grating for the jail were hauled to the town by ox team.

Left: The courthouse, built in 1854, seen here in early spring 1934. The classic white-painted Greek Revival courthouse originally had four columns and an open porch. The porch was enclosed for additional office space sometime after 1900.

Below: A panoramic view of Downieville, circa 1860 to 1870. The courthouse is to the right of the photograph, south of the bridge spanning the North Yuba River.

Above: By the 1920s, when this photograph was taken, the hills surrounding Downieville, stripped bare of trees in the 1850s to build the town, the mines and flumes, were again covered by pines. The courthouse is the building to the right, with the rectangular tower. The small wing was the sheriff's residence.

Left: The current courthouse, built in 1954. The clock over the entryway has not worked for at least 25 years, according to an informed source.

The editor of the *Sierra Citizen*, writing in May 1854, opined: "It is the intention of the contractor to complete the jail entirely and then afterwards proceed with the courthouse and county offices. This we conceive to be the wiser plan as the officers are now put to great inconvenience in guarding prisoners in the rickety log cabin where they are at present confined." The courthouse building housed the jail, with the sheriff's wife preparing food for the jail inmates.

The courthouse burned in 1947 and was replaced on the same site in 1954 by a reinforced concrete building designed by George Sellon. While distinctly modern, the building's gabled front and pitched roof recall the basic form of its classic predecessor. A wooden gallows, built in 1885, survived the fire and remains standing next to the modern courthouse.

County of Tuolumne

Attorneys, county officials and Superior Court Judge George Nicol (on bench, in rear) gather in the courtroom of the old courthouse the day before it was razed in June 1898. The round photograph on the easel to the right depicts Edwin "Ned" Rodgers, a leader of the local bar (he had practiced law in Sonora for nearly 50 years) who had died shortly before the gathering.

old was discovered in August 1848 in what was to become Tuolumne County. The following year, a party of Mexican miners established a camp further up Woods Creek, which they called Sonora, after the state in Mexico of the same name.

The legislature selected Sonora as the county seat of Tuolumne County in 1850 and it has retained that status ever since.

Court sessions were initially held in rented quarters near the original plaza until the town was virtually destroyed by the fire in June 1852. The county then moved into the Masonic Hall, but a few months later a storm so weakened its adobe walls that the building collapsed. The court of sessions (as the board of supervisors was then called) decided a real courthouse was needed.

The first (1853) courthouse was a two-story wooden structure in the Greek Revival style and painted the traditional white. The square observatory tower was later removed.

The location of the new courthouse proved controversial. Property owners at the north end of town persuaded the county to move away from the plaza by donating the land for the site.

The courthouse opened in September 1853 and the center of the town shifted to its vicinity. The Placer Hotel, with room for 175 guests, was built across the street from the courthouse and became a stop for stages passing through town.

By 1898 the wooden courthouse had been outgrown. The county engaged prominent San Francisco architects, William Mooser and Son, to design a building accommodating not only the courts but all departments of county government: clerk, assessor, recorder, sheriff, district attorney, board of supervisors, superintendent of schools, coroner, surveyor, etc. Mooser's plans called for a three-story building approximately 60 feet by 90 feet. The exterior walls are buff-colored pressed Roman brick trimmed with Colusa sandstone. The metal roof is painted red, suggestive of terra-cotta tiles.

The new courthouse was built on the same site as the old. However, the front of the new courthouse was rotated 90 degrees to face north, rather than east as had the old courthouse. According to Sonora legend, this reorientation was due to the influence of S. S. Bradford, a prominent Sonora citizen who owned a house across the street and wanted to gaze out on the imposing main entrance rather than a blank side wall.

The second courthouse, constructed from 1898 to 1900, is still in use. It is on the National Register.

The courthouse clock tower rises 88 feet above street level and shares the skyline with the spires of nearby churches. To the west (left of photograph) and downhill is adjacent Courthouse Square, a much-loved park, scene of outdoor music concerts in the suummer.

Sonora, called "The Queen of the Southern Mines," was a rowdy and dangerous place in its early years. In 1855 a dispute between a mining company and a group of miners drew eminent legal counsel (three per side) from both within and outside Tuolumne County, to the white Sonora court-house. Attorney E. F. Hunter, representing the mining company, was particularly vigorous in his cross-examination of Eugene Drake, a prominent member of the opposing group. Hunter and Drake had a run-in at a nearby saloon after court adjourned, with Hunter coming out the worse. Later that day another "personal collision" occurred when Drake shoved Hunter off the wooden sidewalk. Hunter, enraged, drew his pistol and shot Drake three times, while the latter was struggling to unholster his own pistol. Drake's arm was amputated; Hunter, the attorney, was tried for assault and acquitted.

Above: The courtroom in the second courthouse boasted 16-foot ceilings and elaborate electrical light fixtures.

Left: Ornate lamps on the judge's bench remained in 1975 when this photograph of Superior Court Judge Theodore R. Vilas was taken.

The Sacramento Valley

BUTTE
COLUSA
GLENN
SACRAMENTO
SUTTER
TEHAMA
YOLO
YUBA

County of Butte

The 1903 jail appears to the left, connected to the courthouse by an elevated bridge. Ishi was held in this jail in 1911. The photograph was taken by Dr. F. F. Gundrum, a dentist who traveled the state in the 1920s photographing court-houses.

Butte County takes its name from the distinctive volcanic outcroppings that rise 2,000 feet from the floor of the Sacramento Valley. This impressive landmark may originally have been just within Butte County but, since the legislature adjusted the boundary in 1854, it has actually been just south, in adjacent Sutter County.

Butte County's first courthouse was a private home that the county purchased, transported four miles along the Feather River to Hamilton, the first county seat, and remodeled to serve as the courthouse. Hamilton consisted, in 1850, of two taverns, one store and a blacksmith shop. With the arrival of county offices, another tavern quickly opened.

Within a few years, Hamilton's fortunes waned and the Legislature was persuaded to order the county seat moved to Bidwell's Bar. (The name had nothing to do with taverns; "bar" being a generic term referring to a flat place along a stream or river.) A few years later, Bidwell itself declined, as miners stampeded downstream to the rich diggings at Oroville, where a new boom was underway. Oroville became the county seat in 1856, after a typically irregular election. No trace remains of Hamilton, destroyed by fire and flood, or of Bidwell's Bar, which now lies deep beneath the waters of Lake Oroville, the chief reservoir of the State Water Project.

Oroville in 1856 was California's fifth largest city, boasting a population of 4,000, horse races, two theaters, 65 saloons and numerous brothels and gambling houses. The new courthouse, built on the downtown plaza, was a two-story brick structure, plain and utilitarian, with a jail in the basement.

This courthouse was expanded in 1876, a separate jail constructed in 1903, and another addition tacked on in 1919. In 1946, the board of supervisors embarked on an ambitious plan for an entirely new courthouse and jail on the downtown site. Only the first phase was completed, in 1951. Critical newspaper articles led to a grand jury investigation of mismanagement and possible corruption. Discouraged by the attack on its integrity, the board abandoned the project.

Writing in 1969, Butte County Superior Court Judge J. F. Good concluded that this "pattern of neglect and temporizing, make-shift remedies dodged issues of obsolescence and dilapidation and sealed the fate of the [old courthouse]." Judge Good described the building as "a maze" in which "litigants, witnesses, and even attorneys are occasionally lost."

In 1972, the courts were moved out of the historic downtown park entirely and relocated across the river to join other county offices in a government center in Thermalito. The old courthouse was razed in 1975.

The 1876 expansion added porches on two sides of the building.

Preceding page: Yuba County courthouse, Marysville, 1922.

The Lincoln Street façade of the courthouse circa 1945, shaded by elms in downtown Oroville Park. A long hallway connected this side of the courthouse to the main entrance on Huntoon Street, shown on the facing page.

The December 1855 *Oroville North Californian* reports the following scene. An attorney addressed Judge Moses Bean, holding court in Oroville: "If the Court please, I believe the witness is by his own showing interested in the outcome of this case. I object on that ground to his further testimony. If a man may swear himself into possession of $200 worth of property, all I have to say is that this is a hell-roaring pretty court of justice."

To which Judge Bean is reported to have replied: "This Court permits no profane language in its presence. Your language seems too damned profane. You are fined $5 for contempt of court." The attorney thereupon called His Honor's attention to the fact that the language of the Court was also rather strong and suggested that, in view of that fact, the fine should be remitted. But, instead of remitting the attorney's fine, the court fined itself $5 for contempt of itself, paid the fine and insisted that the attorney do likewise.

In 1972, the courthouse moved across the Feather River to a government center complex in Thermalito. It was expanded in 1996.

Carved wooden staircase in old courthouse.

County of Colusa

n August 1850, the steamer *California* went aground on a sandbar in the Sacramento River and sank. Uriah P. Monroe, an enterprising settler, salvaged timbers from the ship, as well as the lumber in her cargo. With these he built a large two-story structure, which served as a hotel, tavern, store and post office, that he dubbed the Monroehouse. A blacksmith shop, tavern, barn and stable, and a few cabins rounded out "Monroeville," a popular stopping place for miners, hunters, trappers, stagecoaches, wagons and vaqueros. It became the de facto county seat when the county rented one end of the tavern for a courtroom. William Ide, one of the leaders of the 1846 Bear Flag Revolt presided over court proceedings once a week. He also built an iron cage that was used as an open-air jail.

The election of 1853 transferred the county seat to Colusa, several miles down river, which had by then surpassed Monroeville in population. The first courthouse was built the following year, a two-story affair constructed of oak that had been milled from oak trees that then covered the Sacramento Valley and its foothills. The iron cell was moved from Monroeville and incorporated into the courthouse as a jail.

This courthouse was inadequate from the beginning, too small to accommodate any county officers, who were thus scattered throughout town in rented rooms. By 1860, the board of supervisors decided to build on a larger scale. They selected plans prepared by Vincent Brown of nearby Marysville. Brown's courthouse, completed in 1861, is the second oldest courthouse still in use in California. Constructed of brick, two stories high, its Greek Revival style was familiar to the many Southerners who had settled Colusa County.

The first hall of records built in 1882, unusual for its octagonal design. The jail is visible to the rear. The building to the right is the courthouse.

As in other counties, during the early years the courthouse was the center of cultural, social and religious activities in the county. "Political clubs and literary and debating societies met in the courtroom; balls and dances were held there; various church groups conducted religious services there" before they had constructed their own buildings.

The courthouse today appears much as it did in the 1860s. The original dome has been replaced by a cupola, which was later converted to a bell tower. The original brick walls were covered over with stucco by the WPA in the 1930s. Ornamental window moldings were removed and front doors replaced with ones of metal and glass, which are distinctly 20th century. But its Greek Revival façade remains intact and, with its proximity to the river and the huge magnolia trees flanking the path to the entry stairway, it continues to have affinities with antebellum courthouses in the Mississippi Delta. And it remains, as one historian put it, the "architectural gem" of Colusa.

Above: The courthouse, circa 1915. The bear on the triangular frieze has faced both ways over the years as different painters reoriented it.

The gardens surrounding the courthouse complex were a source of particular pride. "There is something inexpressibly gratifying to our county people when they visit their county seat and see the enclosure around the courthouse and the Hall of Records. It is one of the best advertisements our locality has ever had.... Nearly all strangers come here... on such business as calls them within this enclosure where the Orange, the Lemon and the Olive grow... pretty green trees of all seasons and laden with fruit the year round."

Colusa Daily Sun, October 3, 1900

The courthouse façade recalls the architecture of the Southern states from which many of the town's earliest residents had emigrated.

The marble statue of George Washington presented to Colusa County in 1861. County residents had made the greatest per capita contribution of any county in California to the Washington Monument Fund at the 1860 presidential election. The statue stands in the courthouse's main corridor.

The courthouse, flanked by the vaguely Gothic jail constructed in 1878. Note the bridge connecting the jail to the courthouse, over which prisoners were brought to and from jail and courtroom, dubbed "the bridge of sighs," a reference to the famous passageway to the Doge's Palace in Venice. This jail was demolished in the 1960s.

Above: Dedication of the hall of records in 1914. The cupola of the courthouse can be seen in the background.

Left: Unusually styled capitals crown the columns at courthouse entryway. Jane Foster's book *If the Walls Could Talk* identifies them as "Egyptian Revival."

County of Glenn

By the mid-1880s, residents of northern Colusa County had become sufficiently dissatisfied with the policies of the board of supervisors (all elected from the more populous south) to propose separation. It took six years to achieve the goal, but an independent Glenn County was established in 1891. The county was named for Dr. Hugh Glenn, a prominent landowner whose vast holdings (55,000 acres) were planted in wheat and barley.

Willows was chosen as the first county seat. The town drew its name from a large nearby grove of willow and cottonwood trees, fed by springs, which were the most prominent landmark in the flat valleyland between the Sacramento River and the foothills to the west. The town had been founded in the mid-1870s, but had boomed with the arrival in 1878 of the Central Pacific Railroad, which was extending its line to Shasta and on to Oregon.

Hard times arrived shortly after Glenn County was formed. In the panic of 1893, prices for the county's main products—wheat and wool—fell to rock-bottom levels. Foreclosures on farms and ranches were common and bankruptcies rippled through the local economy. It is remarkable that, despite this depression, residents had enough confidence to approve in 1894 the issuance of $80,000 in bonds to construct a courthouse.

The cornerstone was laid in February 1894 amid ceremony and celebration. The parade to the courthouse site was led by Silvey's Cornet Band—a local favorite—followed by the newly formed Company G of the California National Guard. Plans for the courthouse were drawn by John Curtis, who had alone or in collaboration with A. A. Bennett designed courthouses for several other counties. The contract for construction was awarded to California Bridge Company.

According to one local historian, during construction the board of supervisors grew concerned that the contractor would become insolvent and leave the building unfinished. To avoid this, the supervisors ordered the domed cupola added, thereby providing the contractor enough funding to finish the job.

The annex was added in 1968, but the original courthouse, now over 100 years old, still stands facing the town's central square and still serves.

Turned wooden banister and molded plaster ornamentation decorate the central staircase.

The original courthouse in Willows, reminiscent of a Palladian villa, was completed in 1894. An article in the *Glenn County Directory* compiled in 1948 exclaimed, "To many, Willows does not need to have 'her face lifted.' We love her just as she is— courthouse dome and all." Nonetheless, the dome was removed in 1951.

The annex, added in 1968, is similar in appearance to the Lake County courthouse constructed the same year.

County of Sacramento

Sacramento County is one of the 27 original counties. Its first courthouse, completed in December 1851, was a remarkably sophisticated structure for Sacramento, which three years earlier had fewer than 500 residents, most of whom were housed in tents and shacks. The *Sacramento Union*, writing a few weeks before it was completed, was rhapsodic, but accurate:

> Sacramento can now boast of the finest and most commodious courthouse in the State; the building is by far superior to any in the city…. The design of the main entrance is very neat and in good taste. Four fluted columns will support a balcony, surrounding which there will be a handsome iron railing. The building will be ornamented by a neat cupola, in which a bell is to be suspended, and a clock also will show its face and hands to late witnesses and trembling culprits.

After the first wooden courthouse was destroyed in the disastrous fire of July 1854, the county hired one of California's most accomplished architects, the Scot David Farquharson, who designed a two-story brick and granite building in the Greek Revival style. The second courthouse, although twice as large as the first, was completed in little more than three months from the date the construction contract was awarded. It was used by the state legislature until the present capitol building was finished in 1869.

By 1900, the county's population had risen from 9,000 (in 1850) to over 45,000 and talk of a new courthouse began. The site of the new courthouse and the fate of the old one became controversial (see sidebar on page 124). But in 1908, the supervisors decided to demolish the 1855 courthouse and build a much larger courthouse, jail and office building on the same block, bounded by H, I, 6th and 7th Streets, all of which had by then been purchased by the county.

The third courthouse was a somewhat stern, rectangular, granite building designed in a classical style by prominent Sacramento architect R. A. Herold, an early advocate for urban planning and the City Beautiful movement.

While vastly larger than the second courthouse, the 1913 courthouse was itself rendered inadequate by continuous growth in the county's population and the size of its government and court system. In 1910, when the third courthouse was being designed, the county's population stood at 90,000; by 1960, it had risen to over 500,000. When the third courthouse was completed in 1913, it contained 17 offices/courtrooms and only five county offices were located outside the building. By 1965, the total number of offices/courtrooms had grown from 22 to 82, the majority of which, 44, were located in other buildings erected or rented in the vicinity of the courthouse.

A new, still larger courthouse/jail/county office building was completed in 1965. The "old" courthouse stood vacant until 1970 when it was unceremoniously demolished. The designers of the new 1965 courthouse, anticipating continued growth, built in capacity for 45 courtrooms. They were farsighted: Sacramento County's population is now over 1.2 million and 40 courtrooms are now in operation in the main courthouse, with another 15 judges holding court in satellite buildings in Sacramento and three more in other towns within the County.

A great fire swept through Sacramento in July 1854, destroying over 80% of the city, including the first courthouse, whose charred shell is shown in the illustration from the *Pictorial Union*, January 1855. Rebuilding began immediately.

Above: During the winter of 1862, the Sacramento River flooded, devastating the city. Over the next 10 years, the city carried out an astonishing public works program of raising the level of streets and buildings. In 1870, workers installed 400 jacks between the foundation of the second courthouse and the building, then raised it several feet.

Below: The second courthouse and, to the left, the brick hall of records constructed in 1881 to 1882. Note the elevated pedestrian bridge connecting the buildings.

Above: The third courthouse was completed in 1913 on the block that had been the site of the first two courthouses. It was an impressive Beaux Arts structure.

Left: The decorations above the central colonnade, including the head of Justice on the cartouche, were terra-cotta, fabricated at the nearby Gladding, McBean kilns.

Justice overthrown—during demolition of the third courthouse in 1970.

VIEWS ON PRESERVATION VS. PROGRESS, 1908

While virtually everyone agreed that the 1855 courthouse was too small and out of date, there was vigorous debate about whether it should be torn down and a new courthouse constructed on the same site or whether the new courthouse should be located elsewhere and the old courthouse/state capitol preserved. The two Sacramento newspapers took opposite sides, as can be seen from the following excerpts, all of which appeared in September 1908.

The *Sacramento Union,* September 1, 1908, quoting Judge C. E. McLaughlin:

If they do destroy this building, the day will come, and speedily, when the people of Sacramento will be ashamed of their inaction.... Do not lay sacrilegious hands upon the old State capitol, for sentiment is worth something in this commercial age.

The *Sacramento Union,* September 5, 1908:

As time passes the demand that the old state capitol, the present courthouse, shall not be torn down becomes general. The *Union* has been called upon by many citizens, and has received communications from others in protest. There are some, of course, who sneer at it, but such individuals are devoid of sentiment, without home pride, and are entirely lacking in patriotism.

The *Sacramento Bee,* September 19, 1908:

A city of too many landmarks is a city that in this bustling age is a city of oblivion. One or two landmarks are well enough but when you propose to make a landmark out of every second-hand building that is tottering to decay it is time to call a halt.... The march of civilization cannot stop to preserve everything and nothing should be preserved that is based on false assumptions and on mendacious history.... With [the present capitol] and with Sutters Fort... Sacramento is well enough off in landmarks—far better off than if she had a dozen half-baked and partly bogus ones in various stages of decay.

Top: The fourth courthouse was erected on a nearby site in 1965. Whereas the 1913 courthouse was designed with three courtrooms (and eventually remodeled to hold 11), the current courthouse has an ultimate capacity of 45 courtrooms.

Above: Judges Mamoru Sakuma and J. Louis Missal, toting their judicial robes, enter the new courthouse for the first time on October 15, 1965.

Above: The 1965 courthouse reflects the emerging concern for security. An armed guard observes visitors passing through metal detector devices. Above right: Sheriff's Deputy Dwight Trafton works in the heart of the courthouse security system—the control room. Instruments on the panel operate two-way communications and provide electronic control of the doors within the passageways. Right: A parabolic mirror enables the control room operator to observe anyone emerging from the elevator. Here it reflects Sheriff Lt. Edward Bristo.

County of Sutter

During the first six years of Sutter County's existence, its county seat moved five times. Once established at Yuba City in 1856, however, not only the seat of government, but the site of the courthouse on Second Street, has remained unchanged.

The plans for the first permanent courthouse in Yuba City were drawn by builder A. P. Petit, who later designed courthouses for Lake and Mendocino Counties. Completed in 1858, it was destroyed in 1871 by a fire of uncertain origin. According to one history, the "generally accepted version" is that the fire was caused by mice gnawing on the heads of matches left overnight by carpenters working in the county clerk's office.

The second courthouse also burned, in 1899. That fire is known to have begun in the jail cell of a man awaiting transfer to a state insane asylum, who perished in the blaze he had started.

Once again, the courthouse was quickly rebuilt, this time as an almost exact replica of the previous structure. A fine description of the current courthouse, now over a century old, appears in *The Survivors*, a book tracing the architectural history of Yuba and Sutter Counties:

The architectural style of the courthouse—with its two-story Tuscan columns supporting the portico, its tall "eyebrow" windows and its balanced façade—is basically Classical Revival. The second story veranda, which the building possessed until fairly recently, was typical of the buildings in the Old South. But the Italian influence is strong, too, in the elaborately bracketed roofline, the embellishments, and the quoins resembling stone blocks on the corners of the building. The octagonal cupola is an ornamental Victorian addition. And so the courthouse seems to be a rather charming blend of a variety of styles. Best of all, it has been preserved in almost its original state and reflects the nature of civic architecture in the 1870s.

The courthouse rebuilt in 1899, as it appeared in 1975, and as it appears today.

The courthouse after the fire of 1899, started by an insane man being held in a jail cell awaiting transfer to the state mental hospital in Stockton.

A tranquil street scene in Yuba City at the turn of the century. The Romanesque Revival hall of records, built in 1891, is in the foreground, the courthouse behind it to the left.

The handsome Sutter County courthouse built in 1872, seen here in the late 1870s.

The legislature fixed the first county seat at Oro—a nonexistent "paper city." This curious choice was due to the persuasive efforts of State Senator Thomas Jefferson Green—whose district included Sutter County—and who had recently purchased the site for Oro from John Sutter. The four other towns aspiring to be named county seat were all better situated than the imaginary Oro, but the persuasive Senator Green won the day and Oro became the first county seat.

Oro, however, enjoyed the honor for only a short time.

Reminiscing about the county's early days at a Fourth of July celebration 25 years later, Judge Phil Keyser recalled the first, and last, day the court of sessions convened at Oro:

There was not a house or a building in the town for any purpose, much less for holding court, the transaction of county business, and the preservation of public records. Some preparation must be made by the owners of the town to enable the first term, at least, of court to be held at the county seat and to this end they erected, or rather placed upon the ground, a zinc building, about twenty by twenty feet in size, with a floor of rough boards, a roof of zinc—if I remember correctly—and holes cut for the Court, the litigants, the witnesses, the jurors, and the air, but without glass or shutters for the windows, or doors for the entrances. Not a tree, or bush, or shrub grew near enough to give its shade to the building. A May sun poured its rays upon that zinc building, until outside and inside it became almost as hot as the furnace of Shadrach, Meshech, and Abednego. Law and equity, lawyers and litigants, jurors and witnesses, with a spontaneity of action that would astonish nothing but a salamander, rushed out of and fled that building, never again to return.

The "strange, squat Romanesque Revival" hall of records, designed by Curlett and Cuthbertson, built in 1891. It is still in use, newly renovated and serving as meeting chambers for the board of supervisors.

County of Tehama

When Tehama County was established in 1856, the county seat was located in the town of Tehama. The following year county government moved 12 miles north to Red Bluff, then the head of navigation on the Sacramento River and a center of both steamer and stage transportation. County officers and judges spent three years in rented quarters. In 1860, the board of supervisors approved plans for a courthouse drawn by a builder with the memorable name of A. B. C. Nusbaum. The contract to build the courthouse was awarded to Virgil Baker, who completed the two-story structure in only four months.

Judge E. J. Lewis ordered the construction of a tower in 1880 and a bell was purchased and installed a year later. By 1883, a hall of records was built, connected to the north side of the original courthouse.

Walkways were laid out in the town square, by then called Courthouse Square, trees (redwoods and yew trees) and grass planted in 1874. Later a band pavilion was built and Courthouse Square became a center for public life. An astonishingly well-researched term paper written in 1968 by Abby Webster, a senior at Red Bluff Union High School, contains the following evocative passage:

> Mr. Henry Schafer, an old time resident of Red Bluff and a member of the county band since the late 1800s reminisced that the band used to play on the pavilion on the Court House lawn on Saturday evenings to a good sized crowd who lolled on the grass. He recalled that on Saturday, Charles Unash, who with his brother Jim directed the band, went up in the City Hall tower and played "The Last Rose of Summer" and the band accompanied him from the pavilion. The audience was much moved by the soft playing of the band and the echo from the sky.

The original courthouse and hall of records were demolished when the more substantial concrete and brick courthouse was completed in 1922. That building is now itself flanked by later additions: an annex (1979) and a courts building (1988).

Tehama County's first courthouse was built in 1860. It is seen here in 1880, shortly after the tower was added. The building to the left is the jail, built in 1873. The town square landscaping was begun in 1874.

Tehama County Court. House, Red Bluff California

Above: The Beaux Arts Classical courthouse designed by George Sellon and completed in 1922 is the centerpiece of the Red Bluff town square.

Left: In 1883, a hall of records was constructed as an addition to the north side of the original courthouse.

TEHAMA COUNTY

While spittoons are gone from California's courthouses, chewing tobacco remains a custom in rural counties, as shown by this sign, posted above the courthouse's marble drinking fountain in 1999.

The jury deliberation room, visible through the doorway, is flanked by two dormitory rooms, each with six fold-down beds to accommodate sequestered juries.

For over a century, the Tehama County courthouse in Red Bluff was "owned" by the county judge. This peculiar state of affairs arose from the chaotic state of land titles that prevailed in Red Bluff in its early days. All the maps were inaccurate, leading to claims and counter-claims to the town's lots. The solution was to start over, by placing title to all property in the town in the name of the most trustworthy person available—the county judge. And federal legislation enacted by Congress during the administration of President Andrew Johnson (1865–68) did just that. Eventually titles were cleared for all privately held land, but the county judge, and after 1879 the superior court judge, continued to hold title to streets and alleys in the town, as well as to Courthouse Square and the courthouse itself.

An article in the *Los Angeles Times* in 1969 quoted then Tehama County Superior Court Judge Curtis Wetter: "This may be the only county in the country where the judge not only presides in the courthouse but owns the damn thing as well."

In 1988, the California legislature passed a law authorizing and directing the presiding judge of the Tehama County Superior Court to convey title to "Courthouse Square" to the county (Statutes of 1988, Chapter 143). The following year, Superior Court Judges Noel Watkins and Richard Hultgren delivered a grant deed to Courthouse Square to the county. The deed was accepted by the board of supervisors and promptly recorded. After 133 years, the County of Tehama finally owned its courthouse.

A view through the central lobby showing the spiral staircase leading to the courtroom on the second floor.

The courts building, constructed in 1988, provides two additional courtrooms for superior court judges.

County of Yolo

The palm trees surrounding Woodland's newly built Italianate courthouse, seen here circa 1870, add a Caribbean atmosphere.

Yolo County lies near the center of the Great Central Valley. Woodland, the county seat, lies near the center of the county. In the center of Woodland is a square. At the center of the square stands a courthouse. It is rectangular and perfectly symmetrical. The central portico is supported by four columns. On the parapet, directly above each column are four statues of classical figures, two women in the center flanked by a Roman soldier at each end.

The regularity and order of this picture is disturbed only by the street just south of the courthouse square: Dead Cat Alley. A relic of the more boisterous, early days in Woodland, the street is so named because of the town's less disciplined settlers' habit of discarding garbage, including dead cats, in this public thoroughfare.

During Yolo County's first 12 years, its county seat moved four times, renting space for courtrooms in vernacular buildings of which no trace remains. In 1862, the county seat settled permanently in Woodland, a thriving market town serving the farmers and ranchers who were building the area's rich agricultural economy. The first makeshift courthouse was a small frame building on First Street, which later became the Woodland Bakery.

By 1863, however, the ambitious board of supervisors had already hired a well-known architect, A. A. Bennett, who designed an impressive Italianate courthouse set among newly planted palm and shade trees. In 1870, the building was raised eight feet (due to the risk of flooding) and its foundation was strengthened (due to the risk of earthquake).

Nothing Caribbean here! The hall of records built in 1889, is an odd amalgam of Romanesque with a Gothic tower. The couple in the carriage are even more forbidding than the building.

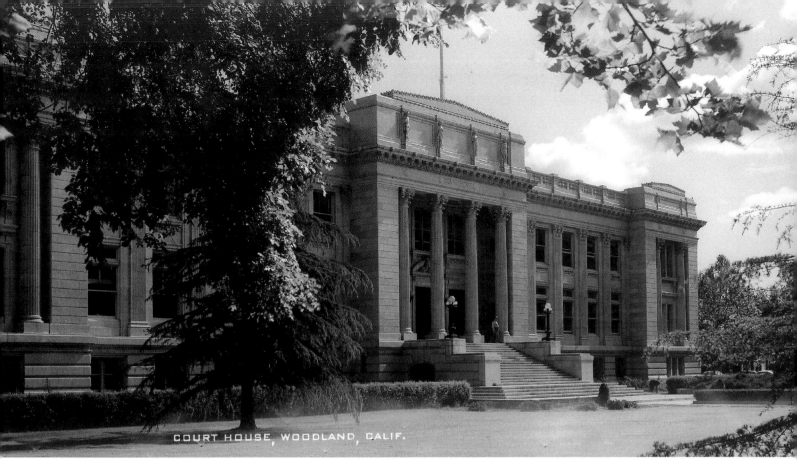

COURT HOUSE, WOODLAND, CALIF.

The precautions were timely. A county history relates that only a few years later, on March 22, 1872, a powerful earthquake shook Woodland while a jury was sequestered. "The jurymen who were locked up in the Jury Room of the Courthouse deliberating upon the case of *Wright v. Laugenour* were immediately scared and clamored to be released from confinement." The sheriff consented to release them, "as they would not agree and the case adjourned for the term."

By 1917, the county had replaced the old and now out-of-date courthouse with a much larger steel frame structure that incorporated the technological improvements (electrical lighting, internal plumbing, temperature control systems) that had become available over the half century since the old courthouse had been built. The building has been well maintained and still inspires admiration in the traveler who ventures off Interstate 5 long enough to visit the pleasant tree-shaded town of Woodland.

County of Yuba

Marysville, located at the confluence of the Yuba and Feather Rivers, has been the county seat since 1850. The town was named in honor of Mary Murphy, a 15-year-old survivor of the Donner Party, who shortly thereafter married town founder Charles Couvillaud.

For the first several years, the county's government and courts were housed in rented quarters and then in the St. Charles Hotel, which the county purchased. In 1854 construction began on what was to be Marysville's most famous building—its fanciful, castle-like courthouse. The building was designed by Warren Miller, who had moved to Marysville from New York. Two angular towers framed the main entrance and rose above the crenellated parapet. The central towers and the smaller towers at the corners were pierced by long narrow openings suitable for archers. If, as reported, Miller drew his inspiration from the stylized castle that is the insignia of the Army Corps of Engineers, it would be appropriate, in light of the corps' important role in later years dredging the rivers and building levees to protect Marysville from flooding.

Stephen J. Field, Marysville's most famous lawyer appeared frequently in its famous courthouse. Field was chosen as the first American alcalde of Marysville shortly after he arrived from New York in 1849. He was elected to the state assembly in 1850. Returning to Marysville the following year, he built one of the most lucrative practices in the state, outside of San Francisco. In the years between leaving the legislature and going on the state supreme court (1857), Field had more cases before the California Supreme Court than did any other lawyer—and won 90% of them! He was serving as chief justice of the state supreme court when President Lincoln appointed him to the United States Supreme Court in 1863, the first Californian to be so honored.

Fear of flooding influenced the design of the hall of records built adjacent to the courthouse in 1895. Architect A. A. Cook placed the offices of the county clerk, auditor and controller on the second floor, safely above flood level, reserving the ground floor for additional jail cells.

Both buildings were razed in 1962. At the time of its demolition, Miller's Gothic fantasy was the second oldest functioning courthouse in California, only a few months younger than its celebrated counterpart in Mariposa.

US Army Corps of Engineers®

The U.S. Army Corps of Engineers' Traditional Castle, said to be the inspiration for the unique Yuba County courthouse.

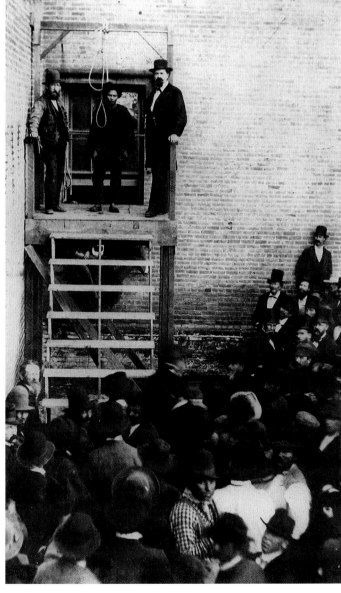

The hanging of Ah Ben, who was convicted of murdering John McDaniels (owner of Marysville's race track) took place on March 14, 1879. Prior to 1889, executions were carried out in the county in which the crime occurred.

Above: The first Yuba County courthouse was built in 1854 to 1855 and used for more than a century. One of the few Gothic Revival courthouses in California, it is said to have been patterned after the insignia of the U.S. Army Corps of Engineers. The hall of records to the right of the courthouse was added in 1895.

Left: The current Yuba County courthouse was built in 1962. Its location on a site that had been laid out as a Marysville city park in 1850 was controversial.

The Bay Area

ALAMEDA
CONTRA COSTA
MARIN
NAPA
SAN FRANCISCO
SAN MATEO
SANTA CLARA
SOLANO
SONOMA

County of Alameda

Alameda County was created in 1853 out of portions of Contra Costa and Santa Clara Counties.

The first courthouse was in Alvarado, now a part of Union City, then the center of the county's population.

Two enterprising sons-in-law of Jose Joaquin Estudillo, holder of the Mexican land grant of San Leandro, persuaded his widow and children to donate land for a county building near the Estudillo rancho, some 10 miles north of Alvarado, in the new town of San Leandro, which they were creating expressly to serve as the new county seat.

By February 1856, San Leandro's supporters had prevailed on the state legislature to declare their town the county seat by law. The following month, the board of supervisors and judges were settled in the new two-story brick Greek Revival courthouse that had been constructed for them on the land donated by the Estudillo family.

By the early 1870s, the center of population had shifted from the agricultural south county to the rising city of Oakland in the north, linked to eastern markets by the transcontinental railroad.

For the first two years, a simple wooden commercial building near the Oakland city limits served as the courthouse. But by June 1875, a much more ambitious courthouse opened on Washington Square in the heart of Oakland, to be joined in 1879 by a hall of records on nearby Franklin Square. The two buildings were much larger and far more ornate than their predecessors. Their scale and elegance provided comfortable associations with European architectural fashions. County historian M. M. Wood, writing in 1883, concluded that the "splendid structures" were ornaments to the city and proud emblems of the importance of the county.

Fifty years later, the county's population having grown from about 30,000 to nearly half a million, the splendid old courthouse was considered inadequate and obsolete. With the depression, ironically, came the opportunity to build anew: Federal money was available from New Deal agencies such as the Public Works Administration, and the goal of "putting men to work" on local projects resonated with taxpayers who approved courthouse bonds in 1932.

Alameda's first courthouse was in Alvarado, now a part of Union City. From 1853 through 1856, county officials met on the upper floor of this two-story wooden building originally constructed as a store. The building is long gone, but the site is a state historical landmark.

Preceding page: San Francisco Civic Center, 363rd Regiment welcomed home from France, 1919.

The courthouse that was built in 1935 to 1936 was, and remains today, one of the most striking in California: an 11-story steel frame/reinforced concrete structure, occupying an entire city block on the edge of Lake Merritt in downtown Oakland. The first three stories and mezzanine form a rectangular base or podium on which is centered a square seven-story tower that terminates in a low-pitched, pyramidal, copper roof and a square observation cupola.

The county seat moved to San Leandro in 1856. The judges were lodged in a newly built two-story brick structure with a subdued but distinctively Greek Revival façade.

One writer says it "rises above the Lake like a Babylonian ziggurat in massive concrete setbacks" (Mark Wilson, *A Living Legacy: Historic Architecture of the East Bay*, p. 245). Another (one of the building's architects) offered a more poetic appraisal: "The upward movement of the design from base to cupola is saved from abrupt breaks by a shallow setback above the first three floors and by two setbacks from the coping of the tower to the pitched roof which carries the eye to the cupola and finial-like flagstaff. Thus the vigorous modern lines modulate as they ascend until the structure asumes, viewed in entirety, a definitely monumental atmosphere" (W. G. Corlett, "Alameda County Court House," *Architectural Concrete*, 1937, vol. 3, no. 2, pp. 6–9).

Now over 65 years old, the depression-era courthouse remains a familiar East Bay landmark with its large scale, distinctive sculpted form, copper roof—now green with verdigris—and its prominent location dominating the southwest shore of Lake Merritt. In those 65 years, the county's population surged from 500,000 to nearly 1.5 million. Thus, while the old courthouse is by no means obsolete, even its five acres of office space were no longer adequate. Additional courtrooms were included in multipurpose facilities built in the 1950s, 1960s and 1980s, none of which are architecturally distinguished, though two are named in honor of two of Alameda County's most distinguished jurists—Wiley Manuel and Allen Broussard, who were, respectively, the first and second African American attorneys appointed to the California Supreme Court.

The San Leandro courthouse was severely damaged by the earthquake of 1868, as this photograph by Eadweard Muybridge shows. It was rebuilt and used until 1873, when another election moved the county seat further north to Oakland.

Above: A simple two-story wooden building in Brooklyn, now East Oakland, served as the courthouse for two years, from 1873 to 1875. The building, shown here in an oil painting by Clifton Dahlgren, survived into the 1990s, being used as a home, a warehouse, and an apartment in an increasingly urbanized neighborhood.

Below: This much more ambitious courthouse opened on Washington Square in the heart of Oakland in June 1875. The building was designed by prominent California architects John and Thomas Newsom. Its lavish references to Renaissance Rome and contemporary Paris made it a symbol of Oakland's prominence as the county's leading city after completion of the transcontinental railroad in 1869. The building was demolished in 1950.

Above: Alameda's fifth courthouse is an 11-story steel frame and reinforced concrete structure occupying an entire block on the edge of Lake Merritt. Opened in 1936, the courthouse is one of the Bay Area's most conspicuous products of the U.S. Public Works Administration, a New Deal agency. The courthouse is a successful example of the combination of classical and Art Deco architecture sometimes called "PWA Moderne"—a style favored for public buildings in the 1930s and 1940s.

Left: Alameda County District Attorney Earl Warren, later attorney general and governor of California and chief justice of the United States Supreme Court, speaking at the groundbreaking ceremonies for the current courthouse in October 1935. In his capacity as grand master of California's Masonic lodges, he laid the cornerstone of the new courthouse.

Shortly after Oakland's imposing courthouse was completed in 1875, a French Renaissance Revival hall of records that nearly rivaled it in ornament was built across the street. Seen here is the central block, completed in 1879, together with the south wing added in 1900. A north wing was constructed in 1916 and the entire complex was demolished in 1964.

10546.   Hall of Records, Oakland, Cal.

Three photographs taken by noted photographer Dorothea Lange of participants in a criminal trial held in Alameda's courthouse in the 1950s. Depicted are Judge Christopher Fox, a witness being sworn in, and Public Defender (later judge) Martin Pulich, conferring with his young client.

Members of the Black Panther Party and their supporters demonstrate solidarity with the party's cofounder and minister of defense, Huey Newton, on trial in 1967 for the killing of an Oakland police officer.

DETAILS OF THE 1936 COURTHOUSE

Right: Twin pairs of concrete eagles perched on all four sides of the flagpole pedestal atop the roof.

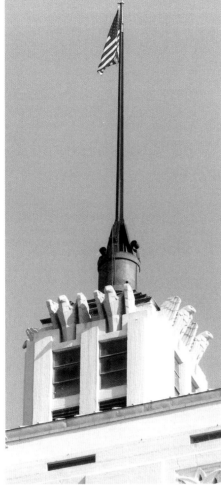

A stylized geometric eagle in carved granite above a side entry door symbolizes the federal government's role in funding construction of the courthouse.

A rosette decoration, trimmed with chevrons, on a spandrel.

The interior of the 1936 courthouse has splendid marble murals designed by Marion Simpson of Berkeley and executed by Gaetano Duccini of San Francisco funded by the WPA Federal Arts Project. The two panels weigh approximately a ton each and contain 400 and 500 pieces.

The south panel (left) depicts the early Spanish history of the county: An explorer on horseback carries the Royal Spanish standard and there is a Spanish galleon in the background. A priest gives benediction to two kneeling Native Americans. Rancheros, representative of such men as Peralta and Castro who once controlled the land now known as Alameda County, complete the tableau.

The north panel (right) represents the American conquest of the area. A pioneer is shown astride a Western pinto pony, his fringed clothing typical of that worn by the early trappers; he holds an American flag with 25 stars. A clipper ship in the background indicates the mode of travel for thousands of the 49ers. A miner studying a map stands behind pioneer mother and child. In the foreground, a man plants a tree, symbolizing the cultivation of the rural land succeeding the rush for gold.

The Wiley W. Manuel Courthouse in Oakland houses 12 courtrooms. It is named for the first African American to serve on California's supreme court. Justice Manuel (1927–81), inset, practiced law in Alameda County as a deputy attorney general for many years before his appointment to the supreme court.

Directly across the street from the Wiley Manuel Courthouse, and connected to it by an elevated pedestrian bridge, is the Allen E. Broussard Justice Center built in 1958 as the hall of justice. Allen Broussard (1929–96) also practiced law in Alameda County and served as a municipal and superior court judge there, before his appointment to the California Supreme Court in 1981.

The severe county administration building, completed in 1964, across Oak Street from the 1936 courthouse (visible in the background), houses 11 courtrooms and offices of the board of supervisors.

County of
Contra Costa

The first courthouse built by the county, completed in 1855, was brick, painted white with a plain Greek Revival temple front and fluted Ionic columns. Early on, the board of supervisors adopted a lenient policy authorizing rental of the large second floor courtroom for plays, dances, etc. After complaints that "mountebank shows" and other undignified uses had turned the courtroom into a "hayloft," however, the supervisors restricted use of the courthouse to county functions and, later, issued an order forbidding removal of furniture from the courthouse for picnics on the surrounding lawn.

By the late 1890s, grand juries were criticizing the building as too cramped. In 1899 the *Gazette* editorialized: "The fact that we have an old building for a courthouse tends to keep people away from the county. It is certainly no credit to the people.... The Supervisors could do nothing that would be of more value to the county than to see that a new courthouse is erected."

The topic provoked a challenge from Concord for the county seat, but Martinez won the election handily. Supervisors then approved plans of architects Havens & Toepke for a dignified, classically inspired building of Vermont granite, four times larger than the old courthouse. The contract for the courthouse and adjacent jail, designed by William Mooser, was awarded in 1901.

The completion of the courthouse in 1903 was celebrated with festivities that drew over 10,000 visitors (more than half of the county's entire population) to downtown Martinez. The town fire truck (with the Fire Queen and her attendants on board) led the parade, followed by the Native Daughters of the Golden West with their white parasols, and sailors in uniform from merchant ships anchored in the harbor. Traditional oratory began at midday, a barbecue was held in the afternoon, and a banquet (for men only) began at 10 P.M. featuring six types of wine, ham, turkey, crab, shrimp, Martinez olives and Cuban cigars.

By 1932, Contra Costa's population had grown from 18,000 to nearly 80,000. The county engaged Edward Geoffrey Bangs, a partner of renowned architect John Galen Howard who designed many buildings on the UC Berkeley campus, to prepare plans for a hall of records to be built just across the street from the courthouse. Bangs's plans envisioned a building that, while contemporary in design, would be compatible with the 1903 courthouse: an almost square, solid Beaux Arts classical structure, with subdued Art Deco embellishments. In nominating the hall of records for inclusion in

The upper floor of the Berryessa adobe was used briefly by the county before the first courthouse was completed in 1855. This photograph was taken at a later date.

The first courthouse shortly after completion. A courtroom and chambers for the county judge and offices of the county clerk and treasurer were on the first floor. On the second floor were the law library and a larger courtroom for the district judge. The jail and sheriff's office were in the basement.

the National Register of Historic Places, the County Historical Society observed: "In feeling and association the Hall of Records expresses its function: to provide a substantial, permanent office and courtroom building to meet the needs of a growing county."

The contracts for construction were awarded in the depth of the depression, so the supervisors were insistent that local labor and local materials be used whenever possible. Indeed, laborers were to be hired equally from each of the five supervisorial districts.

Over the years the courts were moved from the courthouse to the hall of records, a change in use that was given formal recognition in 1966, when the old courthouse was renamed the "Finance Building" and the hall of records redesignated as the "Courthouse." A recent article in the *San Francisco Chronicle* noted the "lofty ceilings, bronze fittings and ornate silver trimmings" that Bangs had incorporated into the interior lobbies of the hall of records. The article continued:

The people most likely to visit the old county courthouse in Martinez also may be the least likely to notice they are passing through one of Contra Costa's most beautiful public places. Overworked public defenders hurry through the halls past parents fighting custody battles and families enduring the trauma of criminal trials. All seem absorbed in their private struggles. But those who take a minute to rest in the building's serene second floor lobby may find solace in the streams of light that pour through the tall windows onto the gray-green marble walls.

In 1986, with the county's population now 10 times larger than it was in 1930, the supervisors constructed the A. F. Bray Courts Building, named for a longtime Martinez resident whose distinguished legal career culminated with 17 years service as judge on the First District Court of Appeal. This newest court building is just across Ward Street from the 1932 hall of records. Thus three buildings that house, or housed, the county's courts now line a three-block stretch of Court Street, so named because the very first courthouse was located there in the 1850s.

Left: The first courthouse in the late 1880s. The structure in the foreground is a water tank. The stone building behind the courthouse is the clerk's and recorder's office building constructed in 1876 and expanded in 1887. All were demolished in 1902 to make room for a new courthouse and jail.

The second courthouse, completed in 1903, was the most prominent landmark in early-20th-century Martinez. For years a beacon shone from the cupola atop the dome to guide fishermen to port. During World War II, civil defense volunteers climbed the narrow stairs to the tower to scan the skies for Japanese planes. The tower and dome were removed in 1957.

The cornerstone of the 1903 courthouse in Martinez, like those of so many 19th- and early-20th-century courthouses throughout the state, was laid under Masonic auspices and accompanied by the traditional rituals of the Masonic Order. In this case, the ceremonies were presided over by William Wells, who was not only the superior court judge of Contra Costa County, but also the grand master of all California Masons. After a representative of the architects' office spread the cement, Grand Master Wells asked each of four Masons to use the symbolic instrument of his office (trowel, square, level and plumb) to see if the cornerstone had been laid in a manner creditable to the ancient craft. Each replied, in turn, that they had found the stone to have been well leveled, plumbed, squared and troweled by the craftsmen. Wells then declared the stone well formed.

The hall of records, built in 1932, is in the foreground and the 1903 courthouse, still sporting its tower and dome, can be seen to the rear. The courts were moved to the hall of records and it was formally designated as the courthouse in 1966.

Left: After the courts were relocated to the hall of records, the old courthouse was renamed the Finance Building. Its main elevation is dominated by the two-story portico whose granite Ionic columns and pilasters support a plain pediment. Other classical details visible include the bracketed cornice and the balustrade above it.

The rusticated Vermont granite of the old jail, also built in 1903, contrasts with the sleek vertical aluminum panels that serve as sunscreens on the 1960s county office building across the street.

Persons entering this building are subject to police search of their person and packages and must produce identification upon request. Contraband, including any weapons, knives, etc. shall be confiscated.

Above: A sign of the times posted on the entrance door to the Bray Courts Building.

Left: The A. F. Bray Courts Building, constructed in 1986, is across the street from the 1932 courthouse and adjacent to a large county detention facility. It contains eight courtrooms and the county law library.

County of Marin

Before 1850, the alcaldes appointed by Spanish authorities and later by the Mexican government conducted their business at the Mission San Rafael Arcangel complex. After Marin's establishment as one of the original counties, the former mission continued to function as headquarters for county officers, its *juzgado* serving as the first American courtroom.

In 1853, the county moved the tribunals to the adobe house that Timothy Murphy had built in 1844 on the grounds of the secularized mission and that had served as headquarters of "Don Timoteo's" extensive ranch lands centered in the San Rafael Valley.

By the early 1870s, the progressive citizens of Marin considered it a disgrace that county business had to be conducted in Don Timoteo's old hacienda. In 1872, the board of supervisors purchased a site for a new courthouse in the center of San Rafael, a town that had grown up around the ruins of the old mission.

The contract for design of the new courthouse was awarded to Kenitzer & Raun of San Francisco. The courthouse they designed for Marin was a sharp departure from the modest adobe. Based loosely on the Virginia capitol building in Richmond, it was a symmetrical structure with a portico supported by imposing Corinthian columns surmounted by a tower and cupola.

Marin County's elegant 1872 courthouse in downtown San Rafael was designed by architects Kenitzer & Raun of San Francisco. Raun, a "49er," had designed Charles Crocker's mansion on San Francisco's Nob Hill the previous year.

A bronze statue of a World War I infantryman stood in front of the courthouse for decades. Marin residents had gathered on the courthouse steps to cheer young soldiers as they marched down Fourth Street to the railroad depot on their way to the trenches in France. The "Doughboy" statue was moved to the new civic center.

The ceremonial laying of the cornerstone in August 1872 was celebrated under Masonic auspices. The first public use of the new courthouse was for a grand social event—the first anniversary party of the Marin Lodge of the International Order of Odd Fellows in February 1873. Less genteel occasions at the courthouse were the executions carried out there until 1893, when they were transferred to San Quentin Prison. Initially, condemned felons were hanged at an outdoor gallows, viewed by spectators perched on a nearby hill. After 1886, when a gallows was installed indoors, executions were witnessed by invitation only.

Despite the addition of a hall of records in 1908, remodeled and expanded in 1949, and a three-story annex in 1958, by the late 1950s the courthouse was viewed as inadequate to house the government of a county whose population had increased from 7,000 in 1870 to over 200,000. In 1956, the board of supervisors authorized the purchase of a 140-acre site two miles north of downtown San Rafael for development of a civic center complex. The site acquisition set off a debate between those who favored hiring a local architect with a traditional style and those who advocated engaging an architect with a global reputation. The latter view prevailed, the board of supervisors commissioning the daringly original Frank Lloyd Wright.

Presenting his plan to several hundred Marin residents in 1958, the great architect, then 91 years old, explained his vision of long, horizontal concrete structures that "will melt into the sunburnt hills.… Instead of slicing away the hills with bulldozers, the buildings will bridge the knolls with graceful arches."

Wright died in 1959, before construction began. The work was completed by his associates, chiefly William Wesley Peters and Bay Area architect Aaron Green. Wright's widow, speaking at the February 1960 groundbreaking, alluded to his goal of an organic architecture, suitable for a democracy: "This historic moment proves that in a government by the people and for the people we can have the finest in the world brought about by the citizens."

Dr. Theodore Gill, president of the San Francisco Theological Seminary in nearby San Anselmo, observed at the 1962 dedication of the administration building that the citizens of Marin had taken a chance on art: "Suddenly we see what one superb dreamer saw. The building is vigorously idiosyncratic like its creator, but it has grace and dignity and power."

Visually, the civic center is composed of three elements. The central focus of the building complex is a rotunda 80 feet in diameter, with a shallow dome, flanked by a slender 172-foot gold tower. This circular central element is the hinge for two wings set at a 120-degree angle to each other: a four-story administration building and the longer hall of justice. The rounded ends of the wings are built into the sides of two low hills. The entire complex is nearly one quarter of a mile long.

The construction combined familiar materials with innovative building techniques. The basic framework is of precast, prestressed concrete floors with steel vertical supports. The barrel arch roof is of reinforced concrete.

Curves predominate. Great arches at the base allow both pedestrian and vehicular passage beneath both wings. The round arches (termed "pendant crescents" by Wright) screen sunlight on the first and second levels. Circular openings along the third level and semi-circular openings in the roof overhang perform the same function. The circular precast ornamental units on the roof were designed to mask imprecise workmanship and the gold spheres along the roof fascias disguise variations in the long straight lines of the roof edge.

The Marin Civic Center is Wright's last major work, the largest constructed public project of his long career, and the only one for a government agency. It represents a partial realization of "Broadacre City"—his American utopia. And the very form of the complex may symbolize his belief in democratic values. The visual dominance of the administrative wing, it has been suggested, places human services above the regulatory functions of government. The elected representatives of the people—the board of supervisors—are placed in the circular central element. Above them, and beneath the dome, is the county library. Thus the library occupies the "Dome of Knowledge" placed over the supervisors' chambers to help influence their decisions. The adjacent tower was meant to allow for county-sponsored radio programs, though this never occured. Thus, the branches of government meet at the place where knowledge is collected and disseminated. More grandly stated, "The power and authority of the state find their raison d'être in the wisdom of the citizenry from which, architecturally at least, their expressions emanate."

The fate of the old courthouse, vacant since the judges moved out in 1969, was vigorously debated in the community. The debate ended abruptly on May 25, 1971, when the building was ravaged by fire, set by an arsonist. Damaged beyond repair, the old courthouse was demolished, to be replaced by an undistinguished office building.

The 880-foot-long hall of justice houses courtrooms, the law library, offices of law enforcement agencies and the county jail.

The circular central building, at which the two long wings converge, houses the county library on its domed top floor, with the chambers of the board of supervisors directly beneath.

San Quentin convict James McClain brandishes a revolver while holding a sawed-off shotgun to the neck of Judge Harold Haley in the August 1970 kidnapping. A second convict, Ruchel Magee, right, holds a revolver on a hostage.

Judge Haley, Assistant District Attorney Gary Thomas and three women jurors are herded to a van in the parking lot as Jonathan Jackson, foreground with carbine, stands guard.

The hall of justice was completed in 1969. Within a year it was the scene of terrible violence, which was to transform the people's access to their courtrooms across the state.

On August 7, 1970, state prison inmate James McClain was on trial for stabbing a guard at nearby San Quentin Prison. Violence within prisons, including assaults on guards, was on the rise and had taken on political overtones. Radical prison leaders were preaching revolution. The charismatic George Jackson, a leader of the militant Black Panther Party and author of *Soledad Brother* had recently been transferred to San Quentin. George Jackson's younger brother, Jonathan, suddenly rose from his seat in the spectator section of Judge Harold Haley's courtroom, brandished a carbine he had hidden beneath his coat and announced "All right, gentlemen, I'm taking over now." Jackson handed a pistol to McClain and, joined by two convict witnesses (William Christmas and Ruchel Magee), took Judge Haley, Assistant District Attorney Gary Thomas, and three women jurors hostage. The assailants bound the hostages with wire, taped a shotgun beneath Judge Haley's neck, and forced them from the courtroom to a van waiting in the parking lot.

As the van pulled away, it was met with a fusillade from police, sheriffs, CHP officers and prison guards. When the shooting was over, Judge Haley, McClain, Christmas and Jackson were dead, Magee seriously injured. A bullet had torn through Prosecutor Thomas' spinal cord, leaving him paralyzed. The jurors escaped with minor wounds. Two months later a bomb destroyed one of the courtrooms; a radical underground group claimed responsibility.

Speaking in 1998, as he prepared to retire from the superior court, then Judge Gary Thomas remarked, "It was the end of one kind of life and the dawning of another era," alluding to the subsequent development of metal detectors, bulletproof judges' benches, and armed bailiffs in courtrooms throughout the state.

After the violence, architect Aaron Green designed a tranquil memorial grove to honor Judge Haley. Incised into the granite rock at the memorial's center is the following statement:

In memory of Hon. Harold Jos. Haley
Judge of the Superior Court
Nov. 14, 1904   Aug. 7, 1970
A just and compassionate man
taken from his bench to his death
lost to his family and community.

The interior atriums widen on each floor as they ascend toward the barrel vault skylight.

County of Napa

Napa County is named for the Native American tribe that lived in the valley before the arrival of Europeans.

The first courthouse was fabricated on the East Coast, brought to California by ship and barged up the Napa River. An unpretentious, two-story, 20-foot by 30-foot wooden building, it was erected early in 1851. The lower floor served as the courtroom, but was also used for church services and entertainments. Prisoners sentenced to lengthy terms were sent to the adobe jail in Sonoma; petty offenders were detained in the upper rooms by being chained to the floor.

In 1856 the board of supervisors awarded a contract for a more substantial building in the plaza that had until then been used as a lumberyard, but that ever since has been the site of the courthouse. The second courthouse lasted only slightly longer than the first—great cracks were appearing in the walls by 1864, and in 1874, Judge Hartson, deeming the building unsafe, refused to hold court in it. By 1878, the supervisors had approved plans prepared by Samuel and Joseph Newsom, architects who were in a few years to design the Carson House, an extravagant Victorian mansion in Eureka. The Napa courthouse, designed in their first year of practice, appears now as a much more sedate building, a fairly plain example of the High Victorian Italianate style. But its present appearance is misleading. When originally constructed, the conventional two-story, rectangular, brick and stucco building sported an audacious tower described as embodying a "Moorish Gothic and Classic motif." The octagonal tower rose from the courthouse roof in two tiers, each pierced by eight windows. A bulb-shaped cupola rested on top of the tower, its gradually tapering spire topped in turn by a golden globe and weather vane. The tower was dismantled in 1931 and a small pediment added to the cornice on the main façade at the same time.

A separate hall of records was constructed in 1916 on the west end of the plaza. Designed by William Corlett, an advocate of new construction methods, the hall of records uses reinforced concrete not only for the walls and floor slabs, but for the exterior detailing as well.

A view of the main façade of the old courthouse illustrates an architectural feature characteristic of the High Victorian Italianate style: tall arched and, on the second floor, pedimented windows.

In 1978, an addition to the courthouse connected it to the hall of records. Although there was some attempt to reflect the architectural character of the courthouse, the infill addition is clearly a different building, detracting from both the Italianate courthouse and the Spanish tile-roofed hall of records.

In the early 1980s, a county administration building was constructed across the street from the plaza and many county offices moved from the plaza complex to the new building. And in 1998, a new criminal courthouse was constructed, once again just across from the plaza. Designed by the Sonoma firm of Ross & Drulis Architects, the new courthouse is the subject of an essay beginning on page 338.

Napa County's third courthouse, built in 1878 in the center of Courthouse Square, is still in use, although sans the outlandish tower, which was dismantled in 1931.

Right: The new criminal courts building (completed in 1999) is directly across the street from the old courthouse.

Below: The 1916 hall of records is now physically linked to the old courthouse. Its proportions are echoed by the new courthouse (above) with the elongated windows above the first floor.

Members of the Native Sons of the Golden West conduct their traditional dedication ceremony for the criminal courts building on March 24, 1999. Left to right, William Hargis (grand second vice president, Solano Parlor), Richard Hoffman (grand president, Nicasio Parlor), Joe Devine (Napa Parlor), James Riley (grand first vice president, South San Francisco Parlor), and Phillip Wong (past grand president, Napa Parlor).

Presiding Judge of the Napa County Superior Court Scott Snowden, left, and President of the County Board of Supervisors Mark Luce participate in the ribbon-cutting ceremony with a formidable pair of scissors.

THEN AND NOW

At the dedication on March 24, 1999, of the new criminal courts building, Napa Superior Court Judge Scott Snowden recalled a similar ceremony over 120 years before—the laying of the cornerstone of the third courthouse. Judge Snowden began:

Ladies and Gentlemen, it has been quite a while since Napa County has had an event such as this one. In fact, I can tell you exactly how long. On September 21, 1878, at around 1:00 P.M., 80 Masons left their hall, up there on the far side of Second Street, and walked across the street to a platform. They were in full regalia, headed by the Napa Band. Photographs were taken. One thousand people were present. The program was commenced with music by the choir, which sang a Masonic hymn to the tune of "Rule Britannia." Dr. J. M. Brown, of the Grand Masonic Lodge of California, spoke, describing the appropriateness of involvement by the Masons in auspicious occasions of the sort, finishing with the hope that "On the edifice about to be erected may symmetry and order rest in each line and curve; may strength and beauty grace each arch and pillar from base to capstone; and may the beautiful proportions of the whole structure be for the admiration of the beholder."

Turning to the events of the day, Judge Snowden concluded:

I suspect, if I may shamelessly borrow a phrase, that "the world will little note nor long remember what we say here." But those of us who are here may note and remember that we are at the dedication of the grandest and finest public building constructed in Napa County in 120 years.

At this dedication, we the judges, Judge Philip Champlin, Judge Ron Young, Judge Richard Bennett, Judge Francisca Tisher and Judge Stephen Kroyer, rededicate ourselves, that this magnificent edifice may endure for generations as a symbol of the principles for which it stands: a public tribunal of strict compassion, ever respectful of the human dignity of every person it touches, vouchsafing to all equal justice before the law.

The ornate entry to the old courthouse.

The City & County of San Francisco

San Francisco is both a city and a county, the boundaries of which are coterminous and the governments of which are consolidated. It is not surprising, then, that for most of the past 150 years the majority of the courts have been housed in City Hall. While the criminal courts have been located in separate halls of justice for nearly 100 years, the civil courts did not gain their own freestanding, dedicated courthouse until 1998. And even then, it's just across the street from City Hall.

During the unsettled years between "the conquest" (1846) and the Constitutional Convention (1849), alcades and other magistrates held court in small buildings on or near the dusty expanse called the Plaza (in the days when San Francisco was a Mexican pueblo known as Yerba Buena) and later renamed Portsmouth Square, after the U.S. Navy sloop *Portsmouth*, which sailed into the bay and claimed the city for the United States in July 1846.

As statehood neared, the courts moved into San Francisco's first substantial city hall, a four-story wooden building fabricated on the East Coast, shipped around Cape Horn and assembled a few blocks north of Portsmouth Square. The "Graham House" served briefly as a hotel and more briefly as city hall and courthouse before it was destroyed by fire in June 1851.

A crowd surrounds San Francisco City Hall on February 22, 1851, during the trial of two men accused of robbing and beating a shopkeeper. Foreshadowing the Committee of Vigilance formed later in the year, the "proto-vigilantes" stormed the courtroom, overwhelmed the authorities, and took over the conduct of the trial, which ended in a hung jury. This city hall was destroyed by fire in June 1851.

In 1852, San Francisco purchased the Jenny Lind Theater (center) for its next city hall and courts convened there for the next 30 years. The building to the left was the El Dorado gambling house/saloon before it was purchased for a hall of records a few years later. The building to the right, formerly the Union Hotel, became the first hall of justice. This photograph was taken from Portsmouth Square in 1865. All three buildings were demolished in 1895 to make way for a new hall of justice.

The courts followed the politicians to the next city hall, which fronted directly on Portsmouth Square. This was the former Jenny Lind Theater, built by impresario Thomas Maguire of yellow sandstone imported from Australia, purchased by the city in 1852 and remodeled at considerable expense. According to architectural historian Harold Kirker, this building was "…the first major piece of construction undertaken in California since the erection of Colton Hall in Old Monterey in 1847. Whereas Colton Hall was designed in the simplest New England academy style, the City Hall reflects, especially in its Doric pilasters and well proportioned arches capped by sculptured keystones, the new architectural cosmopolitanism of the great immigration."

The city grew south and west, away from the old Plaza/Portsmouth Square neighborhood and the city leaders envisioned building on a grander scale. Far to the west, the former city cemetery had been abandoned when shifting sands—blown by the often powerful winds from the Pacific—uncovered its graves. The vacated cemetery was selected as the site for the next city hall. Beginning in the early 1870s, the city embarked on construction of a vast city hall and hall of records complex, designed by Augustus Laver in an ornate Second Empire style. Derided during its long-delayed construction (which extended over 20 years) as the "new City Hall ruin," it became a

JUDGE ALMOND'S COURT—1849
December 12, 1849

The business of the alcalde had so greatly increased, as to render necessary the establishment of another court; and upon application made to the governor, he authorized William B. Almond, Esq., to open and hold a Court of First Instance, with civil jurisdiction only. Judge Almond accordingly organized his court in the old schoolhouse on the plaza, and the novel and summary manner in which he conducted his business and disposed of sometimes very important cases, was a source of as much merriment to some and mortification to others as anything else then transpiring in the town. Many a wag who was fond of fun, and had nothing better to do, would spend an hour in the courtroom to enjoy the satisfaction of observing the chagrin of upstart attorneys, toward whose ora-

torical eloquence and legal knowledge the judge was wont to exhibit the most mortifying indifference. His Honor… had a most sovereign contempt for Buncombe speeches, legal technicalities, learned opinions and triumphantly cited precedents. He was a man of quick discernment and clear judgment, and his opinion once formed, and that sometimes occurred before even the first witness was fully heard, his decision was made. Nothing further need be said…. There can be no reason to doubt that his decisions generally were far more just and equitable than those more recently given in courts claiming greater legal knowledge, where learned judges gravely occupy the bench and tampered juries are influenced more by bribes than testimony.

Upon Judge Almond's refusing to allow him to call another witness, a lawyer protested, "But

you will at least hear us speak to the points of law?" "That would be a great waste of time, which is very precious," replied the judge. "I award the plaintiff $150. Mr. Clerk, what is the next case?"

Young lawyers were not pleased with this summary method of disposing of business. To these, the opportunity of making a speech, the tendency of which is usually to render a clear case obscure, though it doubtless serves to display the extent of their wisdom and intelligence, is of quite as much consequence as meat and drink to other people. They could not live without it. Hence, Judge Almond, who deprived them of this exquisite enjoyment, was no favorite with them.

Frank Soule *et al.*, *The Annals of San Francisco*, (1855), pp. 239–240

ruin in fact one day in April 1906. The courts spent most of the following decade in a hotel on Market Street appropriated by the city for a city hall.

In the aftermath of the earthquake and fire, a coalition of Progressive businessmen, lawyers and educators determined to rid the city of corrupt politicians and to rebuild on the principles of the City Beautiful movement, which sought to support municipal culture and good government with orderly and inspiring city planning. The reformers triumphed with the landslide election in 1911 of James "Sunny Jim" Rolph as mayor. Rolph was the moving force behind both the city hall and the expanded civic center that it anchors. He campaigned relentlessly, writing articles for the newspapers and persuading Luiza Tettrazini, the leading opera diva of the day, to plug the bond issue at her farewell concert just before the election in 1912. The voters approved the bonds by a margin of 11 to 1 and San Francisco had the funding to begin constructing what has come to be regarded as one of the finest ensembles of public buildings in the country. The courts were housed on the upper floors of City Hall, initially on what was expected to be a temporary basis—but which ultimately extended for 75 years.

It was another earthquake, the Loma Prieta quake of 1989, that created the opportunity for the Civic Center to take another step toward realization of its planners' original vision. City Hall was shored up by a forest of wood bracing until it was vacated for remodeling in 1995. The courts dispersed once again. This time, however, they returned to their own courthouse newly constructed across McAllister Street from City Hall, completing the northwest corner of the Civic Center, which had been empty for 75 years. The courthouse is faced with white granite hewn from the same Sierra quarry that supplied the stone for City Hall and all the other buildings that frame Civic Center Plaza. The challenges of designing a 21st-century courthouse to fit harmoniously within a Beaux Arts precinct are discussed in the essay by one of the new courthouse's architects, Charles Drulis, AIA, which begins on page 338.

This photograph was taken from almost the same location in Portsmouth Square some 40 years later. The tower of the new Hall of Justice, completed in 1900 to 1901, is a more muscular version of the tower on the nearby Ferry Building designed by Willis Polk. The slender Ferry Building tower survived the 1906 earthquake, however, while this one toppled.

Above: The hall of records was part of a new Civic Center complex built miles to the west of the old Plaza/Portsmouth Square. Begun in the 1870s, construction stretched over 20 years. The extravagent Second Empire city hall, in the background, housed the courts.

Below: The city hall complex viewed from the west, with the hall of records visible in the background. Courts moved into the city hall gradually, as construction progressed, commencing in the 1880s. The pedimented portico and entry on the right side of the photograph signify the location of the courts.

The "Big One," an immensely powerful earthquake that struck on April 18, 1906, followed by a fire, devastated City Hall (above) and damaged the hall of justice (right). The vast majority of property records, birth and death certificates, etc., were lost as the ornate hall of records burned. Homeless families set up housekeeping in city parks, such as here in Portsmouth Square.

Above Left: Mayor James "Sunny Jim" Rolph, at ground-breaking in April 1913, holds a silver spade made for the occasion by Shreve & Co., the city's most prominent jewelers.

Above Right: The architectural firm of Bakewell & Brown won the design competition for the new city hall; over 100 architects participated. Members of the design team shown here include Jean Louis Bourgeois (second from left), to whom the interior of the dome is attributed and John Bakewell (second from right).

Below: The western façade, with its central pedimented portico, flanking wings with Doric colonnades, and the building's principal design feature, its great dome, which rises higher than the Capitol in Washington, D.C. The buildings in the foreground are the Veteran's Memorial Building (left) and the War Memorial Opera House (right) where the United Nations was formed in 1945, both also designed by Arthur Brown, one of the finest of all American classical architects.

Above: The vast rotunda of City Hall is one of the great interior public spaces in the United States. It is seen here looking upward into the dome from the principal landing, reached by a fan-shaped staircase (not visible) that spills out onto the ground floor.

Left: The hall of justice was rebuilt after the earthquake and fire of 1906 without its central tower, under supervision of Newton Tharp, the same city architect who had designed the former building. The 1960s television drama *Ironsides* had the famous police detective's office, with its distinctive arched windows, set within the hall of justice. It was demolished in 1968, to be replaced by a hotel.

Above: January 14, 1954, Joe DiMaggio and Marilyn Monroe, just after being married by Municipal Court Judge Charles Peery, in his City Hall chambers. The late Art Hoppe, a beloved reporter and columnist for the *San Francisco Chronicle*, observed the next day: "Joltin' Joe DiMaggio wedded the girl of his and many other men's dreams yesterday afternoon in the San Francisco City Hall."

Left: Judge Daniel Shoemaker (later an associate justice on the First District Court of Appeal) helps a workman dismantle the "cage" in which prisoners were held before arraignment in a hall of justice courtroom until 1947.

Above: Pigeons flourish in the Civic Center. Here, an unidentified blue pigeon has just laid an egg on the desk of Superior Court Judge Alfred Fritz. Dick Penland, the judge's court reporter, examines the situation in September 1951.

The current hall of justice, completed in 1960, is a massive, unadorned cube, housing the criminal courts, sheriff's office and jail.

Right: Stainless steel doors at the main entrance to the 1998 courthouse were designed and fabricated by artist Albert Paley.

Below: The 1989 Loma Prieta earthquake forced courts to vacate City Hall, their temporary home since 1916. The new, permanent civil courthouse completes one of the four corners of the Civic Center Plaza as envisioned in the early master plans, the first of which was proposed by Daniel Burnham in 1905. An essay by Charles Drulis, AIA, one of the architects of the new courthouse, appears on pages 338 to 345.

County of San Mateo

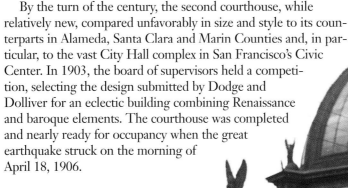

The first courthouse built in San Mateo County was constructed in 1858 in what is now Redwood City, on land donated to the county by the Arguello family and their attorney, Simon Mezes. A courthouse has stood on the site ever since.

The first courthouse was a two-story masonry building. The basement held jail cells; county offices and a courtroom occupied the first floor; the upper floor was one large room used for dancing and social assemblies. A powerful earthquake in 1868 damaged the building to such an extent that the board of supervisors ordered the top floor removed for safety. For the next decade the county made do with a one-story building.

A more substantial brick courthouse was added to the site in 1882, designed by Augustus Laver, architect of the grand mansion recently built in Menlo Park for James Flood, one of the "silver kings" of the Comstock Lode bonanza. The single-story original courthouse continued in use as an annex.

By the turn of the century, the second courthouse, while relatively new, compared unfavorably in size and style to its counterparts in Alameda, Santa Clara and Marin Counties and, in particular, to the vast City Hall complex in San Francisco's Civic Center. In 1903, the board of supervisors held a competition, selecting the design submitted by Dodge and Dolliver for an eclectic building combining Renaissance and baroque elements. The courthouse was completed and nearly ready for occupancy when the great earthquake struck on the morning of April 18, 1906.

The façade of the county's fourth courthouse, seen here in the 1920s, is no longer visible. Its Corinthian columns, ornamental balustrade and triumphal stone eagle were removed in 1939 by a federally financed annex in the PWA Moderne style.

San Mateo County's first courthouse (the two-story building in the center background of the picture) was built in 1858 near the Embarcadero of Redwood City. The stacks of lumber in the foreground were logged in nearby redwood forests from which the city derived its name.

The board of supervisors, while naturally dismayed, were not defeated. Meeting the following month, they enacted a resolution proclaiming:

> Whereas, this board has full faith in our county, its future rapid growth and development, and its proximity to one of the greatest though now stricken cities of the country, and has no fear of any recurrence of any disaster by another earthquake; and
> Whereas, this board has entire confidence in the indomitable courage and energy of the citizens of the county and fully believes that they will work with all the people for a greater and better San Mateo County, a greater and more beautiful city of San Francisco and a greater and more prosperous state of California.
> Resolved and declared that it is the sense and judgment of this board that the public good and welfare requires and demands that steps should be taken to reconstruct and restore [the] courthouse.

The supervisors' confidence was confirmed a few months later in September 1906 when county voters passed, with a greater than two-thirds majority, two bond issues to rebuild the courthouse.

The board selected San Francisco architect Glenn Allen, whose design emphasized structural stability (a steel frame that secured the dome and reinforced concrete), but carried forward many exterior elements of the prior building, including the rotunda dome, the use of green Colusa sandstone and most of the window configuration.

The reconstructed courthouse was dedicated in 1910. It has since endured the indignity of being boxed in by depression-era annexes, being abandoned by the courts, which moved down the street to a massive office complex, and the 1989 Loma Prieta earthquake. Happily it has survived. A sensitive restoration of the dome and rotunda, carried out by architect Adolph Rosecrans, and further seismic and handicapped access improvements were completed in the 1990s. And in 1998, the San Mateo County Historical Association and Museum moved into its new quarters—the old courthouse in Redwood City.

The second courthouse, known as the "Justice Court" because of the large statue of Justice on the roof, was built in 1882. The building immediately behind the new court is the first floor of the original 1858 courthouse, which continued to serve as an annex. The picket fence was necessary to keep cows from foraging on the lawn.

The third courthouse was nearly ready for occupancy when it was heavily damaged in the April 1906 earthquake. Engineers pronounced the dome and foundation salvageable and it was reconstructed.

Far Right: July 4, 1910, was a great day in San Mateo County, as the fourth courthouse, rebuilt from the ruins left by the earthquake, was dedicated. Note the costumed figure at the far left holding both spear and parasol.

Feisty eagles appear on the capitals of exterior pilasters.

The graceful central dome contains 38,240 pieces of stained glass.

The richness of the 1910 courthouse can be seen in these images. This page, clockwise from upper left:

An ornamental light fixture between two of the imitation marble (scagliola) pilasters that line the walls of the rotunda.

The main courtroom lighted by an oval stained glass dome, leaded glass lanterns, simple bulbs and tall vertical windows, appeared in the 1993 movie *Mrs. Doubtfire*.

The Great Seal of the State of California, executed in mosaic tile, on the first floor of the rotunda directly beneath the dome.

Images of California's natural bounty adorn exterior columns of Colusa sandstone.

The second floor balcony in the rotunda.

Left: The 1939 PWA Moderne annex. Long unpopular for having obscured the elegant façade of the old courthouse, it may now, at 60, be appreciated for its own subdued Art Deco touches.

Above: The entry to the 1939 courthouse annex is flanked by bas-relief panels depicting early Californians (left) and American workers (right) in the optimistic style of WPA art.

Right: Courts are now housed in the hall of justice and records, constructed in 1955 and expanded in 1971. The hall of justice and the nearby 1963 county government center led architectual historian David Gebhard to observe, "The latest buildings prove that the course of architecture need not be onward and upward."

County of Santa Clara

The Pueblo of San Jose was founded in 1777—California's first town (as distinguished from a mission or presidio). The County of Santa Clara was organized in 1851. Over the next 17 years, its courts shuttled from one temporary venue to another—seven different locations in all. Most of these were in unremarkable commercial buildings. Those that went beyond merely vernacular architecture are pictured: the short-lived State House built in the Monterey style; the castle-like San Jose City Hall; and the Italianate Murphy Building—nearly identical to the original state supreme court building in Sacramento.

In 1852, the courts moved to the building that had housed the state legislature for the brief time that San Jose was the capitol of California. The State House burned in 1853; seen here is a replica constructed in 1899 to commemorate the 50th anniversary of California Statehood.

But the eighth courthouse was something entirely different—an elegantly proportioned and "vigorously detailed" Renaissance Revival building. An appreciative assessment by Alan Hess, a San Jose architect, observed that its "elongated windows and Corinthian columns swept the eye upward to the fluted, egg-shaped dome and the deep blue of the Santa Clara County sky." It was designed by Levi Goodrich, one of the first professionally trained architects to practice in California and the designer of two other county courthouses (Monterey and San Diego), as well as of the original University of the Pacific buildings in Stockton. His courthouse was not only elegant, it was sturdy. It survived the powerful earthquakes of 1868 and 1906 and has anchored for well over a century the impressive assemblage of public and religious buildings that border St. James Square Park.

After fire gutted the courthouse in 1931, the dome was not rebuilt; a somewhat awkward third story replaced it.

The old courthouse's longtime neighbors, the turn-of-the-century hall of records and hall of justice, were demolished in the mid-1960s to make way for a six-story concrete superior court building. The county executive

This adobe Juzgado, built in 1783, housed the alcade's office, a courtroom and the jail in San Jose under the Spanish and Mexican governments. American authorities continued this use from 1846 to 1850.

Santa Clara County courts used the upper floor of San Jose's Gothic Revival city hall from 1860 to 1862.

recommended that the venerable courthouse be razed as well. But public outcry in favor of the beautiful old building, and opposition by the judges, persuaded the board of supervisors to fund its renovation in the mid-1970s.

The 1989 Loma Prieta earthquake did serious damage, leading the county to close the courthouse because of dangerous breaks in the reinforced brick walls. But instead of demolishing it, the county, with help from FEMA, carried out a sweeping $12-million renovation project. A new steel-reinforced concrete skeleton was constructed within the original 22-inch-thick brick walls. Aesthetics were considered as well, particularly in the restoration of the interior, where courtrooms were refurbished based on the 1931 alterations. Alan Hess applauded the result: "Soft roses, greens, mustard yellows and putties may not be authentic to 1931 but give the courthouse a dignified unity it did not have when the judges in 1971, redecorating for themselves, borrowed all the wrong tricks from the era of green shag carpeting." And, in an unhappy concession to changing times, while most of the original dark oak furnishings were recycled, the judges' benches are new, updated with bulletproofing.

Court was held in the Murphy Building, located in the center of the city's civic and commercial life, from 1863 to 1868.

This courthouse, completed in 1868, was the first building actually designed for the county as a courthouse. Residents could climb the 172 steps within the dome to reach the iron-railed observation deck at its top.

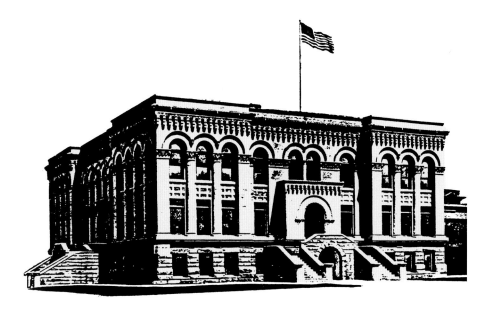

Above and Left: The sand-stone hall of justice was the third county civic building constructed to the west of St. James Park in downtown San Jose. It was finished just in time for the April 1906 earthquake. Rebuilt (shorn of decorative cornices, pediments and balconies), it was eventually razed in 1962.

The interior of the 1893 hall of records, which housed the offices of the county clerk, treasurer, auditor, surveyor, recorder and superintendent of schools.

Right and Below: In May 1931, firefighters battled a fire that raced through the courthouse. This picture was taken just seconds before the dome collapsed. To the right can be seen the Richardsonian Romanesque hall of records, built in 1893.

Below: Young volunteers carry ledgers from the hall of records during the disastrous 1931 blaze.

The 1868 courthouse with its dome and the 1893 hall of records. The two buildings, while distinctively different in style, are a harmonious and impressive pair. Why is it so difficult to accomplish this now?

Above: A forthrightly modernist superior court building was constructed in 1964 adjacent to the old courthouse, whose north wall is visible to the left of this picture.

Above: The main entrance to the 1868 courthouse, as of 1998, shows architect Levi Goodrich's Corinthian columns preserved but recessed back into the façade. The courthouse was seismically strengthened and beautifully restored after the 1989 Loma Prieta earthquake and returned to use in 1994.

Left: A hall of justice, completed in 1991, provided space for 19 new courtrooms in San Jose's new civic center complex, remote from the city's historic center at St. James Square.

County of Solano

Solano County was named in honor of the chief of the Suisun Indians at the suggestion of his friend General Mariano Vallejo. Its first county seat was Benicia, named for General Vallejo's wife. Until the building used briefly as the state capitol was constructed in 1853, county officers and the courts occupied the lower floor of the first Masonic Hall built in California.

The courts' next home was the two-story brick and sandstone Greek Revival temple ostensibly built as Benicia's City Hall but designed to tempt the state legislature to move the capital from Vallejo. The scheme succeeded but Benicia's triumph was short-lived; the legislature returned to Sacramento after only one year. The county occupied the building as a courthouse until 1858, when Benicia also lost its status as Solano's county seat.

As more settlers moved into the eastern sectors of Solano County, demands arose for a more centrally located seat of government. Robert Waterman, an old sea captain and part owner of a large rancho near the center of the county, seized the opportunity. He laid out the town of Fairfield (named for his boyhood home in Connecticut) and offered the county a block of land and temporary quarters if the county seat were moved there. Residents of Vallejo threw their support to Fairfield to spite Benicia, which had wrested the state capital from them six years before. Fairfield prevailed and Captain Waterman's offer was accepted.

A relatively undistinguished assemblage of public buildings was constructed in Fairfield between 1858 to 1887 consisting of jail, courthouse and hall of records. These were replaced in 1911 by a stylish Beaux Arts classical courthouse whose two-story portico and long flight of steps are situated to look down Union Avenue. In 1950, a conventional, but compatibly designed, annex was built to the west of the 1911 courthouse (which housed many county offices in addition to the courts). In

This Greek Revival style brick and sandstone building in Benicia served for a year as the state capitol. When the legislature moved back to Sacramento in 1854, it became the Solano County courthouse. After the county seat was relocated to Fairfield in 1858, it was used variously as Benicia's city hall, public library, police station and dance hall/boxing arena. Seen here in dilapidated condition in the 1940s, it was extensively restored by the State of California in 1956 and 1957 and is now a museum of state and local history.

The one-time State Capitol and county courthouse as it appears after the mid-1950s restoration. State engineer Frank Johnson reported before the work began: "There may be buildings in use for human occupancy in as poor structural shape as this building, but in my experience I have seen no worse. The building has been so weakened by neglect that very little factor of safety remains." The restoration required drastic measures, but has been a grand success.

1976, the courts were removed from the courthouse entirely and relocated across the street to a remodeled high school renamed the "Hall of Justice." An ambitious master-planned government center is envisioned as eventually incorporating the old courthouse, the 1950s annex, the Hall of Justice and a new law and justice center. The first phase of the plan was accomplished in the late 1980s when a new jail and court building, designed by Hellmuth Obata & Kassabaum, were constructed adjacent to the hall of justice.

The first courthouse in Fairfield completed in 1860 is on the right, the hall of records completed in 1878 to the left. Note the iron bridge connecting the two buildings.

An addition to the courthouse built in 1887 joined the hall of records to the courthouse and the iron bridge was removed.

The Beaux Arts Classical courthouse, completed in 1911, shown here patriotically decorated for its dedication ceremony.

Statue of Winged Victory, holding olive branches aloft, was installed in front of the courthouse after World War I. The inscription on the base reads "Solano County's Tribute to its Fallen Heroes."

Above: The October 1917 *Architect and Engineer* issue considered the Solano County courthouse to be one of the best works of its chief architect, E. C. Hemmings of Sacramento. "The main façade of this building is beautified by a series of Ionic columns which give it a monumental feeling and at the same time is suggestive of a public edifice."

Left: A naval gun on the courthouse lawn.

Right: In 1976, the county relocated the courts from the 1911 courthouse, as well as the 1950 annex, to the "Hall of Justice"—a remodeled high school just across the street.

Below: The 1986 expansion of the hall of justice (left) was viewed by its architects as the first phase in a much more expansive governmental complex. The superior court building (right), with an arched skylight atop its lobby, was added in 1989.

Right: Ornate lanterns flank the stairway to the old courthouse's main entry. The courts may return to the venerable building when the board of supervisors moves to a new government center.

County of Sonoma

The county seat fixed by the legislature in 1850 was the town of Sonoma, site of the most northerly of the missions and home to the county's most prominent citizen: former general, now state senator, Mariano Vallejo.

The first courthouse was an adobe building purchased from County Judge H. A. Green, which the 1854 grand jury condemned as "unfit for a cattleshed." The ambitious residents of Santa Rosa solved that problem later that year by persuading the voters to relocate the county seat to their growing young city. Julio Carrillo, owner of thousands of acres surrounding Santa Rosa, and Barney Hoen, one of its first merchants, promised to donate the land necessary for a new courthouse as well as a public plaza, if the voters chose Santa Rosa. Equally persuasive was a free Fourth of July barbecue hosted by Santa Rosa to which all county voters were invited, followed by a dance that lasted until daybreak.

After the election, the court of sessions set the date for the county records to be transferred from Sonoma to the new county seat. As the appointed day approached, talk grew of possible resistance from unhappy residents of Sonoma, who suspected electoral fraud. In response, two Santa Rosans hitched four mules to a wagon and left for Sonoma in the middle of the night, hauled the archives out of the makeshift courthouse while Sonoma slept, and dashed back to Santa Rosa. Their arrival at dawn was cause for another celebratory barbecue. Afterwards, the *Sonoma Bulletin*'s editor remarked, "We are only sorry that they did not take the courthouse along—not because it would be ornamental to Santa Rosa, but because its removal would have embellished our plaza. Alas old 'casa de adobe.' No more do we see county lawyers, and loafers in general, lazily engaged in the laudable effort of whittling asunder the veranda posts—which, by the way, required but little more to bring the whole fabric to the ground."

A courthouse, facing the Santa Rosa town plaza, was completed in 1855 and a second story added in 1859. In 1871 the *Santa Rosa Democrat* was reporting that the loose plaster in the courtroom was "dangerous to bald headed men" and by 1878 the grand jury judged it to be "miserable, dilapidated and a disgrace."

This photograph, taken in the mid-1870s, looking north across the Santa Rosa town plaza, shows the courthouse built in 1856, with its second story added in 1859, on the corner. To its left, is the 1871 hall of records.

The decision to locate the next courthouse, completed in 1885, in the center of the town plaza was controversial. Residents of Santa Rosa, already distressed at the loss of their downtown park, were infuriated by the refusal of the board of supervisors to pay for a clock to be installed in the new courthouse's tower. The Santa Rosa City Council eventually paid for the clock.

The courthouse in ruins after the earthquake of April 1906 toppled its dome and tower. A history written a few years later recalled how everyone pitched in to help rebuild: "Youthful attorneys, with no cases before the court until the insurance companies began to 'welch' on the fire losses, took a summer school course in railroad construction.... Manual labor was the only recognized profession."

The county pressured the city to make the plaza available for a new courthouse. When the city council finally acquiesced in 1883, the county hired prominent architects A. A. Bennett and J. M. Curtis to design a grand courthouse in the popular Italianate fashion. Completed in 1885, it served only until April 1906, when it was destroyed by the earthquake that shattered Santa Rosa as well as San Francisco.

The county moved quickly (remarkably so by today's standards) to rebuild. Plans for a much larger Beaux Arts courthouse were approved by 1907 and the building completed by 1910, on the same site as its predecessor.

In the mid-1960s, the courthouse was relocated to a sprawling county government center at the north edge of town, adjacent to Highway 101. For the first time in over 100 years, there was no courthouse in downtown Santa Rosa.

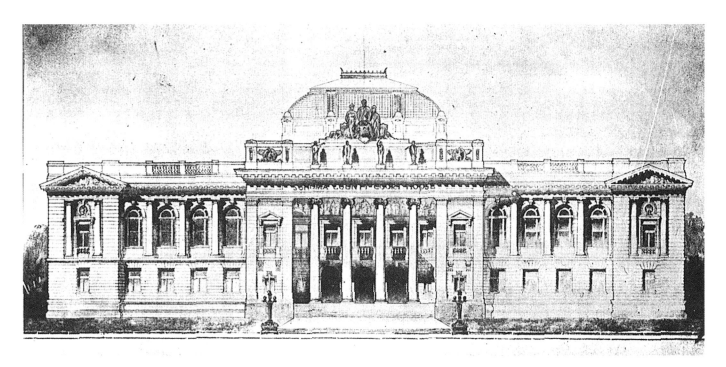

Plans for the third courthouse in Santa Rosa, drawn by San Francisco architect J. W. Dolliver, called for a steel frame building with reinforced concrete walls, faced with locally quarried stone.

Above: The courthouse as built in 1910 closely followed the plans for a symmetrical structure, with slightly less ornamentation over the central colonnade. "It is built for all time and the earthquake" a local historian proclaimed shortly after its completion. In fact, it lasted only slightly more than 50 years, being demolished in 1966.

Left: The first Sonoma County superior court jury to include women sat in 1922. The richness of the courthouse's interior can be seen in the lavish use of marble and bronze.

PEN STROKE HALTS EVICTION AS THOUSANDS JOIN IN PROTEST

A crowd of farmers gathered in front of the courthouse in 1933 to protest a bank's attempt to foreclose on a ranch owned by J. A. Case, a 70-year-old former minister. Superior Court Judge Hilliard Comstock granted an injunction to halt the forced sale.

A happier side of the 1930s —schoolchildren in a maypole dance festival held in front of the courthouse in the early 1930s.

The current courthouse is part of the sprawling county government center campus built in the mid-1960s on what was then farmland at the very edge of town.

The San Joaquin Valley

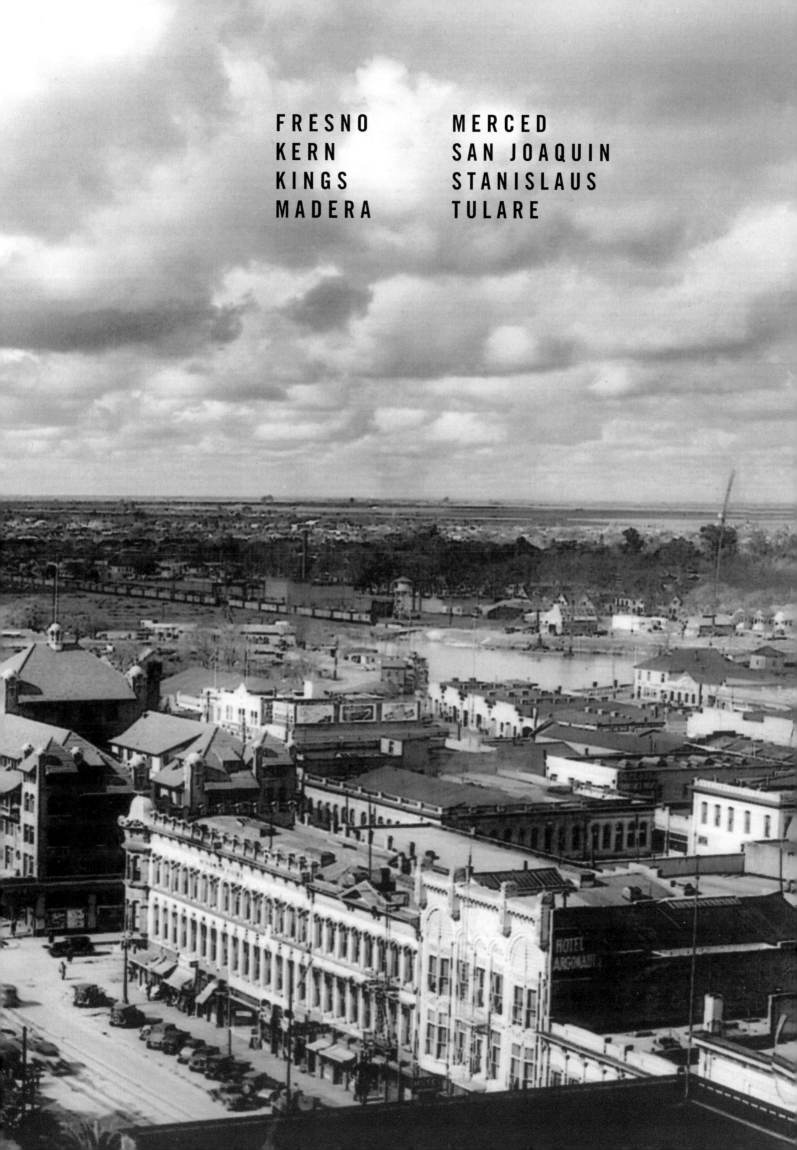

FRESNO   MERCED
KERN   SAN JOAQUIN
KINGS   STANISLAUS
MADERA   TULARE

County of Fresno

Millerton, a gold mining town in the Sierra foothills, was Fresno County's first county seat. After making do with rented quarters for 10 years, the county hired builder Charles Peck, who had recently worked on the classic courthouse in nearby Mariposa, to design its first true courthouse. Peck proposed a similarly plain structure, but to be built of granite and brick rather than wood. Completed in 1867, the courthouse also accommodated county offices and a jail.

The sturdy courthouse withstood a flood during its first winter, but much of Millerton was devastated. In 1872, the Central Pacific Railroad reached Fresno, and two years later, the county seat was moved to the new town growing up around the railroad's Fresno station. Millerton gradually disappeared, many of its buildings being moved to new sites in Fresno. The abandoned courthouse was eventually the last building standing.

The board of supervisors engaged the prominent A. A. Bennett, former state architect, to design their new courthouse in Fresno, making do with a temporary wooden building until Bennett's Palladian vision was completed in 1876. It was similar in style to courthouses Bennett designed for other San Joaquin Valley counties: 60 feet by 95 feet, three stories, with a slender dome and cupola, built of 800,000 bricks and covered by cement.

At the ceremony marking the laying of the cornerstone, District Attorney C. G. Sayle anticipated the courthouse to be "the grandest and noblest edifice that has ever

Fresno's first county seat, Millerton, shown here in 1870, lay on the south bank of the San Joaquin River in the Sierra foothills. The courthouse is the two-story building with a peaked roof at left of center. Native American dwellings line the shore in the foreground.

Preceding page: San Joaquin County courthouse, Stockton, 1930s.

been planned or contemplated in this valley," a building that was "expected to stand the storms of winter and the heat of summer for the period of one thousand years or more...."

The courthouse was expanded (actually transformed) in the early 1890s when two wings, a grand neoclassical style entry and a huge copper-coated dome were added. A spectacular fire in the summer of 1895 destroyed the dome. An account in the *Fresno Daily Evening Expositer* for July 30, 1895, described how "the great mass of copper which covered the dome was melted by the intense heat on the upper levels and poured down in streams of red liquid." According to the reporter the "unanimous feeling of all who saw it was one of pain and sorrow that the grand looking dome should be destroyed."

The damage was repaired and a smaller fireproof dome replaced the grandiose but short-lived copper dome. With periodic improvements, the courthouse stood for the next 70 years, surrounded by the five-acre Courthouse Park, an ornament of Fresno's urban life, whose lawns, walks, and shade trees were the scene of picnics, dances, band concerts, and memorials.

In the early 1960s, the board of supervisors determined to replace the old courthouse, ostensibly because of concerns over its seismic safety, possibly because of the availability of federal funding. A four-year battle ensued. The Fresno Historical Society remonstrated against the plan: "No more beautiful, stately and historic building exists in the County. It represents the very heart and personality of Fresno and... a tie with Fresno's pioneer days. It is more significant and cherished than any museum or gallery could be." The *Fresno Bee*, the San Joaquin Valley chapter of the A.I.A., the Fresno County Bar Association, William Saroyan and thousands of county residents supported saving the old courthouse. But the supervisors persisted, lawsuits failed and the building was demolished in April 1966. An eight-story glass-walled office tower replaced it.

The courthouse and jail was built by Charles Converse. Mr. Converse was also the first occupant of his jail, having been arrested and tried for shooting a man to death during a political rally shortly after the courthouse was completed. This photograph shows the courthouse in 1868, next to the Court House Exchange Saloon.

In the 1940s, community groups rallied to save the first courthouse from being inundated by the waters rising behind Friant Dam. The building was dismantled, the granite blocks and iron bars and shutters moved to higher ground. There they sat until 1965, when the courthouse was rebuilt on Mariner's Point overlooking Millerton Lake, where it now serves as a museum.

Above: The first courthouse in early Fresno as seen from Mariposa Street in the 1870s.

Below: Six young men pose for a photograph with the courthouse in the background. The windmill to the left supplied water to the courthouse.

Above: The courthouse after its transformation in the 1890s. The original courthouse remains as the central core, nearly hidden behind the classical entry façade.

Left: The beloved *Boy with the Leaking Boot* fountain stood in Courthouse Park from 1895 to 1921.

An aerial view of Fresno shows the courthouse (looking much like a state capitol) and Courthouse Park, with the Sierra foothills in the distance.

An illuminated Christmas tree in Courthouse Park, December 1924.

The hall of records, built with federal funding in 1937, exemplifies the Art Deco style.

COURTHOUSES OF CALIFORNIA

Left: A statue of Justice atop the old courthouse regards her successor, nearing completion.

Opposite page: The old courthouse dome toppled in 1966.

Below: The current courthouse reflects the influences of Edward Stone and Minoru Yamasaki,. Architectural historian David Gebhardt dismissed it as "insipid."

County of Kern

K ern County was established in 1866. Its first county seat was Havilah, a flourishing mining town in the foothills of the southern Sierra Nevada. The town had been named for the biblical Havilah—"the land where gold is" (Genesis 2:11)—by Asbury Harpending, an adventurer from Kentucky who was one of its founders. County officers quickly arranged for a jail to be built. The one-story wood frame courthouse took a bit longer, but was ready in June 1867.

As mining activity declined, agricultural interests pressed for the seat of government to be relocated to the more prosaically named, and centrally located, Bakersfield. (The town was named for "Baker's field"—land drained and planted in alfalfa by Colonel Thomas Baker.) The change came in 1874 and by 1876 Kern County had its own A. A. Bennett Italianate courthouse—almost a replica of the courthouse the prolific Bennett had designed for Fresno County a few years earlier.

The first courthouse at Havilah, used from 1867 to 1874. A replica was built in 1966, as part of the County's centennial celebration, and houses a museum.

By the 1890s, the county government's need for space had outgrown Bennett's modestly sized building. San Francisco architects Charles and Barnett McDougall presented expansion plans to double its size. They also transformed it into a much grander structure, with three domes and an almost ecclesiastical appearance.

Only 15 years later the county, whose population had increased from 9,800 in 1890 to 38,000 in 1910, required still larger quarters. Oakland architect Frederick Meyer's plans for a large Classical Revival building reflected both the change in public taste and the county's growing prosperity—with agriculture now supplemented by development of the county's recently discovered oil and natural gas fields.

The courthouse built in 1912 was badly damaged in the earthquake of 1952 and replaced in 1959 by a seven-story concrete and glass curtain wall office building that remains in use, supplemented by the nearby Civic Center Justice Building completed in 1980.

When the county seat moved to Bakersfield, courts were lodged in the city hall for two years.

The architect of the first courthouse built in Bakersfield (1876) was the prolific A. A. Bennett, who designed similiar courthouses for four other San Joaquin Valley counties between 1873 and 1876.

Below: The courthouse, as expanded in 1896. The building served as Bakersfield's city hall when the county built an even larger courthouse in 1912. Both structures were destroyed by an earthquake in 1952.

The first hall of records, seen here in 1908, was directly across the street from the 1876 courthouse.

The hall of records as restored in 1988. The commemorative plaque explains why the building was renovated rather than replaced: "So that a vital link to the past will not be forgotten in future generations."

Frederick Meyer's Classical Revival courthouse. The *Architect and Engineer,* commenting on the plans, in July 1910, saw "a clean cut carefully studied building with an attractive exterior of white Manti stone. The central motif is decorated with free-standing Corinthian columns, while the two end motifs are three-fourths engaged columns with pilaster treatment for the wings. The parapet over the main pavilion is decorated in bas relief figures and ornaments with a rich cresting over the top."

Above: The rotunda of
the 1912 courthouse.

Below: Courtrooms occupy
the functionally designed
building that replaced the
grand 1912 courthouse.

Above: The Civic Center
Justice Building
constructed in 1980.

County of Kings

Hanford, like so many other towns in the Central Valley that became county seats, was established by the Southern Pacific Railroad. (The town was named for James Madison Hanford, a railroad officer who selected the site in 1877.)

Kings County was formed in 1893. Within a few years, the board of supervisors built an impressive courthouse with an eclectic mix of stylistic detail set in Hanford's tree-shaded central square. Two years after the courthouse opened (in 1896), it was joined by a Romanesque jail, whose crenellated octagonal tower suggests a miniature European castle. A 1914 expansion of the courthouse was faithful to the original style and detail.

Even though the county eventually outgrew its original courthouse and jail, both were preserved and converted to other uses in the early 1980s. The courthouse is now home to offices, small retail shops and a cafe; the jail is a restaurant, aptly called the Bastille. Both buildings, in their new roles, continue to contribute to the comfortable small-town atmosphere that makes a visit to downtown Hanford such a pleasure.

In 1976, the county relocated and consolidated the courts, the jail and all county offices to a 110-acre site a few miles to the west of Hanford. The gracefully landscaped college-like campus of one-story buildings was beyond the town's perimeter when it opened in the mid-1970s, but growth has recently leapfrogged beyond the government center; a new shopping mall now represents the westernmost expansion of the town into the surrounding fields.

A preliminary drawing by architect William Willcox shows the principal elevation of the 1896 courthouse. The tall central tower was never built, but the other major features (the two-tiered portico and the corner pavilion towers with their metal pyramidal roofs) were retained.

Severe square columns are topped by Ionic capitals. The upper columns support arches, cornice and an extravagantly decorated pediment.

Portico of the yellow brick courthouse in Hanford's central square, circa 1930.

The 1898 brick and granite jail, adjacent to the courthouse, is now a restaurant.

In the mid-1970s, courts, along with all other county offices, moved to a spacious, landscaped campus at what was then the edge of town. A two-story criminal courts building was added in 1991.

County of Madera

In 1874, two lumber companies completed a 5-foot-wide, 63-mile-long flume to transport lumber from forests in the Sierra Nevada to the Central Pacific Railroad's tracks near the Fresno River. A settlement grew up near the lower end of the flume and in 1876 another lumber company laid out the town of Madera (Spanish for "wood" or "lumber"). When the county was created in 1893 out of northern Fresno County, the same name was chosen for it. The town of Madera became the county seat.

In the early years county government and the courts were housed in a succession of rented quarters. By 1900, the county had acquired suitable land. Advertising for architectural plans, the board of supervisors specified that "the building shall be granite, absolutely fireproof, and not exceed the sum of $60,000." They achieved one out of three of their goals. Fresno architect Hugh Braunton's plans called for the building to be faced in granite. However, it cost $100,000 and, as events were soon to prove, was far from fireproof.

Christmas Eve 1906: The clock tower has already collapsed and flames are consuming the upper floor.

The courthouse completed in 1902 was essentially square (84 feet by 93 feet), two stories in height. The roof and floors were reinforced concrete and steel framing supported the exterior walls, which were faced with granite blocks hewn from the nearby Raymond Granite quarries, which produced granite for construction projects statewide.

On Christmas Eve 1906, Madera firemen were called out to battle a spectacular blaze that threatened to destroy the new courthouse. The fire was controlled but too late to save the clock tower or the courtroom, offices and the library on the second floor. The *Madera Mercury* lamented, "The once beautiful courthouse, the pride of the people of this county is now desolate, the upper floor is a waste of wreck and ruin. The iron forming the dome lies in a tangled mass in the courtroom" (*Madera Mercury*, December 29, 1906).

The first floor survived and the building was structurally sound. It was soon rebuilt and served until 1953 when it was declared unsafe and abandoned. Madera citizens nominated it to the National Register of Historic Places in 1970 and raised funds for its restoration as the Madera County Historical Museum.

The courthouse rebuilt. The hip roof has been replaced and the new clock tower is much narrower than the original but the building is otherwise unchanged. The smoke at the left is from an industrial building alongside the railroad tracks.

COURT HOUSE MADERA CAL

Above: The 1902 courthouse shortly after it was built. The original clock tower was described by an architectural historian as an "octagonal windowed drum" that was "surmounted by a mansard roof dome." A local farmer was more blunt, observing that it looked like a "silo."

A close-up of the courthouse's new clock tower. Though different in style, it houses the clocks that survived the fire. The courthouse is on the National Register and has been restored to serve as the county historical museum.

Below: The present Madera county government center. The county purchased the Mission Revival style Lincoln School in the 1950s and remodeled it for use as a courthouse.

County of Merced

Conditions at the first county seat, the Turner and Osborne Ranch, were primitive when Merced County was established in 1855. The courthouse was a one-story wooden building, 12 by 25 feet, described as "rude and unfinished." A dining table did double duty as judge's bench and clerk's desk; boxes and kegs served as seats. The grand jury met under one oak tree; trial juries deliberated along the banks of Mariposa Creek, beneath another oak.

The spot was one of the windiest in the county, a challenge for the clerk who had no place to store his papers. A county history relates, "At times a sudden gust of wind would get the best of [the clerk] during a session of the court, scattering indictments, warrants, summonses, subpoenas and other legal documents to the four winds. At such times all was confusion and Judge, Jury, Clerk and everyone else turned their attention to hunting and catching papers."

The Courthouse Oaks at Turner and Osborne Ranch, the first county seat, in 1855.

Not surprisingly, within a year county voters had moved the county seat to Snelling's Ranch, where it remained in modest quarters for the next 15 years.

In 1871, however, the railroad arrived in Merced County, platted the town of Merced and set aside four blocks for a courthouse square and buildings. A campaign to relocate the county seat soon began, culminating in 1872. The editor of the *Snelling Argus* lamented: "The county seat goes from Snelling, and with the removal the glory of the place departs."

The board of supervisors engaged A. A. Bennett, whose plan for an elegant eclectic Italian Renaissance Revival (or "Italianate") style courthouse was to set the standard for other counties in the San Joaquin Valley.

The *Merced Tribune*, writing as completion of construction neared in October 1874, described the statue of Minerva atop the dome, "She carries a shield in one hand and a spear in the other—the former for defense and the latter to impale evil-doers. These are fitting insignia of the manner in which Judges Deering and Robertson will mete out justice in the halls below."

There has been only one addition in the 125 years since it was built: a two-story

The courthouse at Snelling's Ranch, built in 1857 and seen here in the early 1930s. The stone walls of the lower floor enclosed the jail; the upper-floor courtroom continued to serve as a justice court until the 1990s, even after the county seat moved to Merced in 1872.

Architect A. A. Bennett designed courthouses for five San Joaquin Valley counties. The Merced County courthouse is the only one that still exists.

annex was added in 1913. Though built of reinforced concrete, its design is compatible with the original building.

The courts moved to new quarters in 1950, but the old courthouse continued to be used by other county officers until the late 1970s. After an extensive exterior restoration in 1975, an additional interior restoration converted the offices for use as a museum operated by the Merced County Historical Society. The museum features exhibits depicting the history of Merced County and the Great Central Valley. The "crown jewel" of the museum is the beautifully restored original courtroom.

Adventurous young people enjoy the view from atop one of the barrel vaults that support the cupola and dome.

The view of Courthouse Avenue from the portico sheltering the main entrance to the courthouse.

One of the three carved wood statues of Justice standing guard on the pediments that decorate the end of the barrel vaults.

The main entrance portico balcony, second floor windows flanked by columns supporting the pediment, surmounted by the cupola and dome.

Opposite page: A close-up of the cupola. The dome rests on two stacked drums. The lower drum is decorated with doubled columns with Corinthian capitals. The upper drum is also pierced by arched windows, which are flanked by pilasters that complement those on the lower drum. The small dome is topped by a laminated wooden statue of Minerva, the Roman goddess of wisdom.

Right: The current courthouse, designed by Walter Wagner & Associates in 1950.

Left: The 1950 courthouse has been outgrown; some superior court judges hold court in portables.

County *of*
San Joaquin

The first courthouse, built in 1854, seen here after the tower was added in 1861, but before the clocks were installed in 1868.

Stockton, which has been the county seat of San Joaquin County since 1850, was founded by Captain Charles Weber, a native of Germany, who named it for Commodore Robert Stockton. From the beginning it has been a commercial city. Thousands of argonauts bound for the southern mines passed through Stockton in the 1850s. Later it became a trading center, as agricultural products of the Central Valley were exported via its deep water port, and after 1869, the railroad.

The first courthouse and jail was the *Suzanne*, a French sailing ship rented by the month from 1849 through 1851. The oak tree to which she was moored was used as a whipping post; those convicted of lesser crimes were punished by dunking in the channel.

In 1850, Captain Weber donated a large block near the head of the main ship channel for use jointly as a courthouse and city hall. After sloughs that crossed the site were filled to create the plaza, plans were drawn by F. E. Corcoran for a two-story brick building, 60 feet by 80 feet, with four entries, one on each side, marked by porticos. The building was completed and jointly occupied by the county and city, in 1854.

The clock/bell tower was added in 1861. The bell, weighing nearly a ton, tolled for court sessions, fire alarms and curfew. The clock was purchased in 1868.

Historian V. Covert Martin observed that "buildings like people, in those early days, were old by their middle age, and in the [18]70s the building was showing such signs of deterioration that plans were being discussed for a new building. In the early 1880s the plaster was cracking and falling and bricks were dropping from the walls due to the faulty mortar. A new Temple of Justice was needed." The courts moved to the old Masonic Temple and then to other temporary quarters. The 1854 courthouse, only 30 years old, was sold for $1,000 for salvage. (The county kept the bell and clock, which are now on display in the Pioneer Museum.)

The new courthouse was designed by the Detroit firm of E. E. Meyers and Son, experienced architects of many Eastern public buildings. After voters approved a bond issue in 1887, construction began the following year on the three-story neoclassical courthouse, built of brick and faced with granite. The imposing tower and dome rose 172 feet above the plaza. The brick was manufactured locally, the granite came from the same quarry in Placer County that had supplied the stone for the state capitol in Sacramento, the slate for the roof came from Amador County, the ironwork from New York and thousands of ornamental tiles for the floors were imported from Belgium. The courthouse was completed in 1890, rapid progress considering that all materials had to be lifted into place by tall wooden cranes with block and tackle powered only by horses.

In 1910, the city was persuaded to move its offices out of the courthouse. The county activities and records grew year by year and over time more county offices were relocated and dispersed throughout Stockton. Sentimental and frugal county voters defeated bond issues for a new courthouse until 1960. The glorious, but inadequate, 1890 courthouse was razed in 1961 and replaced by a seven-story county office building, with glass curtain walls completed in 1964.

The courthouse was only a two-minute walk from the steamer landing. Masts of vessels anchored in the ship channel can be seen just beyond the courthouse roof in this photograph taken between 1868 and 1884.

Below: The grand neoclassical second courthouse was built on the same site, seen here in the 1890s. The ornamental fountain on the plaza, to the right, marked the spot where the well that supplied water to the first courthouse had been drilled in the 1850s.

Above: The second court-house in its prime, surrounded by palm trees and bustling downtown Stockton.

Left: The stately gilded zinc statue of Justice, one and one-half times life size, stood for many years atop the courthouse dome. It is now located on a tall pedestal in the plaza outside the 1964 courthouse.

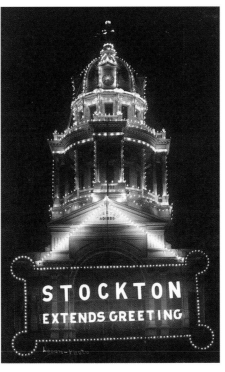

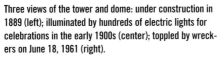

Three views of the tower and dome: under construction in 1889 (left); illuminated by hundreds of electric lights for celebrations in the early 1900s (center); toppled by wreckers on June 18, 1961 (right).

Right: The 1964 courthouse, with a 1957 Chevrolet in the foreground.

County *of* Stanislaus

The first courthouse in Stanislaus County was in Adamsville, a small wooden building previously used as a barn. Within a few months, dissatisfaction with these accommodations led voters to relocate the seat of government 11 miles up the Tuolumne River to Empire City, which served as a point of transshipment of supplies to the southern mines and army posts in the Sierra foothills. The courthouse was once again a modest wooden structure. Little over a year later, in December 1855, the county seat moved again, this time 25 miles upriver to La Grange, a bustling mining town. Here the county first rented and then purchased a private home to serve as courthouse/county offices. The next relocation occurred in 1861, when county offices moved to Knight's Ferry and to more substantial quarters—a two-story brick building, previously the Fisher Hotel, which was first rented and then, in 1864, purchased by the county.

Implacable economic forces at work in the 1860s and 1870s, however, made a final relocation inevitable. The decline of the mining industry and the rise of agriculture (with wheat supplanting cattle on the fertile valley floor), combined with the arrival of the railroad, put an end to foothill county seats such as Knight's Ferry. The Central Pacific Railroad, extending its tracks south from Sacramento, crossed the Stanislaus River in 1870 and purchased a site on the Tuolumne River for its next station. At an election the following year, voters chose Modesto over Knight's Ferry so, after 18 years of travel, the county seat was back within four miles of where it started at tiny Adamsville.

A county history published in 1881 reveals the public's satisfaction with the handsome Modesto courthouse designed by A. A. Bennett and completed in 1873:

> Among the public buildings, the courthouse ranks first…. It is situated in the center of a block 300 by 400 feet and is three stories in height. It presents all the architectural beauty that modern art could apply…. The grounds are tastefully laid out according to the rules of landscape gardening and, as a public park, it is now fast becoming a place of resort for all.

The courthouse was expanded by the addition of an adjacent and stylistically compatible hall of records in 1900. In 1939, it was joined by a four-story county office building executed in concrete, glass and glass block. The old courthouse was demolished in 1958, when the current building, which lacks both the elegance the 1873 courthouse and the advanced styling of the 1939 office building, was completed.

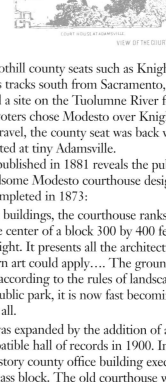

VIEW OF THE COURT HOUSES OF STANISLAUS CO.

The first permanent courthouse in Modesto was designed by A. A. Bennett, who was also the architect for courthouses in other Central Valley counties, among them Kern, Fresno, Merced and Tulare.

The illustration above shows the courthouses in the four towns that preceded Modesto as county seat: Adamsville, Empire City, La Grange and Knight's Ferry.

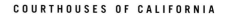

Shady Courthouse Park offered a welcome respite from the heat of Central Valley summers. Young women (left) converse with a stylishly dressed admirer.

Horses enjoy the shade of Courthouse Park while their owners conduct business at the courthouse or in nearby stores and offices in downtown Modesto.

An advanced, Bauhaus-influenced concrete county office building was constructed adjacent to the old courthouse in 1939.

An old man rests against an older artillery piece and regards the new county office building in Courthouse Park.

The Central Pacific Railroad's custom was to name its stations after railroad directors or officers. The site in Stanislaus County was proposed to be named Ralston after William Ralston, the colorful San Francisco banker and member of the railroad's board of directors. When the financier modestly declined the honor, the town was named Modesto (Spanish for "modesty") instead.

The courthouse completed in 1960.

After the old courthouse was demolished, the statue of Justice that had adorned its roof was preserved and relocated to ground level in a small courtyard of the new courthouse.

County of Tulare

Before it was reclaimed (i.e., drained) for agriculture, much of the lower San Joaquin Valley was marshland covered by reeds that the Spanish called *tules*. Thus "Tulare" County connotes a place where reeds grow.

The county was established in 1852; the county seat settling in Visalia the following year. County officers and the court occupied rented quarters until 1857 when the board of supervisors awarded a contract for a 36-feet by 20-feet, one-story pine building. Apparently this was unsatisfactory, for by 1858 the board had contracted for a much larger two-story brick courthouse with over six times the square footage as its predecessor. The upper floor served not only as a courtroom, but as the site for social events, such as dances and meetings, for 20 years.

By 1872, the Central Pacific Railroad arrived in Tulare County. Because Visalia was not willing to grant sufficient subsidies, the railroad decided to bypass the city and to build its station at the town of Tulare, about five miles to the southwest. The railroad and Tulare's promoters envisioned that the county seat would soon be relocated to Tulare, once it was served by the railroad tracks. But, to quell such talk, the board of supervisors hastily secured authority from the legislature to issue bonds and announced plans to build a modern courthouse designed by the famous A. A. Bennett in Visalia. Controversy ensued. The Tulare faction initiated litigation to enjoin issuance of the bonds. But as the grand courthouse rose, the opposition lost steam and the county seat remained at Visalia.

The 1876 courthouse, augmented by two stylishly similar wings built in 1907 and a discordant Art Moderne annex built in 1935, served until 1952 when it was damaged by an earthquake and vacated.

Its fate had already been sealed by demographic forces in any event. The previous year the board of supervisors had purchased a 30-acre site outside of town on which a new county government complex was to be built. According to a contemporary newspaper account:

> The site of the courthouse was chosen in 1951 with the thought being to locate the structure away from the historic downtown site because of the greater availability of land for buildings and parking because the courthouse was to house the governmental functions of a primarily rural county. The location could, therefore, be more readily available to the majority of the taxpayers by being located near the intersection of two of the county's major highways, rather than being in a comparatively congested downtown area.

The courts are now located on the top floor of one of several utilitarian government buildings on the 30-acre campus.

This drawing shows the second county courthouse, a plain two-story brick building completed in 1858.

Construction of this far more grand courthouse in 1876 was prompted in part by the town of Tulare's bid to become the county seat. It was one of five such courthouses designed by A. A. Bennett for San Joaquin Valley counties in the 1870s.

Above: The Italianate courthouse looks almost Venetian during this flood which turned low-lying Visalia's streets into canals. The photo was taken before 1907, when wings were added to the north and south sides of the courthouse.

Right: The main courtroom in the 1876 courthouse was grandly proportioned but simply furnished, with rudimentary facilities for heating and lighting.

Above: This annex to the courthouse was completed in 1935. Originally used as the hall of records, it is now occupied by the county's social services department. The ornamental detailing (streamline edging at corners and cornice, chevron and zigzag panels) is characteristic of the Art Deco period.

Below: The current courthouse was built in the late 1950s as part of a government center on the 30-acre site, still within the city limits of Visalia but far from downtown.

The Central Coast

MONTEREY
SAN BENITO
SAN LUIS OBISPO
SANTA BARBARA
SANTA CRUZ

County of Monterey

Monterey was the capital city of California under Spanish rule and under the Republic of Mexico. After the American conquest, it was reduced to merely a county seat and even that status was lost, to Salinas, in 1872. Between 1850 and 1872, however, the Monterey County courts met in what historian Harold Kirker termed "the most important building erected in the pioneer period"—Colton Hall. This two-story stone building with rudimentary Ionic columns supporting a simple wood pediment also served as town hall, schoolhouse, and public assembly hall. It was completed in 1849 through the determined efforts of Reverend Walter Colton, a U.S. Navy chaplain, who was appointed the first American alcalde of Monterey in 1846 by Commodore Stockton.

The American pioneers who had staked out the site of Salinas in 1868 initiated a campaign to bring both the railroad and the county seat to their town. They succeeded in both ambitions within four years. The seat of government moved from old, Mexican, Catholic and adobe Monterey to new, American, Protestant and wood-frame Salinas, set amid the newly planted fields of grain that stretched from the coast to Soledad.

The courthouse occupied one of those "ramshackle" wood-frame structures in Salinas for five years, until it burned in 1877. At that point the County hired Levi Goodrich, who had earlier designed the impressive courthouse in San Jose. The Salinas courthouse was an altogether more modest affair: a two-story brick building in the Italianate style then in fashion.

The top of the Victorian Era courthouse and its cupola silhouetted at sunset.

By the mid-1930s, the Victorian courthouse was over 50 years old, too small and no longer fashionable. With the help of federal funds, the county replaced it with a reinforced concrete building described by David Gebhard as "a perfect example of the PWA Moderne style of the '30s." To allow courts and county offices to function while the new courthouse was under construction, the county built the new courthouse around the old. When the new building was completed, the old one was demolished and the area it had occupied became the interior courtyard garden of the new courthouse.

The depression-era courthouse is distinguished by its melding of PWA Moderne styling with strong classical overtones and the decorative elements contributed by sculptor Joseph Jacinto Mora. The annex built in 1969 leaves the older building intact but itself contributes little architectural interest to the overall complex.

One of Joseph Jacinto Mora's statues that embellish the courthouse built in Salinas in the late 1930s.

Preceding page: Santa Barbara County courthouse, Santa Barbara, circa 1880.

Colton Hall, the first American public building in California, was the site of California's Constitutional Convention in 1849 and then served as Monterey County's courthouse from 1850 to 1872. California's first jury trial took place here.

Energetic and reflective Reverend Walter Colton is one of the more sympathetic figures of the American conquest. He directed construction of the first American public building, in Monterey, Colton Hall, which served as the county's courthouse from 1850 to 1872. His diary entry for March 8, 1849:

> The town hall on which I have been at work for more than a year, is at last finished. It is built of a white stone, quarried from a neighboring hill, and which easily takes the shape you desire. The lower apartments are for schools; the hall over them—seventy feet by thirty —is for public assemblies. The front is ornamented with a portico, which you enter from the hall. It is not an edifice that would attract any attention among public buildings in the United States; but in California it is without a rival. It has been erected out of the slender proceeds of town lots, the labor of the convicts, taxes on liquor shops and fines on gamblers. The scheme was regarded with incredulity by many; but the building is finished, and the citizens have assembled in it, and christened it after my name, which will now go down to posterity with the odor of gamblers, convicts, and tipplers. I leave it as an humble evidence of what may be accomplished by rigidly adhering to one purpose, and shrinking from no personal efforts necessary to its achievement.

The county seat moved to Salinas in 1872. After temporary quarters burned in 1877, this Italianate building served as the courthouse from 1879 to 1938.

Over 60 of "Jo" Mora's concrete busts decorate the exterior and courtyard walls at regular intervals. A few depict actual historical figures such as Cabrillo, Portola and Father Serra, but most are representative of groups that played important roles in the county's history, such as Native Americans, a Spanish solider, a Yankee sea captain, an American trapper, etc.

COUNTY CO

The Monterey County Co
Salinas, Calif.

Zan H-13

Above: The county used matching funds from the federal Public Works Administration, one of the New Deal agencies, to build a new courthouse on the same site in Salinas.

Left: Architect Robert Stanton engaged well-known sculptor Joseph Jacinto Mora to embellish his otherwise plain building. Seen here is Mora's bas-relief figure of Justice above the eastern side entrance.

MONTEREY COUNTY

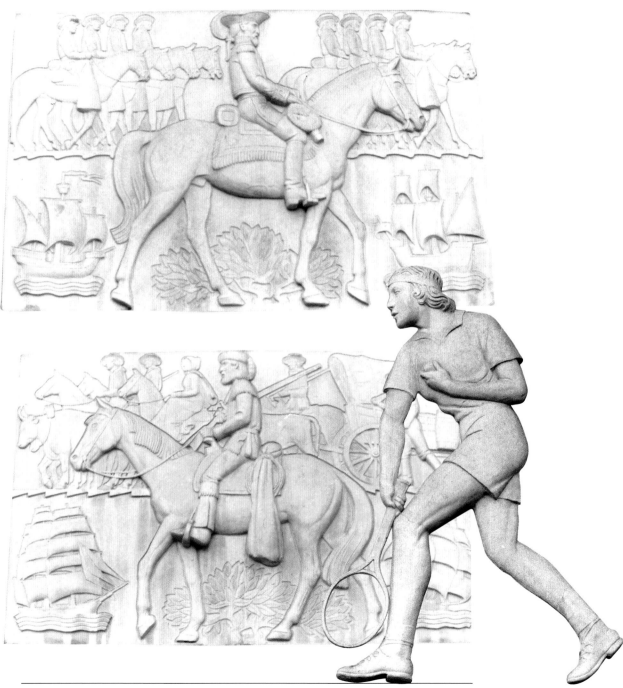

Five travertine bas-relief panels above the main doors to the courthouse represent distinctive eras in Monterey County history. Shown here are the native Americans, the arrival of the Spanish, the American trappers and settlers. The tennis player is the central figure from the panel representing the mid-20th-century American era.

COURTHOUSES OF CALIFORNIA

The capitals of these three-story-high fluted columns depict Native American, Spanish, Mexican and American periods of California.

Right: The 1969 annex that adjoins the 1930s court-house.

County of San Benito

I n 1868, a group of 50 farmers formed the San Justo Homestead Association and purchased from Colonel W. W. Hollister the eastern 21,000 acres of the old Rancho San Justo in what was then the easternmost portion of Monterey County. The land was then divided equally into 50 parcels. Near the center, one hundred acres were reserved for the town site of Hollister.

As an agricultural community grew up in the valley surrounding Hollister, settlers resented making the long journey to coastal Monterey to conduct legal business. While the relocation of the county seat to Salinas in 1873 shortened the trip, the movement toward separation had gained momentum and San Benito County was established as the state's fifty-first county in February 1874, with its county seat at Hollister.

The first courthouse was a modest two-story frame building initially rented from James Hodges, one of the town's founders, for $1.00 per year and later donated by Hodges to the county.

In 1877, the courts and some county offices moved across the street to a one story building. The new courthouse apparently pleased no one. The *Hollister Free Lance* referred to it as "the old rookery that had disgraced the county so long" and "a building that looked more like a dilapidated poorhouse than one devoted to public business."

When the third courthouse was completed in 1888, the paper was content: "Now all this is changed. Instead of being ashamed to speak of our courthouse we can now point it out to strangers with pleasure.… It occupies a commanding position, it is convenient for business, and in every respect is all that could be asked."

In truth, the new courthouse, designed by San Francisco architect John Gash, was a handsome building, Italianate in design, spacious (the courtroom was 52 feet by 35 feet with a 22-foot ceiling) and elegantly appointed. Contemporary descriptions applaud the wide granite staircases leading to the three entries (each sheltered by a porch supported by Corinthian columns), the interior stairways with their elaborate balustrades of polished red cedar, the walnut wainscotting that lined the hallways and courtrooms, the elaborately paneled doors adorned with architraves and fitted with knobs set in ornate escutcheons and swung from silver-tipped hinges.

The courthouse was sturdily built as well. Constructed of brick, covered with Portland cement, it withstood the 1906 earthquake and many smaller ones, for Hollister is located above the San Andreas fault. In the end, an earthquake in April 1961 brought down Hollister's grand courthouse. While the visible damage was not great, the building had been so shaken that it was no longer structurally sound. It was demolished in 1962 and a new reinforced concrete courthouse constructed on its site.

San Benito County's first courthouse was this two-story wood frame building seen here in the 1870s. William McCarthy, the court reporter, stands near the wagon at the left, joined by other county officers.

This sarcastic commentary, indicative of the low esteem in which the second courthouse was held, appeared in the *San Benito Advance* in 1881 under the headline "An Additional Adornment":

> The Court House—that imposing edifice, of which the citizens of San Benito County are justly so proud, has received additional ornamentation in the shape of an elegant sign, which is tacked up in the Superior Court room, warning the public that a fine of $10 will be imposed on any person caught "whistling" or "making litter in this room."
>
> The lettering, which shows an elegance of design and excellence of execution, stamping it as the work of some talented artist, was done with a mixture of lamp black and coal oil on a ragged piece of pine board broken from the top of a dry goods box. The whole affair presents a very handsome and attractive appearance.
>
> If the janitor will only get the rest of the pine box, and use about eight cents worth more of coal oil and lamp black in getting up another sign, warning the public to "comit no nusance under penalty of law," and tack it up directly above the Judge's bench.

Above: The third courthouse with its open cupola surrounded by 12 Corinthian columns and surmounted by a dome, belfry and conical roof. From the cupola one could survey the Diablo Range to the east, the Gabilan Mountains to the south and west, the San Benito River, and the rich wheat fields of the San Juan Valley.

The current courthouse, built in 1963, is a modern adaptation of the Monterey style of architecture with a wide overhanging flat roof sheltering an open second story balcony.

County of
San Luis Obispo

I n 1850, shortly after the county was formed, the court of sessions rented three rooms in the old Mission San Luis Obispo for a courtroom, office and jail.

The following year the court and county offices moved to "Casa Grande," a large two-story adobe built in 1850 by Captain William Dana, a native of Boston and cousin of Richard Henry Dana, Jr., the author of *Two Years before the Mast*.

By the early 1870s, the legal community's dissatisfaction with Casa Grande was rising. Writing in the *San Luis Obispo Tribune* in 1871, District Attorney Walter Murray expostulated: "The old adobe building [Casa Grande] called a courthouse is a marvel of repulsiveness and the courtroom, with its wretched appointments, is a disgrace to the county."

The following year, after the legislature had authorized it, the county sold $40,000 in bonds, purchased a site, and awarded a contract to a San Francisco firm to construct a new, up-to-date courthouse. What they achieved was a stylish three-story neoclassical structure, built of brick, finished in plaster and painted white. Its granite steps, columned portico, pilasters, bracketed cornice and other classical features signified the sea change that had taken place since the days when the mission and the adobe Casa Grande were the most prominent buildings in town. Harold Miossi, writing in 1972, assessed its symbolic significance in these terms: "The great classic white courthouse, then dominating this California town, was a monument to Anglo Saxon ascendancy. Its erection came at the end of a decade that had seen the Mexican land grants drift into American hands, their adobe haciendas replaced by New England style farmsteads."

When it was completed in 1873, the courthouse's neighbors included a hog yard, a hay barn, a saddlery, and a livery and feed store. When it was demolished in 1940, the adjacent properties housed offices, an automobile dealer, a parking garage and a gas station.

The old courthouse was replaced with a much larger county government center, housing not only the courts and board of supervisors, but the many county offices that had previously been dispersed through the town. The federal Works Progress Administration (WPA) and its California analog, the State Relief Administration, provided nearly half the funds. Construction proceeded in stages, over four years. The old courthouse was flanked by new units on the north and south, then razed, and the center unit completed, integrating the three components into one building.

County courts met in the old mission, in a room that had once served as a courtroom under Spanish and Mexican rule. This photograph by Carleton Watkins shows a then-new gaslight installed near the site of the gallows erected by the 1858 Committee of Vigilance.

San Luis Obispo ("Saint Louis the Bishop") is said to have been so named because the two nearby peaks reminded Spanish explorers of a bishop's traditional mitre, or hat. The courthouse is the most prominent building in this pre-1930 view of the town nestled at the base of Bishop's Peak.

An annex was constructed in 1964 with glass curtain walls, aluminum mullions, and "acres of draperies"—"architecturally styleless" in the judgment of one local observer.

Finally, in 1982, the courthouse complex was expanded once again, with the newest component facing Monterey Street and connecting with the rear of the 1941 courthouse and the 1964 annex. The complex now covers the entire city block. The 1941 courthouse remains the visually dominant element, facing the center of town just as did the 1873 courthouse on the same site.

Townsfolk dressed up to celebrate the Fourth of July in 1918 gathered here on the courthouse lawn for patriotic speeches.

The stately 1873 court-house. The iron fence was added to keep wandering cows off the front lawn.

Below: The front entrance of the central unit of the WPA Moderne courthouse complex built from 1936 to 1940. The small lone figure approaching the main door-way and the dark silhouttes of the 1930s automobiles give the scene a quality reminiscent of DeChirico's ominous cityscapes.

County Court House
San Luis Obispo, Cal.

ARTCO 76

Harold Miossi's monograph on the history of San Luis Obispo County's courthouses characterizes the 1940s courthouse as "an assembly of concrete stuccoed units, set in almost pyramidal fashion, which rise to a fourth floor apex. The courthouse attempts to portray simplicity, functionalism and yet the majesty of officialdom."

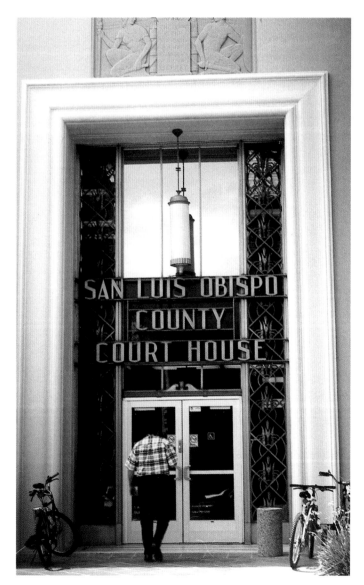

The graceful side entrance to the courthouse from Monterey Street is enhanced by the low relief sculpture over the lintel and by Art Deco metal lettering and grillwork.

Newly installed town clock, with courthouse in background. The admonition on the face reminds passersby to "Spend time with those you love."

Atop the tile roof of the 1940s courthouse tower is the gilded chanticleer weathervane, which once graced the 1873 courthouse and which is the only element of that building that still survives.

Bas-relief over courthouse entryway. The tablet reads, "The law is the standard and guardian of our liberty."

The most recent addition to the courthouse complex is a government center built in 1982, which houses ten courtrooms and a law library, as well as other county offices.

Below: This decorative element near the main entry to the courthouse shows the influence of the "streamlined" Art Deco—the wave of clean lines and subdued angles set in motion by the Century of Progress Exhibition in Chicago in 1933.

Right: The 1964 annex typifies the institutional architecture of the 1960s: glass curtain walls, gray enameled panels, aluminum mullions.

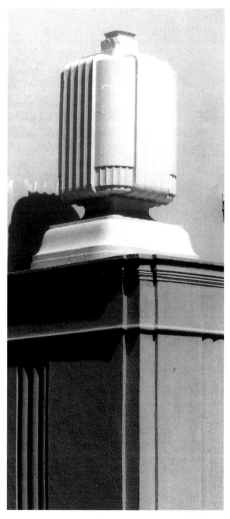

County of
Santa Barbara

Santa Barbara is one of the 27 original counties and the City of Santa Barbara has always been the county seat. The town grew up around the presidio and the mission, both built in the 1780s, and was second in importance only to Monterey during the Spanish and Mexican eras.

By the 1870s, however, the Anglo political and economic ascendancy had become evident in architecture as well. Two-story wooden Victorian frame houses replaced one-story adobes. The 1875 courthouse designed by Peter Barber, in a restrained classical style, was constructed of brick and iron on a stone foundation. It was welcomed in part because it represented such a decisive break with the Hispanic past.

At the turn of the century, however, changing fashions led to a new appreciation of the provincial Spanish adobes now becoming scarcer. The first manifestation took the form of the Mission Revival, with its simple lines and Arts and Crafts movement overtones. After World War I, interest in reclaiming the city's Spanish architectural heritage intensified. The Community Arts Association sponsored a revival of buildings along lines definitely related to the Spanish tradition. The city commissioned competitions in which prominent architects developed plans for resurrecting the downtown core within a unifying Hispanic architectural style.

The old courthouse, though a distinctive piece of architecture when built in 1875, had been outgrown by the 1920s. But no real progress was made in planning for its replacement until matters were brought to a head in 1925 when it was severely damaged by a powerful earthquake. The board of supervisors commissioned William Mooser Company Architects, the oldest architectural firm in the state (having been founded in 1854) to develop plans for a courthouse in harmony with the Spanish origins of the county.

William Mooser, Jr., son of the founder, was an accomplished architect. His son, William Mooser III, a graduate of the Ecole des Beaux Arts in Paris who had lived for 17 years in France and Spain, returned from Europe to assist his father.

They succeeded beyond all expectations. Architectural historian David Gebhard assessed the Santa Barbara courthouse as "certainly *the* public monument from the 1920s Spanish Colonial Revival in California," Charles Moore, in *The City Observed*, deemed it "the grandest Spanish Colonial Revival structure ever built." Harold Kirker praised it as "a beautifully integrated structure... sensitively related to a vast sunken garden of stone terraces and half century old pines, palms and redwoods. The Court House is equally impressive from every vantage point and is rich in wit, fantasy and surprises. It is a treasure house of architectural and decorative devices—archways, towers and loggias; tiled walls, vaults and floors; wrought-iron grills, balconies and landings—in which nothing is repeated or exactly alike."

Santa Barbara's first courtroom was in the adobe built in the early 1840s by Jose Antonio Aguirre, a wealthy merchant and landlord. The county rented space here from 1850 to 1853. The Aguirre adobe was demolished in 1884, after years of neglect.

COURTHOUSES OF CALIFORNIA

The county purchased this adobe building from John Kays, a Yankee trader, in 1855 and used it for the courthouse and offices until 1875 when a neoclassical courthouse (visible to right rear in this photograph) was completed.

The nomination of the courthouse to the National Register begins with a straightforward description of the four buildings that make up the complex (the courthouse itself, a jail, a hall of records and a service building). It discusses how they are arranged in a U shape along three streets, with the partially enclosed gardens occupying the balance of the city block. It identifies the varied architectural influences incorporated to some degree in the building: Spanish, Moorish, Spanish Colonial, Baroque, Renaissance and Romanesque. With a flourish, the nomination then enumerates the courthouse's features:

> It has domes; turrets; loggias; bell ports; terra cotta red tile roofs; curved staircases (one outdoor/indoor); graceful archways; windows enhanced by balconies and grillwork; palacio tile floors; Tunisian tile work; wrought iron chandeliers; decorative lanterns; hand-painted concrete ceilings; panels in polychrome and gilt; counters of panelled walnut; carved walnut jury boxes and rails; carved wood furniture and doors; leather-covered benches and chairs, with brass nails; different colored and sized pots; stained glass panels covering the fire hoses; and hemp handrails.

The board of supervisors prepared an informative booklet on the courthouse in 1929, to coincide with its dedication. The booklet concludes:

> Cleanliness, modernity, permanence, beauty; these are the qualities which the board of supervisors have sought in behalf of the people to give this building. Such a Court House must, in time, attract and hold in the service of the county men and women interested in advancing the science of government. If it does, the people have not built in vain.

The people of Santa Barbara County can best judge whether the courthouse has achieved the particular, idealistic goal set by the supervisors in 1929. But the building certainly succeeds on every other measure. As David Gebhard summed it up: "It [the courthouse] is a building which, along with the distant Mission, dominated the town when it was built and, fortunately, still does."

The transition from one-story adobe buildings characteristic of the Spanish/Mexican era to multistory masonry structures with classical aspirations introduced by Yankee settlers can be seen in this atmospheric photograph circa 1880.

The neoclassical courthouse designed by Peter Barber, Santa Barbara's first architect, who designed many of Santa Barbara's prominent buildings in the 1870s and 1880s and who twice served as the city's mayor.

The hall of records, also attributed to Peter Barber, was built adjacent to the courthouse circa 1890. The steep planes of the roof and the curves of the walls, stairs and arches contrast with the rectangular tower and its pyramidal roof. Both the hall of records and courthouse were damaged in the 1925 earthquake and demolished.

Above: The gardens of the 1929 Spanish Colonial Revival courthouse were designed by landscape architect Ralph Stevens and both incorporate and surround the foundations of the old 1875 courthouse.

Left: Two of the distinctive features of the 1929 court-house: the Roman Anacapa Arch and "El Mirador," the clock tower, from whose balcony one can view the mountains, the city and the Pacific. The inscription in Spanish above the arch proclaims, "God gave us the country, the skill of man has built the city."

The ceiling beneath the main tower is decorated with designs inspired by El Transito, a 14th-century synagogue in Toledo, Spain. A huge Andalusian-style lantern illuminates the space.

Gracefully curving stairway is enlivened by colorful tiles made by Gladding, McBean and Company, columns with stylized acanthus leaf capitals and wall paintings whose patterns suggest Chumash Indian motifs.

Many of the tiles decorating staircases, walls and niches were made in Tunisia, some in Seville.

The walls of the old chambers of the board of supervisors feature murals (among the largest in California) by Dan Sayre Groesbeck that depict a highly romanticized version of the county's history, beginning with Cabrillo's landing in 1542 (left) and ending with the arrival of the Americans, under Fremont, in 1846 (right).

The Anacapa Arch is decorated with sculpture by Venetian-born sculptor Ettore Cadorin. Seated above are Roman goddesses Justice and Ceres; medallions below represent agriculture, and apparently, communications.

One wing of the courthouse complex was originally the county jail. The monumental entrance frames tall wooden gates. The Latin inscription carved in sandstone admonishes prisoner and visitor alike, "Learn justice from this warning."

The bartizan projecting from the sheriff's tower is purely decorative.

Carved wooden doors are typical of those that open onto public spaces within the courthouse.

Old Spanish Days "La Fiesta Time" in California

Court House Grounds

The courthouse is a center for the annual Spanish Days Fiesta.

A mural of painted tiles portrays Jose de Ortega, first comandante of the presidio of Santa Barbara. It was donated by his descendants, many of whom still live in Santa Barbara County.

Former municipal court facility, directly across Figueroa Street from the 1929 courthouse is typical of late 20th-century buildings in Santa Barbara's downtown historic district.

County of Santa Cruz

n 1791, Franciscan padres established Mission Santa Cruz on a mesa overlooking the San Lorenzo River where it flows into Monterey Bay. The mission fell into disrepair after secularization in 1834 and Yankee settlers began converting buildings in the old mission complex to new uses. The largest of the adobe buildings on the mission plaza became the Eagle Hotel, which the court of sessions of the newly constituted Santa Cruz County rented in 1850 for the county's first courthouse.

In 1852, the county purchased a two-story wood frame building that Thomas Fallon had constructed a few years earlier on the mission plaza.

By 1860, it was clear that the center of business activity was moving off the mesa and down onto the "flats." The county rented the top floor of the two-story brick "flatiron" building located in the new downtown. Courts conducted their business here until 1867 when they moved to the county's first "real" courthouse—a two-story Italianate brick structure with gabled roof and adorned with a two-level cupola. It anchored the town's 19th-century civic center until 1894 when it was destroyed by a fire that swept through downtown.

From 1860 to 1867 courts were located on the second floor of the triangular structure called the "flat-iron building" because early residents thought it resembled a clothes iron. Locals liked to point out the bullet holes in the brick exterior: one from the pistol of a judge who in 1862 fired on a rival for the affections of the same 18-year-old woman; many others from an 1871 shootout between the county sheriff and famous bandit Tiburcio Vasquez.

Because the site had been donated by the Cooper brothers on condition it be used for a courthouse, plans for replacement were quickly underway. The county purchased an adjacent lot to accommodate a larger courthouse, and hired prominent architect Nelson Allan Comstock. Then at the peak of his career, Comstock designed a Richardsonian Romanesque courthouse of warm buff-colored brick above rusticated sandstone, which was to become one of Santa Cruz's most beloved buildings. It sustained severe damage in the 1906 quake but was rebuilt and served as the courthouse another 60 years. When the courts moved to the new county government complex across the river in 1967, the old sandstone courthouse began a new career. Sensitively rehabilitated for retail and restaurant use, the Cooper House was a popular landmark until it was damaged beyond repair by the 1989 Loma Prieta earthquake, which devastated the 19th-century masonry buildings built on the alluvial soils underlying downtown.

Courts are now housed in a freestanding county government complex built of precast and prestressed concrete, largely isolated from the rest of the city, within a 10-acre site on the opposite bank of the San Lorenzo River.

"Pictor depictus"—painters pause for their portrait, working on the courthouse completed in 1866.

Water wagon rolls past the elegant 1866 courthouse sometime prior to 1882.

A 1968 article in *Architectural Record* was enthusiastic in its praise of the complex:

In these two buildings for Santa Cruz County, California, the unusual architectural statement results in a lively and highly articulated exterior whose directness and honesty is further expressed in the interior. There, mechanical and electrical systems are treated as elements in the design and are forthrightly left exposed throughout virtually the entire complex. What might have been an uncompromising principle of ruggedness is turned, by precise and elegant detail, into a clear statement of strong conviction. Precast and prestressed elements are used repetitively to achieve an unusual degree of economy.

David Gebhard, writing in 1973, was less impressed, calling it "self-consciously constructivist within the New Brutalist phase of the late '50s and '60s."

In this view the courthouse is flanked by the hall of records, built in 1882.

Southeast corner of Pacific
and Cooper between 1882
and 1894. Left to right:
Mike Leonard's saloon, hall
of records, 1866 court-
house, Ely Block and the
first I.O.O.F building.

The same view after com-
pletion of the sandstone
and brick courthouse in
1894 and before the 1906
earthquake.

Crowd gathers in front of decorated courthouse to greet Teddy Roosevelt's secretary of state, John Hay, near the turn of the century.

Below: The interior of the hall of records. Threatened with demolition in the 1960s, it was preserved and now is the home of the Santa Cruz County Historical Museum.

Right: The main entrance on Cooper Street, with tower as rebuilt more cautiously after the 1906 earthquake.

Below: The tower eventually disappeared entirely, out of concern for its seismic stability. The entire building was damaged beyond repair by an earthquake in 1989.

The courthouse annex built in 1937 in understated WPA Moderne was subsequently converted for use as the county jail.

The 1967 courthouse is the one-story building in the foreground, connected to the five-story administration building by a glass-walled pedestrian bridge.

SANTA CRUZ COUNTY

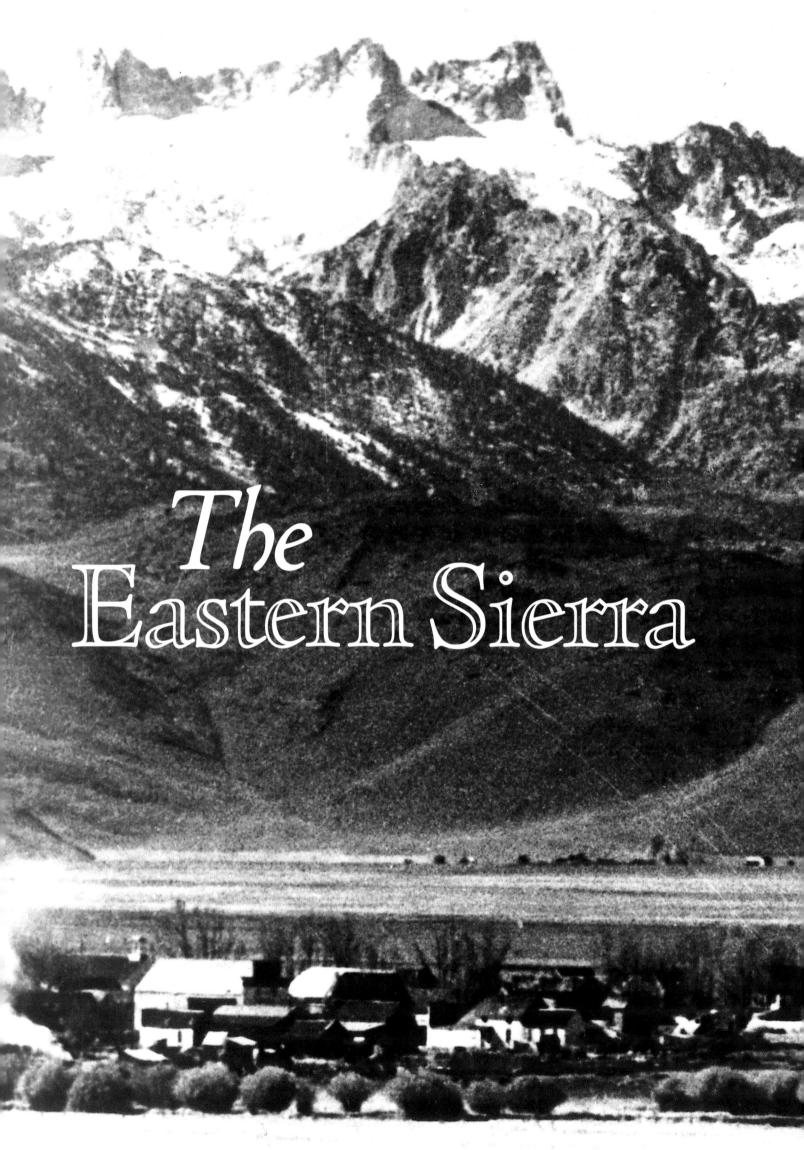

The Eastern Sierra

ALPINE
INYO
MONO

County of Alpine

The 1928 courthouse was designed as a two-story structure, but financial considerations limited it to one story.

With fewer than 1,500 residents, Alpine County is the least populated county in the state. Nevertheless, its courthouse in Markleeville is a handsome stone building designed by one of Nevada's most renowned architects, Frederick J. DeLongchamps.

Discovery of Nevada's Comstock Lode in 1859 drew California miners onto the eastern slopes of the Sierra and into what they assumed was the Nevada Territory. The 1863 survey of the California-Nevada border, however, determined that the mining region was actually in California. Soon thereafter, area residents petitioned the legislature to establish an independent county for them so that they would not have to make the arduous trip across the Sierra crest to conduct official business. Alpine County was established in 1864.

The first county seat was Silver Mountain City, then a thriving mining center. However, its prosperity was not to last. The mines played out and the miners moved on. By the time Congress demonetized silver in 1873, Silver Mountain City was nearly deserted and the county's overall population had plummeted from 11,000 (in 1864 when it was established) to under 2,500 in 1873.

Markleeville (current population: 150) is the smallest county seat in the state. The first courthouse, with adjacent jail, is in the foreground of this photograph, taken circa 1904.

In 1874, Alpine County's remaining residents voted to move the county seat to Markleeville, which had become the largest town. The county purchased the existing Odd Fellows Hall in Markleeville and the two-story wooden building served as the courthouse and county offices for the next 50 years.

In 1927, the county purchased the site on which town founder Jacob Marklee's old cabin had stood and hired architect Frederick DeLongchamps to design a new courthouse. Because of the county's geographic isolation from the rest of California, Alpine County had long turned to nearby and readily accessible Nevada for supplies and professional services. The choice of a Nevada architect was a natural one, and DeLongchamps was an acknowledged master, having designed courthouses for seven Nevada counties, as well as for nearby Modoc County. DeLongchamps did not disappoint; his simple, sturdy stone courthouse in Markleeville is still in service.

Preceding page: Mono County courthouse, Bridgeport, circa 1920.

The I.O.O.F. Hall in Markleeville, which served as the courthouse from 1875 to 1928. The courtroom and other county offices were on the first floor, the second floor was used for dances and traveling shows. It was sold and demolished in 1928.

The Markleeville courthouse was built of native stone, quarried above nearby Silver Mountain City, the first county seat.

County of Inyo

The first white men to settle in what is now Inyo County were miners drawn by the silver in the Panamint Mountains and cattle ranchers drawn to the lush meadows of the Owens Valley. Their encounters with the earlier inhabitants, the Paiute Indians, were violent and the army was called on to subdue the Paiutes. As part of that campaign, a military post was established on the Fourth of July 1862 and called, accordingly, Camp Independence. The town of Independence took its name from the nearby post.

The county was organized in 1866 as the Indian Wars subsided. The first courthouse was built in Independence in 1869 by J. J. Mankin but was destroyed a few years later by the earthquake of 1872. The following year, a second courthouse was completed using the plans of G. Stecker. It burned in the disastrous fire of 1886 that swept through the town. When it became evident that the courthouse would be engulfed, two women, Mrs. R. L. Peeler and Mrs. J. S. McGee, inspired a group of townspeople to carry out the documents and even the furniture from the doomed building. Nearly all the county's records were saved.

A third courthouse was completed in 1887 by M. E. Gilmore, using the plans of W. N. Cancannoh.

The first courthouse was a two-story brick or adobe building with a wooden porch and balcony. It collapsed in the March 1872 earthquake. The entire upper story crumbled, leaving the roof resting on the lower story walls.

The county grew in population and prosperity through the first two decades of the 20th century. When the persistent efforts of the county treasurer to persuade the state to return long-delayed tax revenues paid off with a windfall of over $100,000, the board of supervisors were encouraged to plan in earnest for a new, more spacious and fireproof courthouse.

A committee was formed in 1917 and set off to visit courthouses throughout Northern California and Nevada. While the committee was touring courthouses, they noticed that a large number of public buildings had been designed by Bay Area architect William H. Weeks, a prolific designer and advocate of concrete construction and fireproof design. Weeks was hired to design the new courthouse.

The fourth courthouse, a gleaming white structure built of reinforced concrete, was completed in November 1921. But the dedication was deferred until the spring. At the dedication ceremony in April 1922, Governor William D. Stephens delivered the main address. Music was provided by the Fort Independence Indian Band and the High School Glee Club. The Federated Women's Clubs presented a pageant on the theme of Inyo County. A reception followed the afternoon ceremony at which all were invited to tour the new building. In the evening a dance was held on the courthouse lawn, followed by supper in the

Inyo County's second courthouse served from 1872 until 1886 when it, and much of the town of Independence, was destroyed by fire.

County library, also lodged in the new courthouse.

That April day in 1922 marked, in retrospect, a high point in the public life of Inyo County. Shortly thereafter the Los Angeles Department of Water and Power embarked on its campaign to depopulate the Owens Valley to divert its water resources, both surface flows and groundwater, to the burgeoning city of Los Angeles. By the end of the decade, the county had lost the water wars, and Los Angeles was the major employer/landowner in Inyo County.

The nomination of the Inyo County courthouse for inclusion in the National Register finds the courthouse architecturally significant as the only example of monumental neoclassical Revival public architecture in the county. That unique status is directly attributable to the intervention of Los Angeles. The nomination explains:

> Neoclassical Revival architecture was the style of choice for public buildings during the late Nineteenth through the early Twentieth centuries, and the construction of grand public buildings of this nature are best understood as tangible statements of a community's maturity, optimism, and positive expectations for the future. It was precisely this local mood which was reflected by the construction of the Inyo County Courthouse at the peak of the area's economic prosperity and local autonomy....
>
> That this property represents the only local example of monumental public architecture in the Owens Valley is a direct product of the region's highly unusual political evolution, and the sharp reversal of the patterns of regional growth and development occurring after the mid-1920s. The Owens Valley was afforded only a brief glimpse of the sort of prosperity and community identity that would sustain the construction of grand public architecture.

The third courthouse, built in 1887, was described as too small from the outset but remained in use for 34 years.

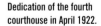

Dedication of the fourth courthouse in April 1922.

The third courthouse in
Independence seen at
night. Moonlight illuminates
the eastern slopes of the
towering Sierra Nevada.

Left and Below: Changing of
the guard. The third courthouse is the background
for miners on horseback in
the photograph below and
for a welcoming committee
of local officials greeting
the "official car" of the
Inyo Good Road Club, circa
1920 (left). District Attorney
F. C. Scherrer, in white
shirt, three members of the
county board of supervisors
and the county clerk greet
the intrepid travelers.

Above: The fourth court-house exhibits many of the distinctive characteristics of the Neoclassical Revival style: symmetrical elevations, classical order columns, portico, monumental stairway and classically derived detailing. The 1965 annex is visible in the background.

Left: The courtroom of the superior court in the 1922 courthouse.

County of Mono

News of rich gold mines near Mono Lake being worked by Mormons reached Sonora in 1857 and a new rush was on. By 1859, hundreds of miners had crossed over the Sierra; boomtowns like Bodie had mushroomed in the high desert. The miners wanted their own county and the legislature accommodated them by establishing Mono County in 1861. Booming Aurora, site of a sensational gold discovery the previous year, was chosen as the county seat. Courthouse and county offices were set up in a rented brick building.

In 1861, President Abraham Lincoln named James Warren Nye as the first governor of the Nevada Territory. In due course Governor Nye and the territorial legislature established Esmeralda County, the western edge of which overlapped Mono County. Indeed the Nevadans claimed that Aurora—Mono County's new county seat—was actually in Nevada.

Confusion and rancor prevailed for two years, until an 1863 boundary survey settled the dispute. The survey confirmed the audacious Nevadans' claims—Aurora was three miles east of the California/Nevada boundary.

County officers quickly vacated Aurora, relocating county records to the American Hotel in Bridgeport, safely within the boundaries of California. After an 1864 election confirmed Bridgeport as the county seat, the county purchased the hotel from J. B. Kingsley and it served as Mono County's courthouse for 17 years.

In 1880, the board of supervisors approved architect J. R. Roberts's plans for a true courthouse. The courthouse is 74 by 80 feet, the latter figure including the wings that project laterally from the rear of the structure. The county offices were on the first floor, with the second floor reserved for court purposes with two courtrooms each 32 by 40 feet. When the present courthouse was completed in 1881, several merchants had their stores moved across town to be near the courthouse, among them a county supervisor, whose tavern was thus relocated.

Architectural historian David Gebhard has observed: "This beautifully kept 1880 wood building has all of the ingredients of the Italiante style: bracketed and pedimented canopies over the windows, engaged columns and quoining at the corners, and a delightful miniature cupola with round headed windows and a curved mansard roof broken by small circular windows."

The courthouse's façade is similar to that of the courthouse built in Virginia City, Nevada, a few years before. That elegant building, which also survives, had been designed by the San Francisco architectural firm of Kenitzer & Raun, who had also designed Marin County's monumental courthouse in the early 1870s.

The two-and-one-half-story wooden courthouse (left) built in Bridgeport in 1881 is an admirable example of High Victorian Italiante architecture popular in the west during the 1870s and 1880s. It was carefully restored to its original condition with the help of a federal grant in 1974 and is now on the National Register of Historic Places.

The courthouse was originally heated by wood stoves. The county clerk was responsible for building the fire. On cold winter mornings he would also have to thaw the ink, which would be frozen if he had forgotten to put the ink bottles in the well-insulated vault. The cannon on the front lawn was cast by a foundry in nearby Bodie in 1881 and presented to the county in 1914. It has been fired only once—by pranksters in the early morning hours of July 4, 1979.

The new courthouse was occupied on April 1, 1881. The *Bridgeport Chronicle Union* reported on the celebration that preceded the move: "Last night was a gala night; citizens formed a procession at twilight and marched to the old courthouse where lawyers delivered humorous speeches and all had a gay time." A booklet issued in 1980 celebrating the courthouse's centennial said it well: "With its green lawns, its lovely wrought iron fences erected shortly after the building and its beautiful silver maple trees, the Mono Courthouse stands as a tribute to the timeless taste of its architect, the foresight of the 1878–1882 board of supervisors, and the support of a populace of visionary pioneers."

When the first county seat, Aurora, was discovered to be in the Nevada Territory, county officials hastily relocated to Bridgeport, purchasing this building, formerly the American Hotel, from J. B. Kingsley in 1864. After serving as the county courthouse for 17 years, it was auctioned off to a rancher who used it to store hay.

Inland Empire and the Desert

RIVERSIDE COUNTY COURT HOUSE.

ERECTED   A.D. 1903

IMPERIAL
RIVERSIDE
SAN BERNARDINO

County of Imperial

IMPERIAL COUNTY COURT HOUSE.

MORT RIESER

IMPERIAL COUNTY FARM BUREAU

The first courthouse was this prosaic building on Main Street, El Centro, seen here circa 1920.

mperial County, formed in 1907, is the newest county in California, the only one created in the 20th century, and most likely the last that will ever be established.

The county is bordered by Mexico to the south, the Colorado River to the east, Riverside County to the north and San Diego County (from which it was formed) to the west. Part of the great Colorado Desert, the land was inhabited only by Native Americans before 1900 when the entrepreneur/engineer George Chaffey completed a canal from the Colorado River to what he called the Imperial Valley. Settlers poured in, and with the Colorado River water for irrigation, "made the deserts bloom." The Imperial Valley is now one of the most productive agricultural areas in the United States.

The centrality of agriculture to Imperial County can be seen in the photograph of the first courthouse, built in 1908. The Imperial County Farm Bureau (a private trade association representing farm owners) shares space, presumably as a tenant, with county officials and the courts.

The first courthouse had been planned as temporary lodgings from the outset and for that reason was designed as a conventional office building to maximize its value when the county moved out. The move came in 1924 when a restrained Beaux Arts building was completed on a 10-acre site to the west of town. This building, designed by Donald Wells and Ralph Swearingen, continues in use today by seven of the county's nine trial court judges. In fact, it withstood a powerful earthquake in 1973 that wrecked the nearly new county administration building directly across the street.

Preceding page: Riverside County courthouse, Ventura, 1998.

Above: A much more
substantial courthouse
and county office building,
constructed in 1924,
remains in use.

Below: The Knights of
Columbus, in full regalia,
stand at attention in front
of the courthouse's portico
at its dedication in
November 1924.

County of Riverside

Riverside County was created in 1893, as the result of a quarrel over a courthouse. The political struggle that led to the county's formation had its origin in decades of small disputes and resentments. But its proximate cause was San Bernardino's plan for a new courthouse.

Between 1886 and 1891, the San Bernardino County Board of Supervisors sought voter approval for three successive bond issues for a new courthouse, hall of records and jail, all to be located in the City of San Bernardino. Each measure failed, in large part due to opposition from Riverside—a rival for the county seat. The board of supervisors, unwilling to abandon its plans, first levied a tax to finance construction of the new buildings on a "pay as you go" basis. Indignant Riverside leaders tried, unsuccessfully, to secede. But then the supervisors went one step further—they lowered property assessments in San Bernardino and raised them dramatically in Riverside and other areas where the bonds had failed. This vindictive measure persuaded the legislature to call an election on the question of creating a new Riverside County. The voters approved it overwhelmingly, naming Riverside as the county seat.

The county's debut coincided with the Panic of 1893 and several years of economic depression. The owner of the new, luxurious (and largely vacant) Arlington Hotel was happy to rent its ground floor to the county for a courtroom and offices.

Prosperity returned with the beginning of the new century. In Riverside County, the wealth being created by the orange groves gave particular encouragement to visionary enterprises. In 1902 voters enthusiastically approved a bond measure for a new courthouse. The board of supervisors launched a design competition, selecting the prominent Los Angeles architectural firm of Burnham & Bliesner. The lead designer was Franklin Pierce Burnham, whose earlier commissions included the Georgia State Capitol. His plan envisioned a classical building in the style associated with the Ecole des Beaux Arts (School of Fine Arts) in Paris, then internationally in vogue.

The courthouse was a hit from the very beginning. The *Riverside Daily Press*, writing in June 1904, deemed it

For the first 10 years of its existence, Riverside County rented the ground floor of the recently built Arlington Hotel for its offices and courtroom.

"a beautiful building and a work of art… a joy forever." Later assessments were equally favorable: David Gebhard declared it to be "*the* complete realization of Beaux Arts design in California" and another architectual historian proclaimed it "an amazingly exuberant Beaux Arts fantasy… an extravagant wedding cake, crisp and sharp-edged, colored in cream and beige with elaborate white decoration."

A major addition, designed by local architect G. Stanley Wilson, was completed in 1933. It is stylistically compatible with the original, but decidedly more subdued.

A series of subsequent remodelings, however, took its toll. Coffered ceilings and even a stained glass dome were covered over by lowered ceilings, fluorescent lights replaced the original Art Nouveau fixtures, decorative pilasters and woodwork were removed to accommodate air conditioning.

And then came the earthquakes. After a quake in 1992, the courthouse was found to be "fragile." Superior Court Judge Victor Miceli described the venerable building as "a heavyweight champion with a glass jaw." The Northridge earthquake two years later forced the courthouse to be closed.

Instead of demolishing the building, the county embarked on an ambitious, $25 million, four-year renovation effort (with a loan from the general fund to be paid back from court filing fees), which has earned admiration statewide. The courthouse reopened in 1998, seismically strengthened, accessible to disabled witnesses, jurors, attorneys and judges, and with its original grandeur painstakingly restored. An essay by Judge Miceli, whose "irrepressible enthusiasm and passion" for the revival of the courthouse was the catalyst for the entire project, appears earlier (pages 2 to 3).

Architect Franklin Pierce Burnham's Beaux Arts design for the courthouse completed in 1904 is thought to have been inspired by the Grand Palais and Petit Palais constructed for the 1900 Paris Exposition.

Right: Judge G. R. Freeman, right, swearing in Judge Oakley K. Morton in Courtroom One, on October 8, 1929. The Latin legend carved on the entablature states, "Justice is the foundation of the Republic."

Right: Residents survey the courthouse colonnade after an earthquake in the early part of the twentieth century. The building sustained only minor damage. The Northridge earthquake in 1994, however, forced it to be evacuated and closed for over four years.

Opposite, clockwise from upper left:

Four groups of sculptures, each consisting of three figures in classical attire, fabricated from pressed zinc and painted to resemble stone, are arrayed atop the courthouse. The two outer configurations represent agriculture and industry, foundations of the economy that depend upon the rule of the law. The two inner groupings, seen here, symbolize constitutional law and criminal law, each essential to the maintenance of a democratic republic.

The sculpture grouping representing constitutional law. The central figure is Justice, holding a sword and scales, symbolizing the judicial branch of government. The seated figure to the left represents the executive branch, and that to the right, holding a quill and tablet, the legislative branch.

A prominent feature of the courthouse is the long vaulted hallway, running the length of the building, lined with pilasters (columns embedded in walls). It is divided by a central rotunda at the main entrance, with a domed ceiling and central columns. A newspaper account of the newly finished courthouse exclaimed of the corridor: "Here all is whiteness, gleaming, almost dazzling."

A postcard view of Riverside, circa 1920, shows comfortable homes on wooded streets in the foreground, then the cluster of commercial and civic buildings (the courthouse is to the right), the orange groves that supported the economy, and the Box Spring Mountains in the distance. In this era Riverside epitomized the California Dream.

The 1933 annex was designed by the accomplished Riverside architect G. Stanley Wilson, whose instructions were to see that the annex blended harmoniously with the original building without copying it. He succeeded admirably.

The family law court across Main Street from the hall of justice was completed in 1998. The landscaped entryway to the right serves dual purposes: a garden-like waiting area and an extension of the court's security zone.

Adult criminal proceedings are held in the Robert Presley hall of justice built in 1991 adjacent to the original courthouse. Underground tunnels connect the hall of justice to both the old and new jails, also nearby.

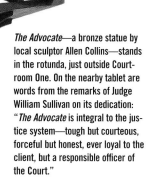

The Advocate—a bronze statue by local sculptor Allen Collins—stands in the rotunda, just outside Courtroom One. On the nearby tablet are words from the remarks of Judge William Sullivan on its dedication: "*The Advocate* is integral to the justice system—tough but courteous, forceful but honest, ever loyal to the client, but a responsible officer of the Court."

County of San Bernardino

San Bernardino is not merely the largest county in California, it is the largest county in the continental United States, larger in fact than seven states.

In 1851, a party of 500 Mormons from Salt Lake City arrived in the San Bernardino Valley. The following year they purchased Rancho San Bernardino from the sons of Don Antonio Maria Lugo and laid out a city along the broad spacious lines of Salt Lake City.

The community flourished, in short order building a sawmill, farms and schools. The Mormon Council House, a two-story adobe, became the first courthouse when the county was created in 1853 (largely due to the efforts of the energetic Captain Jefferson Hunt, an officer in the Mormon Battalion and an early leader of the community, by then serving in the state legislature).

In 1857, Brigham Young recalled the community to Salt Lake because of the threatened invasion of Utah by the U.S. Army.

After the Mormons' departure, county officials moved the courthouse to a house rented from Judge Quartus Sparks from 1858 to 1862 and then purchased the elegant Charles Glasier home, which served until 1874. It was torn down to make way for the first building actually designed as a courthouse. The courthouse built in 1874 was similar in style and scale to that built the preceding year in San Luis Obispo, although San Bernardino's had a flat roof and domed clock tower.

The 1880s were boom times in San Bernardino County, with the arrival of the railroad, the planting of hundreds of acres of orange groves, and the land speculation

The two-story adobe Mormon Council House served as the first courthouse when San Bernardino County was established in 1853.

accompanying the establishment of new communities. The board of supervisors placed a bond issue on the ballot for a new jail and expanded courthouse. The measure failed; the greatest opposition came from Riverside, but other towns opposed construction of a new courthouse in San Bernardino because they harbored hopes of gaining the county seat themselves. After a smaller bond issue for a hall of records also failed, the supervisors imposed a tax to raise funds for a formidable sandstone and marble Romanesque Revival hall of records, completed in 1891. The bold action intensified intercity rivalries and contributed to the formation of Riverside County two years later.

By 1898, the supervisors had their new courthouse as well, another imposing Romanesque Revival structure of sandstone and marble. The 1874 courthouse, the 1891 hall of records and the 1898 courthouse were all demolished in 1928, when the next courthouse was completed.

The new courthouse, nearly 300 feet long, was a sharp departure in both scale and style. Designed by self-taught local architect Howard Jones, it was a rather staid example of Beaux Arts classicism. A contemporary description: "Solidity and simplicity are the outstanding characteristics of the… building, which conforms to no special type of architecture but resembles classical Roman and Italian Renaissance. In outside appearance it is somewhat like Los Angeles' new $6,000,000 Hall of Justice with its massive stone columns and rectangular windows, the former suggesting lofty ideals and the latter a square deal."

The building, expanded with a new wing in 1958, remains in use. It and the by now "old" hall of records (1959), a county administration building (1983) and a new hall of records create a major assemblage of public buildings in downtown San Bernardino.

The building that led to the partition of San Bernardino County. Residents of the Riverside area saw the imposition of a tax to pay for this Richardsonian Romanesque hall of records in 1891 as the last in a series of insults by a board of supervisors dominated by the City of San Bernardino. The southern part of the county split off to form Riverside County two years later, in 1893.

The sandstone and marble trimmed courthouse completed in 1898 illustrates many of the characteristics of the Richardsonian Romanesque—massive columns, arched doorways, rusticated stone facing, turrets, towers and decorative carving.

A parade down E Street, past the formidable 1898 courthouse. The octagonal tower of the 1874 court- house, with four clock faces in its dome, can be seen to the left.

The four-story reinforced concrete classically inspired "courthouse" built in 1928 was really a county administration center, housing the library, assessor, clerk, recorder, tax collector, auditor, treasurer, district attorney, schools and welfare offices, sheriff, board of supervisors and jail, in addition to the courts. It is included on the National Register of Historic Places.

The courthouse as it appears today.

Courthouses and grounds often provide capsule histories of the courthouse site or the early days of the county. A bronze plaque mounted on a granite base on the lawn in front of the San Bernardino courthouse does both. It reads:

Settlement of San Bernardino

In March 1851 Charles C. Rich and Amasa N. Lyman, apostles of the Church of Jesus Christ of Latter-Day Saints, left Utah with 437 people "to establish a stronghold for the gathering of saints in California." Jefferson Hunt, David Seeley and Andrew Lytle were captains of organized companies. They purchased the Rancho de San Bernardino, selected a site for settlement, built a fort enclosing 100 homes and erected an adobe building for church and school. 1,300 acres of grain were planted, grist and saw mills erected, and roads made into nearby canyons. Local government was established, [the] city incorporated and the population doubled before the call back to Utah by President Brigham Young in 1857. Pioneers from Yerba Buena, England and the Pacific had joined the settlement.

Above: The utilitarian 1959 hall of records.

Left: The 1983 county government center, adjacent to the courthouse.

The equally utilitarian courthouse annex, added in 1958, doubled the number of available courtrooms from 12 to 24.

The South Coast

LOS ANGELES   SAN DIEGO
ORANGE   VENTURA

County of Los Angeles

Los Angeles County and its trial court system are remarkable for two very different reasons. The first is their immense size. The second is the surprising continuity of the county courthouse's location. While the county has used at least eight buildings as its courthouse, all have been situated within a mile of each other in downtown Los Angeles.

As of 2000, nearly 10 million people live in Los Angeles County. In terms of population, Los Angeles County, by itself, is larger than 48 of California's 58 counties *combined*. It is larger than 43 of the 50 states in the United States. It is larger than 114 of the 189 countries in the United Nations, including for example, Austria, Ireland, Israel and Sweden.

The trial court system mirrors the population in scale. There are 429 judges serving in Los Angeles trial courts, as well as another 142 court commissioners and 14 referees. These 585 judicial personnel preside at trials and hearings in 58 separate locations distributed throughout the county.

These facilities range widely in size. At one end are small (one or two judges) former municipal court venues. Examples of intermediately sized facilities are the substantial, publicly owned buildings in communities such as Pasadena, Santa Monica and Long Beach, each of which houses 15 or more courtrooms. At the upper end of the spectrum is the mammoth County Courthouse in downtown Los Angeles, which contains 794,459 square feet (about 18 acres) on nine floors, housing 101 courtrooms and 1,000 workers.

The second remarkable aspect of Los Angeles trial courts is the persistence, through 150 years, of the county courthouse and closely affiliated buildings (such as the hall of records and hall of justice) within the same relatively compact area in downtown Los Angeles. The massive courthouse that now serves 10 million people is within a ten-minute walk of the site of the first county courthouse, the adobe Bella Union Hotel.

Each of the six other buildings used as the county courthouse was also situated within the same precinct, south of the original plaza, which has for the past 80 years been called the Civic Center, including

- The home of County Attorney, and later Judge, Benjamin Hayes on Main Street, which the County rented from January 1852 until November 1853
- The Roche (or Rocha) House, an adobe on the corner of Spring and Court Streets, which the county and city jointly purchased from Jonathan "Don Juan" Temple and used from November 1853 to March 1860

The first session of the district court was held in rented rooms in the Bella Union Hotel in June 1852. The Los Angeles County Court of Sessions met here from June 1850 until July 1852. The building, originally constructed in the 1830s as a one-story adobe, served as the government house under Mexican rule.

Preceding page:
Ventura County courthouse, Ventura, circa 1920.

The "Clocktower Courthouse" as viewed from Bunker Hill looking east in May 1869. Said to have been fashioned after the first Faneuil Hall in Boston, the primary architectural feature of the Temple Block was its rectangular tower with one clock face on each of the four sides.

- The building, probably a two-story brick house on Main Street, which the county rented from John Nichols, former mayor of Los Angeles, from 1860 to 1861
- The Temple Market Block, on the site where the City Hall now stands, which the county rented in May 1861, purchased in 1867 and used until 1891
- The red sandstone courthouse on Pound Cake Hill, completed in 1891, damaged beyond repair by the Long Beach earthquake of 1933, demolished in 1936 and now the site of the criminal courts building constructed in 1972
- The hall of records, built next door to the red sandstone courthouse in 1911, used as the courthouse from 1934 until 1959 when the current courthouse was occupied, and demolished in 1973.

With the possible exception of the 140-year-old-clock on an east-facing wall, the current courthouse or the vast assemblage of federal, state, county and municipal buildings that comprise the Civic Center have nothing in the least bit sentimental or romantic. To the contrary, most of the buildings constructed since the mid-1930s are hard-edged examples of efficient modernism, though the Los Angeles City Hall (1928) is a landmark both familiar and imposing.

The farewell to the beautiful but poorly built red sandstone courthouse, however, was unabashedly sentimental. In May 1936, when the building was nearly demolished, the Historical Society of Southern California invited Los Angelenos who had been present at the laying of the cornerstone in 1888 to witness its removal. Among those who attended was former State Senator R. F. Del Valle, a member of a prominent Spanish family and then the oldest practitioner at the local Bar.

"ORDER IN THE COURT"—MORE OR LESS

The etiquette of the frontier courts of Los Angeles County in the 1860s was very informal. The casual style adopted by some attorneys sufficiently annoyed County Judge William G. Dryden, a prominent jurist, that he issued the following proclamation in 1867:

The court, having due regard to the rights of attorneys practicing herein and realizing by experience that a lawyer is but human and subject to the temptation of looseness of habits that are always engendered in a warm climate, has after due consideration of the matter concluded that the proceedings of this court are not conducted in that dignified and orderly manner to which their importance entitles them. That the personal habits of many members of the bar are not suited to lend dignity to the court in which they practice and in view of these facts, it is ordered that hereafter attorneys while in attendance upon court will be required to wear a coat of some kind and will not be allowed to rest their feet on the tops of tables, or whittle or spit tobacco juice on the floor or stove. And the court sincerely hopes that all attorneys will observe this rule and to the end that decent order and decorum may be had without trouble.

Walter R. Bacon, "Pioneer Courts and Lawyers of Los Angeles," *Historical Society of Southern California Quarterly,* 1905, vol. 6, part 3

Jonathan Temple, one of the earliest American settlers in Los Angeles, was already a rich man when he built the Temple Market Block in 1859. Seen here circa 1880 in a Carleton Watkins photograph, the building served as Los Angeles' courthouse from 1861 to 1891.

The original cornerstone was located and the box placed in it nearly 50 years earlier was opened. A contemporary account of the ceremonies reports, "Golden California sunshine poured down, making it a typical California day. As the various mementos, newspapers, cards and programs came out of the box and were read by the Chairman, it was evident that the members of the crowd were stirred; applause and audible comments greeted many of the old mementos. Old men and ladies hugged and nudged each other when a program of a great dance held in Turnverein Hall appeared. The belles and beaux of yesterday certainly remembered that occasion."

Marshall Stimson, president of the historical society, was the chairman of the event. He concluded the ceremony with these words: "The old red courthouse was the pride of our generation. It readily deserved the praise so liberally bestowed on it, for it was a fine example of the best architectural work of the day. As this old landmark disappears from view a definite part of the old days we loved so well passes off the scene… Goodbye, Old Courthouse."

Now that's sentiment worthy of California's largest county!

The aftermath is also instructive. The cornerstone of the old courthouse was kept in storage until the new courthouse was completed in 1959. It was then installed in a place of honor on the lawn of the new courthouse. A subsequent landscaping project removed the lawn and relocated the cornerstone to an elevated planter box. There was nothing to call attention to it or identify it. When someone turned it upside down, the date carved on it (1888) was obscured. There it sat for years, unnoticed. Only the curiosity of Superior Court Judge Gary Klausner led to its rediscovery in 1998. Plans are being made for the old cornerstone to be suitably displayed, perhaps in the criminal courts building, which now occupies the site of the old red sandstone courthouse.

Another recent development illustrates the renewed interest in Los Angeles's judicial and architectural heritage. In 1999, Presiding Judge Victor Chavez arranged for two dozen photographs of the county's historic courthouses to be prominently displayed in a hallway. The collection—the first of its kind—generated an enthusiastic response from judges, attorneys and other visitors. Joyce Cook, directing attorney of the Court's Planning and Research Unit, who had helped assemble the photographs, recalls that visitors were fascinated, and frequently surprised, to discover how Los Angeles appeared in years past.

The "Honeymoon Elevator" carried couples to the marriage license bureau on the third floor of the old red sandstone courthouse for nearly 30 years. It was said that the elevator ascended so slowly that couples could change their minds before it actually arrived at the top.

Below: One of the last photographs of the Clocktower Courthouse, taken after the completion, in 1891, of the "Red Sandstone Courthouse," visible in the distance. The county sold the building in December 1890 and it was razed shortly thereafter. Los Angeles City Hall now occupies the site.

The distinctively colored stone used on its exterior gave the "Red Sandstone Courthouse" its nickname. Public buildings in Los Angeles were frequently decorated with flags and bunting to welcome conventions at the turn of the century.

The courthouse viewed from the west. The clock in the tower had been salvaged from the old Clocktower Courthouse. When this courthouse was later demolished in the 1930s one face of the clock was preserved and later incorporated into the current courthouse.

The hall of records served as the seat of county government from 1911 to 1960, housing the board of supervisors, recorder, auditor, treasurer, assessor, tax collector, county counsel, law library and four superior court departments. Arnold Hylen appreciatively observed its "Mondrianesque exterior design… an exercise in the subtle organization of rectangular shapes." (Los Angeles before the Freeways.) It was demolished in 1973 as part of the redesign of the Civic Center.

Below Left: One of the ten murals created during the mid-1930s as part of the Federal Art Project of the Works Progress Administration. This painting is by Buckley Mac-Gurrin and depicts the founding of Los Angeles in 1781.

Below: The murals were located in the room for the board of supervisors on the fifth floor. This painting by Helen Lundeberg shows the signing of the Treaty of Guadalupe Hildago in 1848, which ended the hostilities with Mexico.

Right: The neoclassical hall of justice near completion of construction in 1926. The imposingly solid, 14-story gray granite tower—surmounted by a classical temple— was designed by Allied Architects of Los Angeles, and partially carried out their Beaux Arts plan for the Civic Center. The site of the trials of Sirhan Sirhan and Charles Manson, it is now the oldest structure left in the Civic Center.

Below: William Davidson, chief mechanical engineer, of Los Angeles County, uses a mason's trowel to place mortar at the cornerstone laying ceremonies for the hall of justice in January 1925.

Below Right: Detail of decorations on entablature at ninth story of hall of justice.

COURTHOUSES OF CALIFORNIA

Above: The three principal buildings that housed courts in Los Angeles during the first half of the 20th century. Only the hall of justice, far right, remains. Vacated in 1993 for seismic safety reasons, its future is uncertain.

Left: A new civic center has risen to the west of the old. Clockwise from bottom left are the county law library, county courthouse, music center complex, Los Angeles Department of Water and Power, County Hall of Administration, hall of records and (partially visible) criminal courts building.

U.S. Supreme Court Chief Justice Earl Warren, with gold-plated shovel, breaks ground for construction of the new county courthouse, on March 26, 1954. From left: California Court of Appeal Associate Justice John Shenk, District Attorney Ernest Roll, Municipal Court Presiding Judge Clarence Stephens, Superior Court Presiding Judge Phillip Richards, County Supervisor Herbert Legg, the chief justice, Sheriff Eugene Biscailuz, and Supervisors John Anson Ford, Roger Jessup, and Kenneth Hahn—who watches the ceremonies with his three-year-old son, James Hahn. James Hahn later served as city attorney and mayor of Los Angeles. The courthouse was designed by a team of architects including Paul Williams, one of the first African American architects in Southern California to achieve prominence.

Right: East entrance to the current Los Angeles County Courthouse. Bitter political controversy over its location culminated in a decision by the California Supreme Court holding that a county board of supervisors has a legal duty to provide for a courthouse and that the decision of where it should be sited is not subject to initiative.

Far Right: Detail view of a 24 foot by 24 foot sculptural group of figures above eastern entrance designed by Donal Hord. Justice is flanked by two male figures holding tablets that read in Latin, "Law" (left) and "Light and Truth" (right).

A corridor in the Central County Courthouse gives a sense of the building's scale. Containing over 790,000 square feet, it is the largest county courthouse in the state. While designed in the plain International style, the materials used in the courthouse were rich: Italian marble in the corridors, eastern white oak paneling in the courtrooms and white bronze entrance doors.

Three stern figures above the western entrance to the courthouse represent three pillars of American jurisprudence: (left to right) the Ten Commandments; Magna Carta; and the Declaration of Independence. Designed by sculptor Albert Lewis, the heroic figures were executed by Gladding, McBean & Co. in ceramic veneer sections.

Left: Parking near the courthouse is priced, like many lawyers' services, in increments of 10 minutes. The Civic Center is enjoying a renaissance, with a new Roman Catholic cathedral and the Walt Disney Concert Hall, designed by Los Angeles architect Frank Gehry, under construction. Scenes like this will soon be a thing of the past.

The Court of Flags with the courthouse in the background. The numerals on the clock face have told the time on three successive Los Angeles courthouses, for 140 years.

Below Left: The hall of records, built in 1962, was designed by Richard Neutra, one of Los Angeles's best-known architects. The vertical aluminum louvers shield the south facing glass wall (left) from the sun.

Below Right: The criminal courts building, rear, was constructed in 1972 on the site of the old Red Sandstone Courthouse. Site of the 1995 O. J. Simpson trial, the building was recently renamed in honor of Clara Shortridge Foltz, California's first female attorney and Los Angeles County's first woman prosecutor.

County of Orange

I n 1889, after 20 years of trying, residents of what is now Orange County finally succeeded in separating from Los Angeles. When Judge James Towner first convened court in Santa Ana, a local newspaper exclaimed that the proceeding "marked the end of servitude and almost foreign courts." The *Los Angeles Express* was wistful, its headline reading "Wayward Sister, Separate in Peace."

Ten years later county voters approved (by a five-to-one margin) a bond issue for a new courthouse. The board of supervisors hired Los Angeles architect C. C. Strange, who had proposed a three-story Richardsonian Romanesque courthouse. The style had been popular for government buildings in the Midwest in the 1870s and 1880s but had fallen out of fashion. However, it was well received by Orange County residents, many of whom had moved to California from the Midwest and were familiar with the horizontal lines, rusticated stone and rounded arches characteristic of Romanesque Revival from the town halls and courthouses they had grown up with.

August 1899: Court first convened in Orange County in J. R. Congden's building, left, rented by the county for 50 cents a year. Workers are laying ties for streetcar tracks on Fourth Street.

The hall of records, built in 1924, was connected to the courthouse by an elevated iron bridge. It is shown here after suffering superficial damage in the 1933 Long Beach earthquake. It was demolished in 1975 as part of a street-widening project.

The materials used in the old courthouse are rich but by no means luxurious. The exterior walls are sheathed in red Arizona sandstone and locally quarried granite. Inside, blue and white or cream colored tile was widely used on floors and landings; marble only sparingly. The wood was oak. Budget-minded supervisors also scrapped the elevator and a clock for the clock tower, which was deemed "a luxury this county can live without."

The building's dedication on November 12, 1901, was marked by an all-day celebration. Festivities extended into the evening when the building was lit inside and out, from basement to cupola, by electric lights. The press reported that "flood lights and Republican speakers radiated at the courthouse for the 'grand illumination' and dedication."

In the 1960s, as Orange County's population rocketed past one million, the county and the city embarked on an aggressive building program at the Santa Ana Civic Center just to the west of the old courthouse. In 1968 the new Richard Neutra–designed, 11-story courthouse was completed. Proposals to convert the old courthouse to a museum were delayed by the need for a costly seismic stabilization. Closed for safety reasons in 1979, the courthouse reopened in 1987 after a four-year $4.5 million structural and aesthetic restoration. The courthouse was rededicated on November 17, 1987, the occasion marked by a marching band, a barbershop quartet and history buffs dressed in period costumes. It now serves as a museum and as a venue for conferences and receptions. And, just as 100 years ago, it is still home to the county clerk's marriage license bureau.

The brand-new courthouse stands ready for its dedication on November 12, 1901. The distinctive tower, constructed of sheet metal formed and painted to look like sandstone, was removed after an earthquake in 1933. The building is now the oldest surviving courthouse in Southern California.

Richard Nixon, born in nearby Whittier, comes home to campaign for vice president of the United States in 1952.

The old sandstone courthouse has been featured in numerous movies and TV shows. Here MGM is filming *Twilight of Honor* in 1963.

Two artillery pieces, one from World War I and the other from World War II, stand on the courthouse lawn.

The beautifully restored main floor lobby. The central staircase features Corinthian capitals on the columns, Tennessee marble stairs, ornate ironwork and oak handrails, tile flooring and bronze chandeliers (originally designed to operate on both gas and electricity).

The old courthouse underwent a $4.5 million restoration during the 1980s, culminating a 14-year battle to save the building, which county officials once planned to raze for a parking lot.

The restored courtroom of Department One looks much as it did when the courthouse opened. The judge's bench and most woodwork is original.

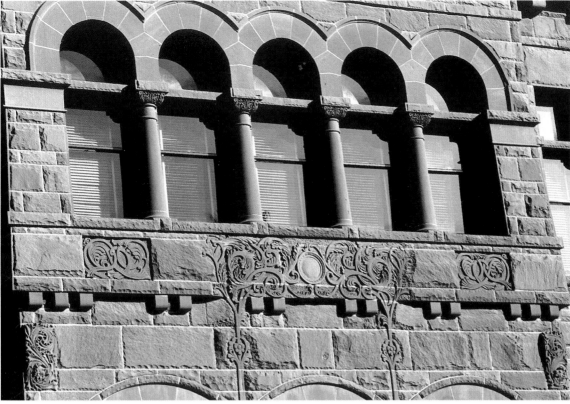

The round arches and carved stone tracery, characteristic of Romanesque Revival architecture, are evident above the main entry.

The distinctive columns and arches that frame the main entry, left, are featured on a banner, above, announcing the beloved courthouse's first centennial.

In the mid-1960s, the county built a huge new courthouse designed by internationally renowned architect Richard Neutra. The 11-story building is part of a vast government center west of the old courthouse.

The New Orange County COURTHOUSE

HIGH TECH IN THE COURTROOM: 1901 AND 2001

Orange County is building a new high-tech Complex Litigation Center in Santa Ana. The center will include five courtrooms equipped with monitors and imaging devices for displaying evidence during trials as well as links from the judges' desktop computers and attorneys' laptops to the court reporters' computers, allowing the judge and counsel to see testimony displayed on screen immediately after it has been given. Judge William McDonald hopes the new computer-friendly courthouse will encourage attorneys to present evidence via CD-ROMs, rather than generating the huge piles of paper that now characterize complex litigation such as construction defect, environmental tort and intellectual property cases. "During a trial so much time is taken up sifting through files for a misplaced document," said Judge McDonald. Also, due to the reams of paper, "Our courtrooms have gotten messier and messier over the years." The judges who will preside at the new Complex Litigation Center hope that clutter and delay will be things of the past.

Orange County deployed state-of-the-art courtroom technology in 1901 as well. On display in the old courthouse museum is the equipment used by the county's first court reporter to record and transcribe trial proceedings. The reporter read his shorthand notes into the horn of the Edison dictating machine, which would record the words onto wax cylinders. The transcriber would then transfer the cylinder to a similar machine, don earphones, replay the cylinder and type. The cylinders were reusable; they could be "erased" by using a third machine to shave off a very thin layer of wax (actually resin).

The hall of finance and records built in 1961 as part of the sprawling Civic Center complex.

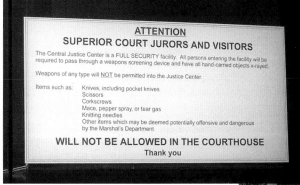

ATTENTION

SUPERIOR COURT JURORS AND VISITORS

The Central Justice Center is a FULL SECURITY facility. All persons entering the facility will be required to pass through a weapons screening device and have all hand-carried objects x-rayed.

Weapons of any type will NOT be permitted into the Justice Center.

Items such as:
Knives, including pocket knives
Scissors
Corkscrews
Mace, pepper spray, or tear gas
Knitting needles
Other items which may be deemed potentially offensive and dangerous
by the Marshal's Department

WILL NOT BE ALLOWED IN THE COURTHOUSE
Thank you

SIGNS OF THE TIMES (clockwise from above):

Broad prohibition on weapons greets entrants at the courthouse door.

New approach to criminal justice is advertised at a bus stop outside the courthouse.

Bilingual directory to the Civic Center's acres of buildings and grounds.

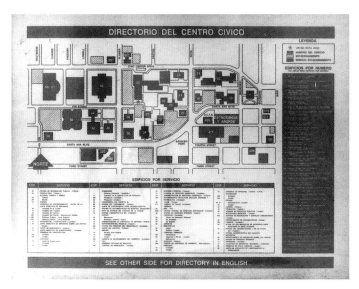

County of San Diego

n January 1847, the volunteers of the Mormon Battalion arrived in San Diego after a 2,000-mile march from Council Bluffs, Iowa. They had set out six months earlier to support the American military garrisons in Southern California in the Mexican War. The war was over by the time they arrived in the tiny pueblo of San Diego, so the soldiers began working in the community, mending fences, whitewashing adobes, improving wells. They built the first brick kiln in California and used about 40,000 of those bricks to construct the small building on the plaza that was to be used as the first courthouse of the American era. The building served a range of other functions: the city council and the board of supervisors met there, as did the grand jury, the Masonic Lodge and the Boundary Commission, charged with surveying the boundary line between the United States and Mexico. The building was destroyed in the fire that swept through Old Town in 1872. Local citizens, persevering through a series of bureaucratic delays that would have strained the patience of a saint, succeeded in reconstructing a faithful replica on the exact site of the first courthouse. Completed in 1992, the Old Courthouse Museum is an important element in the Old Town State Historic Park.

By the late 1860s, San Diego County's population had grown from the 800 or so present when California joined the United States to nearly 5,000. The tiny brick courthouse had been outgrown, and in 1869, the board of supervisors rented Thomas Whaley's larger and more substantial brick house that stood nearby, only a few blocks from the plaza.

But larger forces were at work. In 1867, Alonzo Horton, an enterprising business-man who had purchased much of what is now downtown San Diego, began a campaign to move the business district, and county seat, from Old Town south to his rapidly growing "New Town." The contest grew bitter. Old Town residents feared such a change would mean ruin for them. The ambitious newcomers to Horton's addition, however, were growing in numbers and influence. In July 1870, Horton's allies on the board of supervisors directed that all records be moved from the Whaley House to a new site in New Town. County Judge Thomas Bush countermanded the supervisors, ordering the sheriff to use force, if necessary, to prevent the move. A posse of Old Towners was summoned, a cannon positioned and a guard posted in front of the jail.

The first courthouse was a small (27 feet by 16 feet), one-story brick building that faced onto the plaza of Old town. It was built in 1847 with help from soldiers of the Mormon Battalion. Photograph is circa 1867.

The *San Diego Union* reported, "Old Town has seceded." In September, Judge Bush ordered the three Horton allies on the board of supervisors removed from office and replaced them with three Old Town loyalists. But in January 1871, the California Supreme Court ruled that Bush had no authority to remove or appoint supervisors. With the previous board back in power, it was only a matter of time; the axe fell on the night of March 31, 1871, when the newly appointed county clerk and a party of Alonzo Horton's friends loaded the county's records on wagons and moved them from the Whaley House to rented space in New Town.

Within a few months, Horton had donated land for a new courthouse and the supervisors had hired a prominent architect to draw up plans and awarded a contract to build it. At the ceremonial laying of the cornerstone, in August 1871, the president of the board of supervisors, Dr. E. D. French, expressed the hope "that all ill feelings that have existed between Old and New San Diego might be buried in the stone…."

Less than 20 years later, the Santa Fe railroad had arrived, the port expanded, and the county's population increased sevenfold. The 1872 courthouse had been out-grown, but the real estate boom of the 1880s had ended and the supervisors were reluctant to present a bond issue to the voters, many of whom were facing hard times. The county commissioned the San Francisco architectural firm of Comstock & Trotsche to prepare plans for "repair projects," to be financed on a pay-as-you-go basis. Two wings were added on either side of the original building. When it was dis-covered that the original structure would not bear the weight of a third floor and clock tower, it was demolished on another "repair order" and completely rebuilt, the overall project lasting from 1888 to 1890. As thus "repaired," the courthouse was an impressive Italian Renaissance structure, replete with Victorian embellishments

The Whaley House was built in the 1850s by New Eng-lander Thomas Whaley. The county rented it in 1869. The one-story addition to the left was used for a courtroom and records were stored on the second floor of the main building.

The interior of the room in the Whaley House used for a courtroom from 1869 to 1871. The woodwork was of eastern white cedar brought around Cape Horn. The restored Whaley House is part of Old Town State Historical Park.

A 1960 reenactment of the midnight raid on March 31, 1871, which moved the county's and court records from the Whaley House to New Town.

including 42 stained glass windows representing each of the states of the Union as of 1890, a Seth Thomas clock, and a dozen statues of allegorical figures and American presidents adorning the roof, bell tower and cupola.

The balance of the city block occupied by the courthouse was developed with ancillary buildings—a hall of records in 1911 and a jail in 1913.

By the end of World War II, the county was facing unprecedented growth—its population passing the half-million mark by 1950. The grand Victorian courthouse was now itself insufficient. A jarringly modern annex, built on the front lawn in 1950, was a mere stopgap. When two bond issues failed, San Diego boosters complained that the venerable courthouse "squats like an ugly toad on choice downtown property."

The voters ultimately approved a bond issue at an election in 1954 and ground was broken in 1958 for a combined county office building (seven floors), courthouse (three floors) and jail (eight floors). The complex extended across two city blocks, including that previously occupied by the old courthouse, hall of records and jail, with an elevated two-story bridge spanning C Street to connect the two units. At nearly $9 million, the contract was the largest ever awarded for a public building in San Diego County.

Speakers at the 1958 groundbreaking and the 1961 dedication ceremonies were enthusiastic: "A great day for San Diego City and County," said Dean Howell, president of the board of supervisors. "A monument to public spirit," according to Judge Eugene Daney, Jr. "A marvelous new tool to facilitate the administration of justice in San Diego," said Court of Appeal Justice Lloyd Griffin.

But with spectacular growth rates continuing relentlessly throughout the 1960s,

The first building actually designed as a courthouse was constructed in New Town, completed in 1872. Designed by San Jose architect Levi Goodrich, built of brick, finished with plaster, it was far larger (60 feet by 100 feet) and grander than its makeshift predecessors.

COURTHOUSES OF CALIFORNIA

A panorama of New Town San Diego, circa 1876. The newly built courthouse is the large building in the center, middle distance.

1970s and 1980s, it was inevitable that the "glistening courthouse" of 1961 would in its turn be viewed as "cramped and old and simply inadequate" as it was described in a 1995 article on the $61 million, 13-story hall of justice then under construction across the street.

The newest courthouse, the hall of justice completed in 1996, differs from its predecessors in several respects, including its financing. The original plan envisioned traditional bonds to be repaid from a new sales tax. The tax increase, however, was held to violate state constitutional limits on taxes. So the bonds were restructured to be secured by revenues generated from the building's 500-space parking garage, rental income and traffic fines. In addition, a major contribution from the City of San Diego's redevelopment agency was necessary. As explained by County Supervisor Ron Roberts, "The county told the city that if it helped finance the hall of justice, it would keep its main courtroom presence in the downtown area." Since it has been estimated that 40 percent of downtown San Diego offices have some connection to the county justice system, the argument was persuasive. According to Supervisor Roberts, "The fact that the City's economic base would gain from the county's decision to keep its principal court and detention facilities in the downtown area helped the City Council agree to a deal."

The courthouse in 1889, after two flanking wings had been completed and during the "repair" (actually a total reconstruction/expansion) of the original courthouse. The overall project was finished in 1890. The uniformed men in the foreground are Knights Templars.

The 1990 courthouse complex at the height of its glory—April 1929. The automobiles lined up in front were the "Silver Fleet," which drove across the country as a promotion for a particular brand of tires.

Statues congregated around the central clock tower of the 1900 courthouse. Most (including those of presidents Washington, Lincoln, Grant and Garfield) were removed after the 1906 San Francisco earthquake. The tower itself and the remaining figures were removed in 1939.

FROM THE DEDICATION BALL TO THE WRECKER'S BALL

It was the night of the Grand Dedication Ball, when the city was young, the Courthouse was new and booted men and slippered ladies swung into the District Courtroom with high spirits to the inspiring strains of the Grand March Militaire.

A Brilliant Affair and grand success…." bouqueted *The Daily Union*, a cute little four page tabloid-size sheet. The *Union* went on "At a moderately early hour the guests began to arrive at the front entrance of the handsome new building… the airs, many of them new, were thoroughly enjoyed by the dancers who tripped the light fantastic to the enlivening strains until an early hour of the morning… quadrilles, waltzes, schottisches, redowas, lancers, Portland Fancy, gallop, Virginia Reel, mazurka….

Since that memorable warm evening in June 1872, the building has borne without plaint or collapse the buffeting of storm and quake and the hollered arguments and oratory of politicians and lawyers… For this edifice that has cradled the dramas of almost every experience in human life and human laws there must be veneration—there must be a respectful farewell.

San Diego Evening Tribune, July 11, 1959

The courthouse annex/hall of records, foreground, was built in 1911 on the same block as the courthouse; a third floor was added in 1927. A jail (to left of photo) built in 1913 rounded out the block. All were demolished in 1959.

VIGNETTES FROM THE OLD COURTHOUSE TAKEN IN 1948: A man leans against wall waiting outside municipal court; two men (attorneys? detectives?) confer outside superior court; revelers, some the worse for wear, are arraigned in municipal court before Judge Brennan.

The 1961 courthouse complex that replaced the 1910 courthouse extends over two city blocks. An object of awe and admiration when it was completed, it has recently been called "a dump," "archaic" and "pathetic."

Above: Photographs of earlier courthouses line the walls of a courtroom in San Diego's 1960s courthouse.

Right: One of dozens of leaded "art glass" windows preserved when the 19th-century courthouse was demolished, now displayed behind the bench in presiding judge's courtroom.

The newest courthouse building, completed in 1998, provides space for 16 courtrooms with the top seven floors occupied by the District Attorney's offices. It towers over the 1961 courthouse, right, to which it is linked by an elevated pedestrian bridge.

Right: The formal entrance to the 1998 hall of justice.

Above: The elevated pedestrian bridge linking the 1961 and 1998 courthouses. Such bridges have been employed in California courthouses since the 1850s.

County of Ventura

For the first year after the creation of Ventura County in 1873, its courts convened on the second floor of the Spear Building, directly above one of the county's most popular saloons. In May of 1873, the board of supervisors committed $6,000 "in gold coin" toward construction of a courthouse and jail, on two conditions: first, that $4,000 in matching funds be raised by the public, and second, that a suitable site be donated. Both conditions were soon met, Roman Catholic Bishop Thaddeus Amat offering a portion of the old mission gardens.

A simple two-story brick building with a small wooden porch was completed by early 1874. It was expanded in 1879 and again in 1884, and sometime thereafter a clock tower was added. By 1910, the tower had developed a noticeable tilt. Fearing collapse, the board of supervisors commissioned a young Los Angeles architect, Albert C. Martin, to design a new courthouse. Architect Martin was to have a distinguished career, founding a firm that designed many of the most notable buildings in Southern California, among them Los Angeles City Hall and Union Station. Martin proposed a much larger Beaux Arts classical structure, 280 feet long, an ornamental main entrance flanked by rows of fluted Doric columns and gracefully arched Roman windows, faced with glazed white terra-cotta. The materials to be used inside and out were rich: a granite staircase led to ornate bronze doors; the interior lobby floor was marble; carved oak and mahogany lined corridor and courtroom walls. Three leaded stained glass windows were set into the coffered ceiling of the main courtroom and depicted symbols of the law: scales, a book and a sword.

In the mid-1950s, Albert Martin, by then an old man, visited the chambers of the board of supervisors unannounced. Introducing himself—no one recognized him—Martin told the board that, after a long career, the Ventura County courthouse was one of the buildings in which he took "particular pride."

The county's first courthouse was built on a portion of the old Mission San Buenaventura gardens, donated to the county by Bishop Amat. As initially constructed in 1874, the courthouse consisted only of the square central block. This view shows it in the mid-1880s after wings had been added on both sides.

The clock tower was added in the late 1880s. When cracks appeared 20 years later and the tower began to lean, county supervisors decided it was time to move.

After an earthquake in 1968, concerns about safety led the county to vacate the courthouse. It was saved from demolition by the City of Ventura, which purchased it in 1970, and carried out an extensive and sensitive restoration program to convert it to use as Ventura's city hall.

The county moved the courts and most county functions to a government center complex completed in 1978, which is designed for functionality and efficiency in handling the demands of a population that has increased from 20,000 when the old courthouse was completed in 1913 to over 500,000 in 1980, and to nearly 750,000 today. But it will never become a tourist attraction, nor win the community's affection, as Albert Martin's gleaming white temple of justice, set on a hillside overlooking the old town and the Pacific, has done.

The spacious main courtroom, seen here in 1913, now serves as the Ventura City Council chambers.

July 12, 1913: Dedication day ceremonies at the splendid new courthouse. Board of supervisors Chairman Adolfo Camarillo presided. Speeches were followed by sports events in the afternoon and, in the evening, a fancy ball at the new courthouse.

Marble Stairway Courthouse.

The central stairway to the second floor was built of Cararra marble imported from Italy, and for many years, was flanked by brass spittoons.

The annex added in 1932 was designed to complement the architecture of the original 1913 courthouse. Subsequent additions to the rear of the courthouse built in the 1940s and 1950s made no such attempt.

A night view shows the massive central section of the 1913 courthouse.

The stately colonnade features monks' heads on the spandrels between first- and second-floor windows.

Three of the 24 terra-cotta monks' heads created by the Gladding, McBean and Company are reminders of the Franciscan padres who founded the mission and city in 1782.

In 1978, the county moved to a new county government center, comprising five buildings and vast parking lots on an 80-acre campus. This building, part of the hall of justice, houses the courts.

The Appellate

Courts

The Appellate Courts

Litigation in the trial courts generally produces winners and losers. Not all parties who lose in the trial court are content—a significant percentage are sufficiently unhappy, and determined, to take their case to a "higher court." From the outset, California has provided a forum for such disappointed litigants to obtain review of a trial court decision.

The Constitution of 1849 established a supreme court with three members to hear appeals from trial courts. The court was enlarged to five in 1862 and to seven (its current complement) in 1879.

An intermediate court of appeal was not created until 1904. The constitution adopted that year initially provided for three court of appeal districts: one in San

The California Supreme Court and the First District Court of Appeal share this subdued Beaux-Arts building in San Francisco's Civic Center. Constructed in 1923, it was renamed the Earl Warren Building after extensive renovations completed in 1999.

Francisco, one in Los Angeles, and one in Sacramento. The notion was that these new courts were to handle appeals in the "ordinary run of cases," thus freeing the supreme court to concentrate its energies on "the great and important cases" (Blume, "California Courts in Historical Perspective," *22 Hastings Law Journal*, 1970, pp. 121, 173–174). And so they have. With the exception of appeals of death sentences, the supreme court's jurisdiction is discretionary; it decides which cases to accept. In exercising this jurisdiction, the Court seeks to settle important legal questions of statewide concern and to secure uniformity of decision among the various court of appeal districts and the trial courts.

In 1928, a constitutional amendment authorized the legislature to create "divisions" within the existing court of appeal districts and to establish additional districts. Since then both new districts and new divisions have been created to keep pace with increases in caseload. A fourth district was created in 1929. Initially, it was a circuit court, sitting in Fresno January through April, in San Diego May through August, and in San Bernadino September through December. Hon. Gerald Brown, who served as presiding justice of the Fourth District, Division One, for 20 years, observed wryly, "It is apparent the senators were well aware of weather, in providing for the summer months in San Diego."

In 1961, a new fifth district was created. Sitting in Fresno, it siphoned off the Central Valley counties from the Fourth District. Separate divisions within the Fourth District were subsequently established, in San Bernadino in 1965 (relocated to Riverside in 1999) and in Santa Ana in 1982. Most recently, a sixth district was created, based in San Jose.

Cumulatively the court of appeal has grown from nine judges in 1904 to 93 as of 2000—a 10-fold increase, but less than half the rate of increase necessary to keep pace with growth in the state's population over that time.

Preceding page: Third District Court of Appeal, Sacramento, 1938.

The appellate courts are busy—25,000 appeals and petitions were filed in courts of appeal in a recent year; over 8,000 petitions for hearing were filed in the supreme court. But they are also very quiet places. The courtrooms are configured differently than those in trial courts: There is no witness stand (because new evidence is not presented) and there is no jury box (because there is no jury). Instead, there is simply a podium at which the attorneys for each side present their legal arguments and attempt to answer the questions posed by the panel of judges seated at an elevated bench a few feet away. The atmosphere is restrained, almost academic. The audience is small—often the parties themselves don't attend. The decision is not announced the day that argument is held; instead it emerges in the form of a written opinion days or weeks later. But it is in these dignified courtrooms and quiet chambers that decisions of great importance, not merely to the parties but to the entire state, are routinely made.

The buildings in which these proceedings occur vary widely in scale and style. Some are overtly classical and clearly governmental in nature. Others are conventional office towers in which the court of appeal is simply a tenant, perhaps one of many. But they are all open to the public just as the trial courts are, and all Californians are welcome to visit and observe their outstanding appellate judges at work.

Below: The newly restored courtroom of the supreme court once again displays the coffered dome and skylight (left) and paneled walls (right) of the original, obscured for nearly 50 years by a 1950s remodeling that lowered the ceiling and covered the walls with blue leather.

Right: Six divisions of the
Second District Court of
Appeal occupy a portion of
the Ronald Reagan State
Office Building in downtown
Los Angeles.

Above: One division of the Second District Court of Appeal is
located in Ventura, in this two-story building distinguished
by the projecting corner entryway with its Monterey style
balcony.

The Third District Court of
Appeal courtroom is in the
monumental neoclassical
Courts and Library Building
just west of the state
capitol in Sacramento,
built in 1928.

ARCHITECTURAL EMBELLISHMENTS AT THE THIRD DISTRICT COURT OF APPEAL

Six carved panels on the bases of the colonnade depict an odd array of classical figures, Spanish explorers and a Buddha with an ample, well-rubbed belly.

Above: Mosaic tile designs on the lobby floor.

A formal garden separates the Courts and Library Building from its twin State Office Building directly opposite. The fountain in the center is a popular site for wedding portraits.

Right: An elegant vase and bronze lamp greet visitors in the entry hall.

Division One of the Fourth District rents space in the Symphony Towers high-rise in downtown San Diego.

Below: A bronze tablet in the entry of the new Riverside Appellate Court Building acknowledges the leadership role of Presiding Justice Manuel Ramirez: "He attended to its completion with firm resolution. And now we may all delight in it.… Without his dedication this courthouse would have been only a building, like any other."

Division Two of the Fourth District in Riverside occupies the only building constructed specifically for, and used exclusively by, a court of appeal. Completed in 1999, it is a handsome combination of classical and modern elements.

Right: Division Three of the Fourth District rents the entirety of this office complex in Santa Ana, which was recognized with an architectural society award when it was completed in 1989.

Below: The most recently created Sixth District rents space in this high-rise tower in downtown San Jose.

Above and Right: The Fifth District is also a tenant; it occupies a brick and glass office building in Fresno.

Preserving *the* Old

By Chris VerPlanck and Jay Turnbull, FAIA

This essay examines the recent rehabilitation of two of California's most significant courthouses: the United States Ninth Circuit Court of Appeals and the California State Building, both in San Francisco. These courthouses, one part of the federal judiciary and the other contributed by the State of California to San Francisco's developing Civic Center, have many similarities. They were designed by master architects and built during the first quarter of the twentieth century. They share a monumental scale and the classical language of the Ecole des Beaux Arts. Both buildings sustained major damage during the Loma Prieta earthquake of 1989. Our office participated in rehabilitating and altering the buildings. Changes in use and program, a full-scale seismic retrofit, and system replacement were coupled with comprehensive life safety, code and accessibility upgrades. To integrate these many requirements, we needed to first analyze the buildings and identify their most significant features. Then, appropriate treatments could be found to repair or restore significant features, to protect valuable finishes during construction, and to accommodate new programmatic or code-generated needs without destroying historic material, workmanship or detail.

REASONS FOR PRESERVATION

Why bother to preserve and rehabilitate historic courthouses such as these? Four answers suggest themselves.

Continuity

In a secular society the judicial/governmental complex is often the principal symbolic precinct in the community. California has been characterized by rapid and ceaseless change. Continuing to use substantial public buildings such as courthouses for their original purpose (or at least preserving them from demolition and adapting them to new uses) allows them to serve as tangible links to our past.

Carved detail of Union Shield, Postmaster's Office, Court of Appeals.

Material and Craft Conservation

Preservation of 19th- and early 20th-century courthouses can often be justified by the simple fact that buildings such as these will, realistically, never be constructed again. Many of the materials and labor-intensive craftsmanship employed in the construction of the Ninth Circuit Court of Appeals and the California State Building are now either too costly to obtain or no longer available. If carefully conserved, both buildings will continue to illustrate these "lost arts," rare materials and craftsmanship to future generations.

Historic Significance

The siting, scale and style of courthouses often reveal events or trends of historic significance. The location of the California State Building and the Ninth Circuit Court of Appeals in San Francisco, for example, signifies the primacy of that city during much of the 20th century. San Francisco was the undisputed commercial, cultural and administrative center of the Western states and Pacific territories until the rise of Los Angeles at mid-century. The location of the California State Building, with the state supreme court as its principal occupant, in San Francisco's Civic Center underscored the statewide importance of the city. Likewise, the location of the chief courthouse of the Ninth Circuit (which has appellate jurisdiction over nine Western states) in

Pilaster, second floor corridor, Court of Appeals.

San Francisco reinforced the city's position as the de facto capital of the West.

The grandeur evident in the design and construction of these two courthouses was reserved for comparatively few buildings of their era, whether public or private. The investment of such significant resources illustrates the respect accorded to legal institutions. In the case of the Ninth Circuit, it may also reveal the desire of Washington, D.C., for an impressive federal presence on the western edge of the continent.

Architectural Singularity: American Renaissance and the City Beautiful Movements

In their architecture and planning, the California State Building and the Ninth Circuit Court of Appeals are premier examples of the American Renaissance and City Beautiful movements. Both movements became popular at the end of the 19th century, a time when the United States was beginning to assert its cultural and political influence in the world. Inspired by the "White City" at the 1893 World Columbian Exposition in Chicago, and carried out by American architects trained at the Ecole des Beaux Arts in Paris, the American Renaissance consciously harnessed the language of the Italian and French Renaissance to demonstrate America's growing cultural and political prestige. Meanwhile, adherents of the City Beautiful movement sought to create beauty and civic order in America's fast-growing but chaotic urban areas by encouraging the construction of imposing Renaissance Revival public buildings, grand boulevards and public monuments. The Ninth Circuit Court of Appeals has been widely recognized as one of the most important monuments of the American Renaissance. Richard Guy Wilson of the University of Virginia has observed that the luxurious appointments of this building demonstrated that "America had become Europe's immediate successor in the march of civilization." Likewise, the California State Building, an integral component of San Francisco's Civic Center, is an important contributor to what most architectural historians consider to be the "finest and most complete manifestation of the City Beautiful Movement in America."

NINTH CIRCUIT COURT OF APPEALS

The Ninth Circuit Court of Appeals is located south of Market Street, about a quarter mile from the Civic Center.

Exterior Description

The building consists of two interconnected structures surrounding a one-story in-fill courtyard. Exterior walls are primarily granite ashlar. Both primary public elevations are symmetrical and designed in a manner consistent with the American Renaissance style. Each is embellished with Italian Renaissance–inspired detail, including rusticated stonework, pedimented window hoods, consoles, cartouches, a denticulate cornice and a roof-mounted balustrade.

Interior Description

Many of the interior spaces of the court of appeals are decorated with expensive marble finishes and exquisitely carved stucco and woodwork produced by Italian artisans. The ceiling of the 260-foot-long first-floor corridor consists of a series of ornamental ribbed groin vaults. Arches spring from the bracketed entablature, which is supported on paired, half-round Doric columns. The walls are paneled with Pavonazzo, Alaskan Gravina and Italian Cippolino marbles. The floor consists of small ceramic tiles laid in a mosaic pattern. Courtroom Number One is the pièce de résistance, featuring mosaic murals and a grandly ornamented plaster ceiling with three leaded skylights. Walls are paneled with Pavonazzo marble and crowned with a bracketed entablature.

History

The final design of the combined Ninth Circuit Court of Appeals and Main Post Office was developed in the late 1890s by James Knox Taylor, supervising architect of the United States. Construction began 1897. When the building was dedicated in August 1905, it became the focus of national attention. The *San Francisco Call* asserted that the building represented "the expression of the highest art in architecture." *Sunset* magazine declared it "the best constructed public building in the country." The court of appeals elicited favorable comparisons with its contemporary, the Library of Con-

gress in Washington, D.C. However, not all were delighted with the sumptuously appointed 326,500-square-foot building that had taken eight years to construct and seemed to have a limitless budget. The editorial staff of the *San Francisco Chronicle*, unhappy with the expense and delays, grumbled about the "gaudy" finishes.

The court of appeals was one of the few major downtown buildings to escape the 1906 earthquake and fire relatively unscathed. Postal employees saved the building from the firestorm that swept down Stevenson Street, engulfing the neighboring frame buildings. When the fire entered the court of appeals through a window in the northeast corner of the building, postal workers kept it from spreading by ripping out wood doors and moldings and extinguishing the flames with water-soaked mail sacks. Within a few days, the main post office was back in business and delivering mail to the outside world.

In October 1930, local architect George Kelham was chosen to design an addition to the east elevation. Completed in October 1934, Kelham's exterior elevations imitated but simplified those of the 1905 structure. The interior spaces were much more restrained than the original interior, a result of depression-imposed budget constraints and changing tastes. New courtrooms display a "stripped" variety of classicism popular for the design of depression-era federal buildings.

From 1934 until 1989, the court of appeals operated with relatively few program or design changes, although over the years incremental modifications, such as the installation of surface-mounted conduit and fluorescent fixtures, had taken their toll on the building's appearance.

The Loma Prieta earthquake of October 17, 1989, caused extensive damage and the building was immediately vacated. After several years of planning, a $91 million rehabilitation began in the spring of 1993. The project was divided into two components: first, the seismic upgrade; and second, the rehabilitation of the structure, bringing the building up to code while preserving its significant historic features. Additionally, the main post office was converted into a law library. Seven years after the earthquake, the court of appeals reopened, on October 19, 1996.

CALIFORNIA STATE BUILDING

The California State Building is located on McAllister Street, facing the northern boundary of Civic Center Plaza.

Exterior Description

The original portion of the building is a six-story, 372-foot by 52-foot structure, with a northward-projecting central wing housing the courtroom shared by the California Supreme Court and the First District Court of Appeal. Two wings added in the

Above: Medallions on west elevation (education, labor, justice, agriculture), California State Building.

Right: California State Building McAllister Street elevation, 1930s.

1930s project from the north elevation of the building, connecting it to the newly constructed, 14-story Hiram Johnson Office Building. Designed in the American Renaissance style largely consistent with other major Civic Center buildings, the California State Building is constructed on a steel skeleton and clad in gray California granite and terra-cotta simulating granite. The façade is composed of a three-story base surmounted by two stories of alternating arched and pedimented windows, separated by composite pilasters. These floors are surmounted by an entablature and an attic story with an ornamental terra-cotta cheneau. The long façade facing the Civic Center is bowed in plan, advancing 18 inches at the centerline; this optical innovation allows the lengthy elevation to appear flat. The McAllister Street elevation is dominated by three monumental entrance arches at the center of the façade. A profusion of architectural elements inspired by the Italian Renaissance ornament the façade, including Corinthian pilasters and cartouches enclosing symbols of labor, justice, education and agriculture.

Below: Ceiling detail, main lobby, California State Building.

Bottom: Pilaster detail Governor's Office, second floor, California State Building.

Interior Description

The interior of the California State Building is not as extravagant as that of the court of appeals. Designed by Bliss & Faville, a firm known for its conservatism, and constructed with a lower budget, the interior was quite restrained and utilitarian. Over the years some interior spaces, particularly the courtroom, were remodeled, removing much of their original character. Clad in terrazzo and embellished with fluted pilasters and an ornamental plaster ceiling, the main lobby is the primary public space in the building. The offices on the upper floors, including those of the governor, the chief justice, and the attorney general, are paneled with gumwood and mahogany and ornamented with fluted Ionic pilasters but are otherwise very simple.

History

In 1914, California voters approved a bond issue to finance a new home for the California Supreme Court, to be constructed on the site of the previous California Supreme Court building, which was destroyed in 1906. Many distinguished firms submitted designs to the competition jury formed in 1916, including Bakewell & Brown who had designed the adjacent city hall.

In 1917, the jury selected the prominent San Francisco firm of Bliss & Faville to design the new building. Bliss & Faville's design aroused the opposition of several local architects, including Willis Polk, who contended that the façade's massing was ill proportioned and the details too small for a large building. Despite the controversy, the state supervising architect upheld

The courtroom of the California Supreme Court, as remodeled in 1950s.

the jury's decision and the state building was constructed according to Bliss & Faville's original design.

The building was completed in 1923. In 1930 two additions were constructed on the north side of the building. Throughout the 1930s and 1940s, aesthetic and mechanical changes were made in the appellate courtroom, offices and other interior spaces, altering many beyond recognition. A large modern annex to the north, facing Golden Gate Avenue, was completed in 1960.

In October 1989, the Loma Prieta earthquake damaged the state building so substantially that it was immediately vacated. Five years later, the General Services Administration sponsored an architectural competition for the rehabilitation and seismic upgrade of the original building and the replacement of the 1957 addition with a new, multistory office building. Work began April 1996 and was completed in December 1998.

Reconstructed courtroom, California State Building, 1998.

SPECIAL CONSTRUCTION PROBLEMS AND ISSUES
Seismic

The Ninth Circuit Court of Appeals presented significant challenges after the Loma Prieta earthquake had heavily damaged the venerable old building. Shear wall installation, used in many seismic upgrades, normally involves the temporary removal

of historic fabric before shear walls can be poured. The potential for accidental damage is always present when materials are removed and stored elsewhere during construction. This risk was especially high with the irreplaceable mosaic murals, plaster vaulting and marble wall finishes of the court of appeals. As a result, the friction pendulum base isolation system was selected as the preferred solution.

Base isolation is an expensive but very effective method that substantially reduces the amount of force transmitted to the structure during an earthquake by installing giant shock absorbers underneath the structural columns. The foundation is separated from its superstructure, allowing it to "float" above any seismic-induced ground movement with minimal oscillation. To allow for horizontal movement, a moat is excavated around the perimeter of the building. Prior to the rehabilitation of San Francisco's city hall in 1998, the court of appeals was the largest base isolation project in the United States.

For the California State Building, a steel-frame structure with nonload-bearing, unreinforced-masonry walls, extensive seismic strengthening was necessary. The work involved the installation of a concrete mat foundation and the construction of new concrete shear walls along the perimeter and at key locations within the courthouse. This more traditional and invasive method was selected because the building's historic interior finishes were neither as extensive nor as unique as those of the court of appeals. When the seismic work was completed, all significant historic interior finishes were reinstalled in their original locations.

PRESERVING THE OLD

First floor corridor during restoration, Court of Appeals.

First floor corridor restoration complete, Court of Appeals.

Systems and Codes

Both the Ninth Circuit Court of Appeals and the California State Building required upgrades to their electrical, mechanical, conveyance and communications systems. Over the years both buildings had undergone piecemeal installation of new mechanical systems, electrical and telephone wiring/conduit and modifications to the elevators. In both buildings a congested network of ducting and surface conduit wiring was concealed behind dropped ceilings. As part of the rehabilitation of both courthouses, wiring and mechanical systems were completely replaced and installed where they would no longer be visible, allowing the dropped ceilings to be removed and historic ceilings restored.

Life safety issues were resolved in both the court of appeals and the California State Building, in some cases utilizing the State Historic Building Code. The SHBC is an alternate to the Uniform Building Code; it allows alternate methods or materials to be used when architecturally significant features would be negatively affected by strict adherence to standard building codes. The SHBC was invoked to resolve a problem encountered during the rehabilitation of the court of appeals. Here, the issue involved a decorative wire elevator cage. Typically, elevator shafts are enclosed but this one was clearly designed to be open. The cage was retained but care was taken to ensure that no opening into the cage was more than four inches in width or height thus protecting children from injuries. In the rehabilitation of the California State Building, the SHBC was invoked to avoid the walling in of architecturally significant elevator and stair lobbies by fire separation walls. Typically, open stairwells are not permitted by fire safety regulations. Here, however, because the stair and elevator lobbies are the primary public spaces on the upper floors of the building, an alternate system involving special smoke removal and fire suppression systems was utilized.

Historic Fabric

One of the more formidable challenges encountered during the rehabilitation of both courthouses was protecting historic materials and features during construction. All interventions, (seismic, mechanical, conveyance, electrical and life safety) were carefully planned to avoid as much negative impact as possible. However, some impact was inevitable. One of our most important responsibilities was to develop methods for protecting existing fabric from damage, preferably in situ, or if necessary, temporarily relocating it during construction. Another issue involved repair versus replacement of decayed or damaged historic elements. Using the Secretary of the Interior's Standards for the Treatment of Historic Properties as our guide, we formulated strategies for repairing deterio-

Marble panels stored in Courtroom Number 15.

Keystone volute with classical mask during (left) and following (right) restoration, California State Building.

rated historic features whenever possible. If the decay had become too advanced methods for replicating deteriorated elements were identified.

The court of appeals, with its exceptional and delicate finishes, required that as much fabric as practicable be repaired and left in place during the seismic upgrade and rehabilitation. On the exterior, granite blocks and terra-cotta elements that had been cracked and dislodged were repaired in place instead of being removed and replaced. Minor cracks were repaired with cementitious mortar. If the cracks presented a potential life/safety problem, stainless steel pins, set in epoxy, were countersunk into the stones and the holes filled with repair mortar.

The terra-cotta cheneau presented one of the most significant preservation/conservation challenges associated with the California State Building. The cheneau is a decorative frieze of 264 terra-cotta units running along the top edge of the attic story. During the early phase of the project, a survey revealed that approximately 90% of the individual units were in poor condition, exhibiting cracks, spalling and delamination. The salvageable units were repaired by removing the rusted anchors and injecting epoxy into small cracks. Large cracks were repaired with pins and epoxy. Delaminated areas on the cheneau were recoated and water repellent was applied to all surfaces. The nonsalvageable units were replicated.

Terra-cotta cheneau, California State Building.

Conservation of terra-cotta cheneau, California State Building.

Building *the* New

By Charles Drulis, A.I.A.

The courthouse has long been a powerful symbol in our society. Traditionally, given its role as an important public building, the courthouse was located in the center of a town or city. In California, until the 1950s, county courthouses were invariably built "downtown." Moreover, with the exception of the Art Deco–influenced, WPA-funded courthouses of the 1930s and 1940s, they were distinctively governmental buildings, generally designed in a classically derived style.

During the last 50 years, however, new courthouses in several counties (Marin, Tulare and Ventura, for example) have been constructed at the edge of town, where land is more readily available and the building accessible to a more dispersed population. The courthouses built in these suburban campuses did not need to consider the context of surrounding buildings, because there were none. Even those counties that rebuilt their courthouse in a downtown center often abandoned classical architecture. The newer courthouses in counties such as Mendocino, Humboldt, Fresno, Orange, Kern and San Diego, while still in the city center, were virtually indistinguishable from commercial office buildings.

Recently, two counties chose to construct new courthouses in their historic city centers. The function, setting and scale of the two buildings are quite different. Despite these differences, many of the design issues and goals in both projects are similar, and together, they offer a case study of the challenges and opportunities encountered when designing a modern court building in a traditional setting.

The San Francisco Civic Center courthouse is a civil courthouse that does not require direct physical connection to the county jail, although it does have a vehicular sallyport and limited holding cells for witnesses who are incarcerated. The new Napa County courthouse is a high-security criminal facility with secure holding cells adjacent to all courtrooms and a tunnel linking it to the county jail.

The San Francisco courthouse is located in a major city, within a grand Beaux Arts Civic Center Plaza recognized as one of America's great urban public spaces. The Napa courthouse is in a town center that is the seat of government for a small agricultural county. The nearby buildings, with the exception of the existing Victorian-era courthouse, are not historically significant. However, the downtown square in which the old courthouse is set, flanked by turn-of-the-century commercial buildings, follows the model of many California rural town centers.

San Francisco's new courthouse as viewed from across the Civic Center.

In terms of scale, the San Francisco courthouse is 230,000 square feet on seven levels, one below grade, and contains 38 courtrooms. The Napa courthouse is 48,000 square feet on four levels, one below grade, containing five courtrooms.

Schematic view of two courtrooms adaptable to use as a single "megacourtroom."

EXPECTATIONS FOR THE 21ST-CENTURY COURTHOUSE

Judges, attorneys and court administrators have heightened expectations for designers of new court facilities. Aspects in which these new demands are evident include security, accessibility for persons with disabilities, flexibility (i.e., the adaptability of space to multiple and/or changing uses), enhanced concern for the convenience and comfort of courthouse users, and effective utilization of new information and communication technologies.

In terms of security, older courthouses sometimes required criminal defendants to be transferred from jail to the courtroom in chains, through public corridors. Now dedicated pathways, completely separate from both public spaces and those accessible to court officers and staff, allow secure and dignified entry and exit.

An example of design flexibility is the ability to easily convert two adjacent courtrooms into one "megacourtroom" to accommodate complex, multiparty cases.

User-friendly jury assembly room provides comfortable seating, rich cherry paneling and computer-ready workstations.

The impact of the Americans with Disabilities Act and its California counterpart has been pervasive. Ramps, wider aisles, and braille directional signage, for example, are routinely incorporated into courthouses, just as they are in other types of buildings. There are some unique adaptations as well, such as incorporating assisted-listening devices using infrared transmission into the courtroom's sound system thereby allowing headphone amplification of proceedings for hearing-impaired participants. Another innovation allows vision-impaired visitors to carry an electronic sensor that, at the touch of a button, will announce where they are in the building.

Some examples of greater sensitivity to the needs of courthouse users are (1) the incorporation of computer-ready individual carrels in the jury assembly room so that jury candidates may work while awaiting assignment to a jury, (2) provision of staffed child waiting/playing areas, for children of participants in court proceedings, and (3)

New courthouse, center, relates to both City Hall, left, and the state supreme court building, right.

New courthouse, center, relates to both City Hall, left, and the state supreme court building, right.

private attorney conference rooms so that lawyers and clients don't need to hold whispered conversations in the hallways.

In addition to standard power, voice and data distribution, many new capabilities are available in the modern courthouse environment as a result of evolving technologies. Technological advancement has influenced the presentation of evidence; the recordation of testimony; the filing of briefs, motions and other "papers"; and the communication between the courts and the public.

In the courtroom, the use of increasingly sophisticated evidence display systems has improved the clarity with which evidence can be presented. Display systems allow for presentation of computer-generated information (text, graphics, data spreadsheets, etc.), in addition to handwritten notes, drawings and objects. Components of these systems typically include a podium-mounted overhead projector for use by the attorneys, a podium-mounted flat screen for attorney viewing and annotation of the projected images, flat screens on the judge's bench and in the witness box, rail-mounted flat screens in the jury box, and ceiling- or wall-mounted flat screens in the gallery area to display evidence to the public.

The use of video testimony provides for remote participation in trial proceedings, either within a courtroom or in the judge's chambers. Possible applications include child testimony and arraignments conducted remotely from jail.

Recordation and transcription of testimony normally requires at least a day for preparation of a typed transcript. Computer-assisted "real time" recording equipment now makes the text of testimony accessible to the judge and counsel almost instantaneously on a computer screen.

Electronic filing of documents promises advantages in terms of speed, cost, efficiency and convenient public accessibility. In September 2000, San Francisco Superior Court Judge Stuart Pollack ordered attorneys in two major class action cases being tried in the new Civic Center courthouse to file all documents electronically. Judge Pollack was quoted in an article by Dennis Opatrny in the September 12, 2000, *Recorder*: "It's going to save a whole lot of paper and make service a lot easier.... People won't have to clutter their files with stuff until they have a need to use it.... It gives instant access to the file by the judge, the law clerk and people outside the courthouse."

Both the San Francisco and Napa courthouses incorporate these features to different degrees. Clearly, integrating technology with support spaces and required infrastructure is essential in the design of new facilities. Planning for flexibility, adaptability and access to the vertical and horizontal cabling pathways is necessary to accommo-

Detail of stainless steel entry doors designed by Albert Paley.

date the continual evolution in technology. All building systems must be designed to support the loads required by electronic technologies.

However, most of the impact of technology occurs in the interior and does not influence, much less dictate, the exterior appearance of the building. There is no reason why a courthouse that incorporates the full range of new technologies cannot also be a distinctively governmental building and one that fits comfortably within a traditional architectural setting.

SAN FRANCISCO CIVIC CENTER COURTHOUSE
Historical Context

When the current city hall was completed in 1916, the civil courts were given "temporary" quarters on the third and fourth floors. They were still there in 1989 when the Loma Prieta earthquake struck, bond issues for a new courthouse proposed in the 1950s and 1970s having failed to gain the necessary two-thirds vote. When it became evident that City Hall would have to be vacated to construct the necessary seismic upgrades, judges seized the opportunity to plan for a new courthouse within the Civic Center. Funding was available from a variety of state and local sources, eliminating the need for voter approval of a traditional bond issue.

Exterior Architecture

The overall goal was to design a "modern" building that recognizes the formal composition and character of the historic Civic Center district.

City Hall is the focal point of the Civic Center Plaza area; it establishes the primacy of the east-west circulation and approach axis. The buildings along this axis are City Hall to the west and the old and new city libraries to the east. All have a monumental scale, colonnades and a dramatic play of light and shadow on the entry façades that signal their importance. The buildings along the north-south axis (the Civic Auditorium to the south and the California State Building to the north) frame City Hall and create the edge or boundary that defines the grand public plaza. The four corner buildings envisioned in the master plan (of which only one existed prior to the new courthouse) are intended to serve a similar design function, as a "wall" in

Arched and vaulted ceilings in top floor courtrooms were a response to structural constraints on height.

relation to the landscaped plaza. The exterior architecture of the new courthouse acknowledges this role and relationship.

Courthouse designers sought to develop a scale and architectural vocabulary that is contextually appropriate. Decisions about the courthouse's height, roof lines, roof type, cornice lines, belt courses, corner elements, bay modules and materials were all influenced by the surrounding buildings. Some examples:

- The use of a corner entry to the building responds to the master plan vision. Only one of the four sites at the corners of the plaza, the Public Health Building to the south of City Hall, had been fully developed. The new courthouse would "bracket" City Hall to the north. This relationship to City Hall and the Public Health Building was the determining factor in the location (corner) and form (chamfered) of the courthouse entry, both of which mirror those of the Public Health Building and thus help "frame" City Hall.
- The predominant exterior material, Sierra white granite, is the same as that used on the other Civic Center buildings. In fact, it was hewn from the same quarry near Raymond, California, that supplied the stone for the earlier buildings. The quality of its detailing firmly establishes the courthouse as "colleague" of those earlier formal buildings on the plaza. This was accomplished by installing the stone skin of the building as individual blocks in traditional offset masonry patterns as opposed to a pre-cast concrete panel system with granite "tiles." This allowed narrower, staggered joints between the large blocks of granite. The technique required a six-story concrete shear wall to be poured in place for seismic resistance. The four-inch thick blocks of granite were then craned and welded into place individually. Each block has four stainless steel clips embedded into the back of the stone and these were welded to stainless steel brackets embedded in the shear wall.
- The height limit at the site established by zoning was 70 feet. The California State Building, directly across Polk Street from the new courthouse, however, is 80 feet in height. As noted previously, it was important for the courthouse to relate harmoniously to neighboring buildings. A variance of 10 feet was sought; the consistent height allowed other elements of the new courthouse (the roof line, cornice line, etc.) to match those of the state building, while not competing with City Hall.
- The new courthouse references its neighbors in other ways. The first two floors comprise the rusticated base course with the small, deeply set windows characteristic of both City Hall and the state building. Floors three, four and five establish the prominent arched window composition that references the similar windows on the state building. The mansard roof is clad with lead-coated copper, similar to that of City Hall.

Interior Spaces

A significant challenge for the designers of the courthouse was to accommodate the program within the envelope dictated by site constraints. The entire 33,000-square-foot lot is covered by the building footprint. Six floors above grade were required to house the programmed spaces. This limited the floor-to-floor heights to 13 feet, 6 inches to meet the city-mandated 80-foot building height limit. The 13-foot, 6-inch height is very low for a court facility. Traditional courtrooms often have ceiling heights of 20 feet or more.

The design challenge was to give the major spaces, in particular the courtrooms, a sense of dignity and volume within this framework. This was accomplished by articulating and up lighting the ceilings to create an enhanced experience of "lift" in the rooms. Two of the courtrooms on the sixth floor have very low ceilings (7 feet, 6 inches and 10 feet) in response to the penetration of structural beam elements from the roof. The ceilings in these courtrooms were designed as arched planes with recessed panels. Their success is measured by their popularity with judges and the public.

The interior public spaces are organized around a three-story rotunda, which provides a single, secure entry point into the building. The rotunda reinforces the vertical exterior corner element of the building and is a dignified entry space. The perimeter public spaces on the first, third, fourth and fifth levels provide natural light and views to the Civic Center. The primary interior materials, cherry wood and Beauharnais French limestone, are "warm" in contrast to the "cool" exterior granite.

The spirit of the exterior architecture was the basis for the interior detailing, which is a hybrid of traditional references and modernist sensibilities. For example, the "cornice" on the judge's bench and the bar railing cap in the courtrooms are an interpretation of the exterior cornice on the building.

The new Napa County courthouse completed in 1999 as viewed from Old Courthouse Square.

NAPA COUNTY CRIMINAL COURTHOUSE
Historical Context

The San Francisco Civic Center was envisioned from the outset as a unified array of public buildings by a group of talented architects planning on a grand scale. Development in the vicinity of the Civic Center Plaza has been guided by their planning over the past 85 years.

By contrast, Napa's courthouse square was set aside by the town's founders, but the surrounding blocks developed organically without rigid design guidelines. Change has been continuous throughout the 20th century. Some turn-of-the-century commercial buildings remain almost intact. Others have been remodeled extensively; still others replaced entirely. The result is that the old courthouse has been (and the new courthouse would be) surrounded by a great variety of land uses and architectural styles. Immediately to the west of the new courthouse site is a 1970s county administration center, a bit further is a homeless shelter and a block beyond that is the First Presbyterian Church, built in 1874, still in use and a State Registered Landmark. To the east is the Napa River, a nearby shore recently developed into a riverfront park. To the south is the existing hall of justice, containing the county jail, the sheriff's department and other law-enforcement-related offices. To the north is the old courthouse set amid the lawn and trees of Courthouse Square, which in turn faces commercial buildings ranging from the 19th century to the 1950s.

The challenge presented was to design a high-security criminal courthouse that related to its diverse neighbors, contributed to the city's efforts to foster a renaissance in its historic central district, and adhered to a strict budget.

Exterior Architecture

The absence of architectural unity in the existing context and the idiosyncrasies of the site in relationship to the existing buildings was a clear design challenge. The

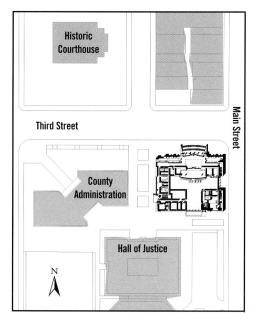

Site plan shows new courthouse in relation to existing hall of justice, county administration building and old courthouse.

strategy used to address these conditions was to treat each side of the courthouse as a major or minor "front" with its own unique identity. These asymmetrical elevations reflect the context that each faces and relate to each other without combining into a single, monolithic statement. The elevations respond both to their contexts as well as their uses: courthouse entry, river façade, judges' entry and courtyard. Each façade contributes to the overall experience of the building and is both a "front" (for itself) and a "side" (for its neighbors). The courthouse does not turn its back to any side.

The north, courthouse entry façade of the building has an important relationship to the historic courthouse across the street. This major elevation uses scale, entry steps and three-story transparent elements to establish its importance. The scale suggests archetypal courthouse elements and the prominent center bay functions as a "lantern" for the building at night.

To the west, the building bookends the path to the hall of justice in conjunction with the mid-'70s administration building, which was replastered to be compatible with the new courthouse. This façade combines with the administration building to form a courtyard on axis with an existing street right-of-way. This elevation has larger scaled elements and is "public," but it is secondary in relationship to the entry elevation.

The site was originally planned as a ceremonial front lawn for the existing hall of justice and the new courthouse stands in front of this building. This relationship dictates that the "back" of the courthouse is a significant elevation. The elevation acknowledges its relationship to the hall of justice by providing a large bay element for interest.

To the east, the courthouse stands at the edge of downtown along the Napa River and contributes to the character of this edge condition. The elements on this elevation are scaled to be visible from a distance while approaching the building from the east, one of the main thoroughfares into the city center.

Since both of its immediate neighbors are distinctively modern in style, the courthouse uses scale elements, rather than highly articulated detailing, to establish its

South (judges' entry) façade is on the right.

image and relationship to classical traditions. The exterior materials are Sierra white granite, precast concrete, stainless steel, aluminum and glass. The budget did not allow for granite to be used on the entire building, so it is strategically located at the building's major focal points and around the entire base, where people will come into contact with the stone. Precast concrete panels, using a mix that complements the adjacent granite, cover the rest of the building.

Where a traditionally styled building might rely for detail on fine stonework and colonnades, the courthouse employs contemporary details such as the metal solar shading devices, stainless steel guardrails and the curved entry canopy.

Complexity is added to the dignified monochromatic stone and concrete exterior by the transparency of the public entry

West (courtyard) façade is on the right.

façade. This is achieved by the three-story windows that border the public area, affording a clear view to the nearby Courthouse Square and its Victorian courthouse. The interior wall of the public space is covered by a three-story cherry wood paneling that is visible from the street.

Courthouse main entry.

Courthouse entry façade at dusk.

The courthouse has characteristics of strength and dignity, yet is accessible; it is secure and yet visually open.

Interior

The courthouse provides space for five courtrooms, accompanying holding cells, judges' chambers, jury deliberation rooms, and the clerk's function for the criminal courts. The jury assembly room for both civil and criminal trials is located in the recently renovated hall of records, adjacent to the old courthouse. The structural bay and the mechanical system are designed to allow for the future conversion of existing space into up to three additional courtrooms.

The interior detailing introduces cherry wood paneling in the public areas and courtrooms. The wood grain patterns reference the proportions of traditional coffers, pilasters and stiles while maintaining the relatively smooth planer surface of the building's exterior. As in San Francisco, the proportion of courtroom space dedicated to spectators and participants has been reversed. Whereas traditional courtrooms provided a large amount of seating for the public, new courtrooms enlarge the "well": the area within the bar in which the trial activity occurs.

The courthouse has three levels of circulation: public; restricted for judicial officers and staff; and secure for prisoner transfer and holding. The building is connected to the hall of justice and jail via an underground tunnel with a holding area in the basement. On the court floors, the holding area is a centralized "single core" serving courtrooms on the second and third floors. The use of a single secure elevator with a centralized holding area reduces initial and long-term staff and maintenance costs for the facility. A prisoner "dock" is provided in the high-volume arraignment courtroom. Additionally, a vehicle sallyport for prisoner transportation is provided on the ground level.

Visitors first entering the building are afforded a "through building view," in contrast to the inward focus of more traditional buildings. This "transparency" is accomplished through the layering of walls of glass on the north (courthouse entry) façade, the clerk's area and the south (judges' entry) façade. Ample natural light and views to the outside are available throughout the clerk's area and the public corridors and waiting areas. This strategy provides a secure yet open and pleasing environment for court personnel and the public. The goal is to present the courthouse as a "public" building that provides important but difficult services to citizens in a relatively stress-free environment.

Hallway and public entrance to courtroom.

Treasured Courthouses

COURTHOUSES LISTED IN THE NATIONAL REGISTER OF HISTORIC PLACES

California trial courts now occupy approximately 450 separate buildings. Of these, 13 are listed in the National Register of Historic Places, established under the National Historic Preservation Act of 1966. In addition, 12 buildings that previously served as courthouses but that have since been converted to other uses are also listed in the National Register. Finally, there are a handful of other buildings that now are, or once were, county courthouses that are not listed in the National Register but that have received formal recognition as a California State Historic Landmark (CSHL).

All of the buildings that have been designated in one or more of these categories (and which still exist) are listed below. The list is by no means exhaustive; many county courthouses of great architectural merit and with rich historical associations are not included. The courthouses in Alpine, El Dorado, Glenn, Imperial, Modoc, Plumas, Riverside, Solano, Sutter, Tehama and Yolo counties, for example, all appear to be eligible for the National Register. One reason for the incompleteness of this roster is that the nominating process for inclusion in the National Register typically begins at the local level. While both the State Historic Preservation Office and historians at the National Park Service (which maintains the National Register) evaluate all nominations, local communities must take the initiative to get the process started.

COUNTY	CITY	DATE BUILT	ORIGINAL USE	CURRENT USE	STYLE/ IMAGE	ARCHITECT/ DESIGNER	RECOGNITION
Calaveras	Mokelumne Hill	1855	Courthouse	Hotel (Since 1866)			California State Historic Landmark (No. 663)
Calaveras	San Andreas	1867	Courthouse	Museum (Since 1966)	Greek Revival	Morrill, D. L.	National Register
Colusa	Colusa	1861	Courthouse	Courthouse	Greek Revival	Brown, Vincent	California State Historic Landmark (No. 890)
Contra Costa	Martinez	1903	Courthouse	Finance Building (Since 1966)	Neoclassic/ State Capitol	Havens & Toepke	National Register
Contra Costa	Martinez	1932	Hall of Records	Courthouse (Since 1966)	Beaux Arts Classical	Bangs, E. G.	National Register
Inyo	Independence	1921	Courthouse	Courthouse	Beaux Arts Classical	Weeks, W. H.	National Register
Kings	Hanford	1897	Courthouse	Retail/Office (Since 1979)	Renaissance/ Victorian	Wilcox, W. H.	National Register
Lake	Lakeport	1870	Courthouse	Museum (Since 1968)	Italianate	Petit, A. P.	National Register, CSHL (No. 897)
Lassen	Susanville	1917	Courthouse	Courthouse	Beaux Arts Classical	Sellon, George C.	National Register
Madera	Madera	1902	Courthouse	Museum (Since 1971)	Renaissance/ Victorian	Braunton, Hugh	National Register
Marin	San Rafael	1962/1969	Government Center/ Hall of Justice	Government Center/ Hall of Justice	Modern	Wright, Frank L., Taliesen Associates	National Historic Landmark, National Register, CSHL (No. 999)
Mariposa	Mariposa	1854	Courthouse	Courthouse	Greek Revival	Fox, P. V. and A. F. Shriver	National Register, CSHL (No. 670)
Merced	Snelling	1857	Courthouse	Courthouse	Greek Revival		California State Historic Landmark (No. 409)
Merced	Merced	1874	Courthouse	Museum (Since 1973)	Italianate	Bennett, A. A.	National Register
Mono	Bridgeport	1880	Courthouse	Courthouse	Italianate	Roberts, J. R.	National Register

COUNTY	CITY	DATE BUILT	ORIGINAL USE	CURRENT USE	STYLE/ IMAGE	ARCHITECT/ DESIGNER	RECOGNITION
Monterey	Monterey/ Colton Hall	1849	Town Hall/School (Served as Courthouse 1850–1872)	City Museum	Federal	Colton, Walter	National Historic Landmark, CSHL (No.126)
Napa	Napa	1878	Courthouse	Courthouse	Italianate	Newsom Bros. & Ira Gilchrist	National Register
Orange	Santa Ana	1901	Courthouse	Museum/County Offices (Since 1987)	Richardsonian Romanesque	Strange, Chas.	National Register/ CSHL (No. 837)
Placer	Auburn	1898	Courthouse	Courthouse	State Capitol	Curtis, J. M.	National Register (as part of Old Auburn Historic District)
San Bernardino	San Bernardino	1926	Courthouse	Courthouse	Beaux Arts Classical	Jones, Howard E. & Dewitt Mitcham	National Register
San Diego	San Diego	1847	Office of Alcade (Served as Courthouse 1850-1869)	Reconstructed 1992; Part of Old Town State Historic Park	Vernacular		National Register (as part of Old Town Historic District)/ CSHL (No. 830)
San Diego	San Diego/ Whaley House	1856	Private Home (Served as Courthouse 1869-1871)	Museum	Monterey		California State Historic Landmark (No. 65)
San Francisco	San Francisco	1916	City Hall/ Courthouse (Served as Civil Courthouse 1916-1989)	City Hall	Beaux Arts Classical/ State Capitol	Bakewell & Brown	National Historical Landmark, National Register (as part Civic Center Historic District)
San Mateo	Redwood City	1908	Courthouse	Museum (Since 1998)	Renaissance	Allen, Glenn	National Register
Santa Barbara	Santa Barbara	1929	Courthouse	Courthouse	Spanish Colonial Revival	Mooser, Wm.	National Register
Santa Clara	San Jose	1868	Courthouse	Courthouse	Neoclassic	Goodrich, Levi	National Register (as part of St. James Square Historic District)
Shasta	Shasta	1855	Store (Served as Courthouse 1861-1888)	State Historic Park	Vernacular/ Italianate		National Register
Solano	Benicia	1853	City Hall (Served as Courthouse 1854-1858)	State Historic Park	Greek Revival	Rider & Houghton	National Register, CSHL (No. 153)
Trinity	Weaverville	1856	Saloon	Courthouse (Since 1866)	Vernacular/ Italianate		National Register (as part of Weaverville Historic District)
Tuolumne	Sonora	1900	Courthouse	Courthouse	Eclectic	Mooser & Son	National Register
Ventura	Ventura	1913	Courthouse	City Hall (Since 1973)	Beaux Arts Classical	Martin, Albert C.	National Register, CSHL (No. 847)

Anyone interested in a particular courthouse's history can obtain a copy of the materials submitted in support of its nomination to the National Register from the National Register Reference Desk, National Park Service, 1849 C Street NW, Washington, DC 20240. (The website for the National Register is www.cr.nps.gov/nr.)

As a part of his contribution to this project, architectural historian Michael Corbett prepared a much more comprehensive table of courthouses, including over 200 buildings and containing more detailed information about each. A copy has been lodged with the California Historical Society and plans are underway for the society to make the table available through its website (www.calhist.org) and periodically to update and expand it as new information is furnished by visitors to the website.

Bibliography

Introduction

Ellis, Joseph, *American Sphinx: The Character of Thomas Jefferson* (1998)

Howell, Benjamin; Rosenthal, Deborah; and Steele, Jeanna, "Liti-gators," *California Lawyer* (May 2001)

State of California, Task Force on Court Facilities, *Preliminary Determinations: Trial Court Facilities Guidelines* (October 1999)

State of California, Task Force on Court Facilities, *Second Interim Report* (March 2001)

Tansey, Bernadette, "Martinez Courthouse," *San Francisco Chronicle*, July 16, 1999

Vallejo, Mariano G., "Recuerdos Historicos y Personales Tocante a la Alta California" (1875) excerpted in *Gold Rush: A Literary Exploration* (1997)

History

Bakken, Gordon Morris, *Practicing Law in Frontier California* (1991)

Beck, Warren A. and Hasse, Ynez D., *Historical Atlas of California* (1974)

Brett, C.E.B., *Court Houses and Market Houses of the Province of Ulster* (1973)

Brewer, William, *Up and Down California in 1860–1864* (1930)

Browne, J. Ross, *Report of the Debates in the Convention of California on the Formation of the State Constitution* (1850)

Burns, John F., Ed., *Sacramento: Gold Rush Legacy, Metropolitan Destiny* (1999)

Carpenter, John W. and Emerick, Michael, *Tennessee Courthouses* (1996)

Caughey, John Walton, *The California Gold Rush* (1948)

Coleman, William, "San Francisco Vigilance Committees," *Century Magazine* (1891), excerpted in *Gold Rush: A Literary Exploration* (1997)

Coy, Owen C., *Guide to the County Archives of California* (1919)

Ellison, William Henry, *A Self-Governing Dominion: California, 1849–1860* (1950)

Field, Stephen J., *Personal Reminiscences of Early Days in California* (1880)

Greiff, Constance M., Ed., *Lost America: From the Mississippi to the Pacific* (1972)

Grenier, Judson A., *Golden Odyssey: John Stroud Houston, California's First Controller and the Origins of State Government* (1999)

Grivas, Theodore, *Military Governments in California, 1846–1850* (1963)

Hall, Frederick, *History of San Jose and Surroundings* (1871)

Hawke, David Freeman, *Everyday Life in Early America* (1989)

Historical Activities Committee of the National Society of Colonial Dames of America Resident in the State of California, *Counties and Courthouses of California: A Survey* (1964)

Holliday, J.S., *Rush for Riches: Gold Fever and the Making of California* (1999)

Ignoffo, Mary Jo, *Gold Rush Politics: California's First Legislature* (1999)

Jackson, John Brinckerhoff, *Discovering the Vernacular Landscape* (1984)

Kirker, Harold, *California Architecture in Perspective* (1991)

Kirker, Harold, *California's Architectural Frontier: Style and Tradition in the Nineteenth Century* (1986)

Langum, David J., *Law and Community on the Mexican California Frontier* (1987)

Royce, Josiah, *California From the Conquest in 1846 to the Second Vigilance Committee in San Francisco* (1886)

Taylor, Bayard, *El Dorado: Adventures in the Path of Empire* (1850), reissued by Heyday Books and Santa Clara University (2000)

Weese, Ben, "The County Courthouse: rediscovering a national asset," *Architectural Record* (June 1975)

Architecture

In addition to the specific sources listed below, several general types of sources also provided important background for the architectural essay. Several regional and national architectural journals, notably *California Architect and Building News*, *Architect and Engineer*, and *American Architect and Building News*, provided information on specific courthouses, and on courthouse issues and architects. Numerous 19th-century patternbooks, available from Dover Publications and on the shelves of the Environmental Design Library at the

University of California at Berkeley, were searched for courthouse plans. Guidebooks and other publications on the courthouses of many other states, including a series by Albert J. Larson in *Pioneer America Society Transactions/ Material Culture*, helped to place California courthouses in a broader context. Finally, the material cited below in the bibliography for individual counties provided much information for this essay.

American Bar Association and American Institute of Architects, Joint Committee on the Design of Courtrooms and Court Facilities, *The American Courthouse: Planning and Design for the Judicial Process* (1973)

Architect and Engineer, "The Kern County Court House," Vol. 21:3 (July 1910)

Architectural Record, "Santa Cruz County Governmental Center," Vol. 144:2 (August 1968)

Benjamin, Asher, *The American Builder's Companion*, unabridged reprint of the sixth (1827) edition (1969)

Bicknell, A. J. & Co., *Bicknell's Victorian Buildings* (1979)

Brownell, Charles E.; Loth, Calder; Rassmussen, William M.S.; and Wilson, Richard Guy, *The Making of Virginia Architecture* (1992)

Coy, Owen C., *California County Boundaries: A Study of the Division of the State Into Counties and the Subsequent Changes in Their Boundaries* (1923)

Craig, Lois and the staff of the Federal Architecture Project, *The Federal Presence: Architecture, Politics, and Symbols in United States Government Buildings* (1978)

DeLappe, Russell Guerne, "Functional Design in Modesto County Building," *Architect and Engineer*, Vol. 141:1 (April 1940)

Eisen, Theodore, "The Consistency of San Francisco Architecture," *California Architect and Building News*, Vol. 3:4 (April 1882)

Finney, M. MacLean, "The Court House Beautiful," *Architect and Engineer*, Vol. 98:1 (July 1929)

Gebhard, David and Von Breton, Harriet, *Architecture in California: 1868–1968*, catalog of an exhibition organized to celebrate the Centennial of the University of California (1968)

Gebhard, David; Sandweiss, Eric; and Winter, Robert, *The Guide to Architecture in San Francisco and Northern California*, revised edition (1985)

Goodsell, Charles T., *The Social Meaning of Civic Space: Studying Political Authority Through Architecture* (1988)

Gowans, Alan, *Styles and Types of North American Architecture* (1992)

Green, Aaron G. and DeNevi, Donald P., *An Architecture for Democracy: The Marin County Civic Center* (1990)

Gundrum, Frederick F., *California's Courthouses: Photographed in Passing During the Years 1918 to 1926*, (photographic album on file at the State Library of California, Sacramento)

Hamlin, Talbot, *Greek Revival Architecture in America* (1964)

Hines, Thomas S., "Richard Neutra," *Macmillan Encyclopedia of Architects*, Vol. 3 (1982)

Hoover, Mildred Brooke; Rensch, Hero Eugene; Rensch, Ethel Grace; and Abeloe, William N., *Historic Spots in California*, 4th Ed., revised by Douglas E. Kyle (1990)

James, Ronald M., *Temples of Justice: County Courthouses of Nevada* (1994)

Kelsey, Mavis P., Sr. and Dyal, Donald H., *The Courthouses of Texas, A Guide* (1993)

Kirker, Harold, *California's Architectural Frontier: Style and Tradition in the Nineteenth Century* (1973)

Kirker, Harold, *Old Forms on a New Land: California Architecture in Perspective* (1991)

Lardner, Lardner Architects and Associates, *The American Courthouse: Northern and Central California Historic Courthouses* (1975)

Lounsbury, Carl, "The Structure of Justice: The Courthouses of Colonial Virginia," *Perspectives in Vernacular Architecture, III* (1989)

Lowell, Waverly B.; Hardy, Mary; and Downey, Lynn A, *Architectural Records in the San Francisco Bay Area: A Guide to Research* (1988)

Lowry, Bates, *Building a National Image: Architectural Drawings for the American Democracy, 1789–1912* (1985)

National Society of the Colonial Dames of America Resident in California, Historical Activities Committee, *Counties and Courthouses of California: A Survey* (1964)

Neutra, Richard, *Survival Through Design* (1969)

Oxford, June, *The Capital That Couldn't Stay Put: The Complete Book of California's Capitals* (1995)

Pare, Richard, Editor, *Court House, A Photographic Document* (1978)

Price, Edward T., "The Central Courthouse Square in the American County Seat," *Common Places: Readings in American Vernacular Architecture* (1986)

Rawls, James T., *California: An Interpretive History*, 7th Edition (1998)

Taylor, Katherine Fischer, *In the Theater of Criminal Justice: The Palais de Justice in Second Empire Paris* (1993)

Upton, Dell, *Architecture in the United States* (1998)

Willis, Ray, "Alameda County Hall of Justice: A New Trend in Governmental Buildings, Oakland, California," *Architect and Engineer*, Vol. 215 (October 1958)

Woodbridge, Sally B., *California Architecture: Historic American Buildings Survey* (1988)

Individual Counties

From about 1880 through the 1920s, several commercial publishing companies produced histories of nearly all counties in California. These were typically underwritten by subscription, i.e., local merchants, farmers and professionals made advance contributions to cover the cost of production, in exchange for the inclusion of short, complimentary biographies—sometimes with illustrations of the donor or his ranch/farm. William Henry Chamberlain's *History of Yuba County, California: with illustrations descriptive of its scenery, residences, public buildings, fine blocks and manufactories*, published by Thompson & West in 1879 is representative. Many libraries have extensive collections of these commercial county

histories. They are a wonderful source of information, though historians today caution that their anecdotes and accounts of local lore are not always reliable. Several of these volumes were consulted, but not systematically, nor so extensively as to warrant including them all in a bibliography. Those that provided significant and specific information are noted.

Two categories of sources provided particularly useful. The first was the series on the history of courthouses in each county that was published by the *Los Angeles Daily Journal* during 1975 and 1976. The Daily Journal Corporation's archives do not extend back to the 1970s; however, the series (or at least the great majority of articles) is available on microfilm at The Bancroft Library, University of California, Berkeley. The second category was the National Register Nomination Forms (now called "Registration Forms") submitted to the National Park Service. These exist for 26 courthouses; copies are available from the National Park Service in Washington, D. C. Copies of all the *Daily Journal* articles and National Register forms that we obtained are also included in the materials which will be archived by the California Historical Society, as explained in the following paragraph.

In addition, copies of several hundred documents were assembled from libraries and historical societies statewide. Most of these are empheral materials, such as newspaper articles, unpublished pamphlets, programs produced for courthouse celebrations (groundbreakings, dedications, anniversaries, etc.), lists of the contents of courthouse cornerstones, etc. In the vast majority of cases, these materials are available only in the local library/archive. Rather than generate a bibliography of virtually inaccessible sources, it seemed more helpful to donate them to the California Historical Society, which will be able to organize, catalog and preserve them as a specialized archival collection. Readers interested in reviewing these materials should contact the librarian at the California Historical Society in San Francisco. In some cases, however, architects and local historians have produced articles, pamphlets or books of high quality that are likely to be available in bookstores or library collections or through local historical societies. These are listed below. (Those previously cited in the bibliography are not repeated here.)

Alameda

Hadley, Homer, "Oakland's Monumental Court House," *The Architect and Engineer* (September 1936)

Williams, Frederick, "Noble Structure Dominates City Skyline," *The Architect and Engineer* (September 1936)

Amador

Cenotto, Larry, *Logan's Alley: Amador County Yesterday in Picture and Prose* (1988)

Butte

Good, James Francis (Hon.), "Butte County Courthouses and Jails," Vol. 13, *Butte County Historical Society Diggin's* (Summer 1969)

Calaveras

Kennedy, Lorrayne, "An Old Courthouse With a Lively Past," *Las Calaveras-Quarterly Bulletin of the Calaveras County Historical Society* (July 1991)

Colusa

Patton, Richard E. (Hon.), "The Colusa County Courthouse and Jail," *Wagon Wheels-Colusa County Historical Society* (February 1969)

Fresno

"A History of Fresno Courthouses and Jails," Vol. 10, *Fresno Past and Present*, No. 3 (1968)

Humboldt

Melendy, Howard, *The Construction of Humboldt County Courthouse at Eureka, California 1883–1889* (January 1953)

Inyo

Inyo County Board of Supervisors, *Inyo 1866–1966* (1966)

Lassen

Purdy, Tim I., "Lassen County Courthouse Complex" (November 11, 1994)

Los Angeles

"Goodbye, Old Courthouse," *Historical Society of Southern California Quarterly*, Volume 18 (1936)

Barrows, H.D., "Recollections of the Old Courthouse and Its Builder," *Historical Society of Southern California Quarterly*, Volume 3 (1893–96)

Hylen, Arnold, *Los Angeles before the Freeways* (1981)

Moore, Charles et al., *The City Observed: Los Angeles* (1998)

Waldron, Granville A., "Courthouses of Los Angeles County," *Historical Society of Southern California Quarterly*, Volume 41 (1959)

Madera

"Madera County's Historic Courthouse," *The Madera County Historian*, Vol. 9, No. 1 (January 1969)

Marin

Donnelly, Florence, "The Story of Marin's Courthouses," *Marin Independent Journal* (February 5, 1966)

Dunham, Judith, *Details of Frank Lloyd Wright: The California Work, 1909–1974* (1994)

Marin County Historical Society Bulletin (March 1990)

Park, Helen Van Cleave and Trudell, Clyde, "Old Courthouse History," *Marin Independent Journal* (November 8, 1975)

Twombly, Robert C., *Frank Lloyd Wright: An Interpretive Biography* (1973)

Mariposa

Pinkerton, Scott and Radanovich, Leroy, *Mariposa County Courthouse: Shrine to Justice* (1989)

Mendocino

"Mendocino County Dedicates Her New Courthouse," *Redwood Journal Press Dispatch* (Courthouse Dedication Supplement, April 7, 1951)

Merced

Radcliffe, Corwin, *History of Merced County* (1940)

Modoc

Laird, Irma, *The Modoc Country* (1971)

Monterey

Monterey County Board of Supervisors, "Legacy: Joseph Jacinto Mora—A Celebration of Sculptures" (1998)

Ware, Richard. et al., "Poured Around Its Predecessor," *Architectural Record* (August 1943)

Nevada

Davis, H.P., *Gold Rush Days in Nevada City* (1948)

Starkey, Marilyn and Browne, Juanita, *Sketches of Yesterday and Today in Nevada County* (1988)

Orange

Brigandi, Phil, *Old Orange County Courthouse—A Centennial History* (2001)

"Rock of Ages," *Orange Coast Magazine* (November 1988)

Sleeper, Jim, "Portrait From the Past—A Historical Profile of Orange County's Old County Courthouse" (1979)

Placer

Placer County Historical Society, "The Placer County Courthouse" (1994)

Riverside

Fitch, Robert, "A Historical Look at the Courthouse," *Riverside County Bar Association Bulletin* (November 1991)

Moses, Dr. Vincent and Fron, Heidi, "Justitia Rei Publicae Fundamentum," Brochure for Rededication of Courthouse (1998)

Patterson, Tom, *A Colony for California: Riverside's First Hundred Years* (1971)

Patterson, Tom, "Underlying Issues in the Creation of Riverside County," in *Historical Portraits of Riverside County*, John Brumgard, Ed. (1977)

Sacramento

Sacramento County, Jackson Research Projects, *The Old Courthouse Block 1848–1983* (1983)

Severson, Thor, *Sacramento—An Illustrated History 1839 to 1874* (1973)

State of California, Department of Finance, "California's State Capitol" (1956)

San Benito

Thomas, Mark (Hon.), *Wielding the Gavel: The Story of the Courts of San Benito County from 1874 to 1994* (1996)

San Bernardino

Ingersoll, L.A., *Ingersoll's Century Annals of San Bernardino County 1769 to 1904* (1904)

Schuiling, *San Bernardino County: Land of Contrast* (1984)

San Diego

Board of Supervisors, "Justice: The Story of San Diego County Courthouses in Word and Pictures" (1979)

Smythe, William, *History of San Diego 1542–1907* (1907)

Van Housen, Caty, "Order in the Court—New Hall of Justice Will Be $61 Million Change of Venue," *San Diego Union Tribune* (August 20, 1995)

San Francisco

Hansen, Gladys, Ed., *San Francisco: The Bay Region and Its Cities* (1973)

Howard, John Galen, "San Francisco's Civic Center," *Architect and Engineer* (July 1913)

Soule, Frank et al., *The Annals of San Francisco* (1855)

Watkins, T.H., *Mirror of the Dream* (1976)

San Joaquin

Martin, Covert et al., *Stockton Album Through the Years* (1959)

Wood, R. Coke and Covello, Leonard, *Stockton Memories—Pictorial History of Stockton, California* (1977)

San Luis Obispo

Miossi, Harold, "The San Luis Obispo County Courthouse" (1971)

Tritenbach, Paul, *San Luis Obispo Discoveries* (1989)

San Mateo

Edmonds, John, "The Early Courts of San Mateo County" (1986)

Regnery, Dorothy, *An Enduring Heritage* (1976)

Santa Barbara

Board of Supervisors, "The Santa Barbara County Courthouse" (1929)

Conrad, Rebecca and Nelson, Christopher, *Santa Barbara: A Guide to El Pueblo Viejo* (1986)

Palmer, Kevin L., "Courting the Civic Image," *Noticias* (Spring 1991)

Spaulding, Edward Delden, *A Brief Story of Santa Barbara* (1964)

Santa Clara

Butler, Phyllis Filiberti, *The Valley of Santa Clara: Historic Buildings 1792–1920* (1975)

Hess, Alan, "Courthouse Restoration Becomes Gift to Street," *San Jose Mercury News* (May 8, 1994)

Muller, Kathleen, *San Jose: City With a Past* (1988)

Santa Cruz

Chase, John, *The Sidewalk Companion to Santa Cruz Architecture* (1979)

Koch, Margaret, *They Called It Home* (1974)

Souza, Margaret, "The History of the Santa Cruz Courthouse" (1966), unpublished paper on file at Santa Cruz Public Library

Shasta

Allen, Marion, *Redding and the Three Shastas* (1989)

Bisbee, Cliff, "The Courthouse at Shasta," *The Covered Wagon—Shasta Historical Society Yearbook* (1954)

Eaton, Richard (Hon.), "The Four Courthouses of Shasta County," *The Covered Wagon—Shasta Historical Society Yearbook* (1958)

Peterson, Albert, "Excerpts From My Court Reporting Career," *Shasta County History—An Original California County*, H. McKim, Ed. (1985)

Siskiyou

Meamber, Fred and Bernice, "The Court House Building in Its Early Days," *Yreka Echoes* (August/September 1975)

Solano

"Recent Work of Mr. E. C. Hemmings—Solano County Courthouse," *Architect and Engineer* (October 1917)

California Department of Parks and Recreation, "Benicia Capitol State Historic Park" (1985)

Sonoma

Hansen, Harvey and Miller, J., *Wild Oats in Eden: Sonoma County in the 19th Century* (1962)

LeBaron, Gaye, *Santa Rosa, A Nineteenth Century Town* (1985)

… *Santa Rosa, A Twentieth Century Town* (1993)

Thompson, Thos., *Atlas of Sonoma County* (1877)

Stanislaus

Elias, Sol, *Stories of Stanislaus* (1924)

Elliot & Moore, *History of Stanislaus County* (1881)

Herndon, Carroll Ray, *Stanislaus County 1854–1954* (1955)

Sutter

Delay, Peter, *History of Yuba and Sutter Counties* (1924)

Sullivan & Zall, *The Survivors—Existing Homes and Buildings of Yuba and Sutter Counties' Past* (1974)

Tehama

Webster, Abby, "Tehama County Court House, Red Bluff, California" (1968), research paper with illustrations on file at Tehama County Library, Red Bluff

Trinity

Cox, Isaac, *The Annals of Trinity County* (1940)

Miller, Dorothy, "The Old Courthouse," *Trinity County Historical Society Yearbook* (1980–1981)

Tulare

Mitchell, Annie, *Sites to See: Historical Landmarks in Tulare County* (1983)

Mitchell, Annie, "Tulare County Courthouses," *Los Tulares—Quarterly Bulletin of the Tulare County Historical Society* (December 1970)

Small, Kathleen, *History of Tulare County* (1926)

Tuolumne

DeFerrari, Carlo, "The Tuolumne County Courthouses, Part One" *CHISPA—The Quarterly of the Tuolumne County Historical Society* (July–September 1999), "Part Two" (October–December 1999)

Marovich, Sharon, "Courthouse Square—Sonora's First Park," *CHISPA* (January–March 1988)

Ventura

Bandurraga, Peter et al., *Ventura County's Yesterdays Today* (1980)

Sheridan, Sol, *History of Ventura County California* (1926)

Yolo

Illustrated Atlas and History of Yolo County, California, DePue & Co. (1879)

Russell, William, ed., *History of Yolo County* (1940)

Yuba

Schuck, Oscar, *History of Bench and Bar of California* (1901)

History of Yuba County, California, Thompson and West (1879)

Photographic & Artistic Credits

At the heart of this book are the graphic images: architectural plans, drawings and photographs. They were created by the artists, and made available through the courtesy of the institutions, listed here.

Alpine County Museum: pp. 260; 261 (top)

Amador County Museum: pp. 77 (top); 78; 79 (top)

Balcher, Alan: pp. 61 (bottom); 67 (bottom); 107; 131 (top); 156; 261 (bottom)

Bancroft Library, University of California at Berkeley: pp. 9, 16 (top); 104(bottom); 139 (bottom); 140 (top); 141 (center)

Calaveras County Archives: pp. 80 (top); 82

Calaveras County Historical Society: p. 81 (center and right)

California Historical Society: pp. 63 (bottom) FN-31672; 64 (top) Ralph H. Cross Collection, FN-31669; 94 (top left) FN-31671; 109 (top) GN-03483; 119 (top), Ralph H. Cross Collection, FN-31673; 139 (top), FN-31458; 148 (top), FN-25682; 161, FN-16842; 162, FN-31437; 178 (top), FN-31456; 182, FN-31457; 207 (bottom left), FN-31773; 210 (bottom), FN-01366; 231, FN-00765; 232 (top), FN-09449; 251 (top), FN-31772; 254 (bottom), FN-31670

California State Library, Sacramento; California History Room: pp. 15; 17 (top); 79 (bottom); 95 (top); 105 (top); 110-111; 112 (top); 121; 122 (bottom); 123 (top); 136-137, 160; 163 (bottom); 164; 165 (bottom); 197 (bottom); 263 (bottom); 270; 320-321; 324 (bottom)

California State University, Chico; Special Collections, Meriam Library: pp. 64 (bottom left); 65 (top) (and Judge Richard Eaton); 73 (top and middle) (Hal Goodyear Collection); 100 (with Plumas County Museum); 112 (bottom); 128 (bottom); 129 (bottom) (and Ruth Hitchcock)

California State University, Fresno; Special Collections Library: p. 198 (top)

Colusa County Archives: pp. 114; 117 (top)

Community Memorial Museum of Sutter County: p.126 (bottom)

Contra Costa County Historical Society: 146; 147; 148 (bottom)

Corbett, Michael: pp. xi (top); 33 (top); 47 (bottom right); 83 (top left); 127 (bottom)

County of Inyo, Eastern California Museum: pp. 262 (top); 264; 265

Court of Appeal, Fourth District: p.327 (top)

Covello & Covello Photographers: pp. 252; 257 (top)

David, Robert E.: pp. 152 (bottom); 173 (bottom right-courtroom)

Davis•Davis Architects: p. 313 (top)

Del Norte County Historical Society: pp. 46 (bottom); 47 (top, middle)

El Centro Public Library: p. 271 (bottom)

El Dorado County Historical Museum: pp. 84; 85 (bottom); 86

Elderman, Michael J.: pp. 268-269; 275 (top right)

First American Corporation History Collection: pp. 298 (top); 300 (bottom)

Fresno Bee, Editorial Library: pp. 200; 201 (top)

Fresno Historical Society: pp. 195 (bottom); 196; 197

Fresno Department of City Planning: p. 30 (top)

Historia, Ltd.: pp. 11, 81 (left inset); 189 (bottom); 190(bottom); 191 (top, middle)

Humboldt County Collection, Humboldt State University: pp. 44-45; 49; 50; 51 (top)

Huntington Library, San Marino, California: pp. 239 (top); 280

Imperial County Historical Society, Pioneers Museum: p.271 (top)

Kern County: p.205 (inset)

Kern County Museum: pp. 202; 203; 204 (top left, bottom); 205 (top)

Lake County Museum: pp. 52; 53

Lange, Dorothea, The Oakland Museum of California, City of Oakland, Gift of Paul S. Taylor: p. 142 (three images)

Laws Railroad Museum: pp. 262 (bottom); 263 (top)

Lewis Kostiner, Seagram County Courthouse Archives, Library of Congress: pp. 248 (top); 249 (top)

Library of Congress: pp. 18; 46 (top); 65 (lower left); 104 (top); 106 (bottom); 115 (top); 174; 198 (bottom); 315 (top)

Los Angeles Public Library/Photo Collection: pp. 286; 291 (bottom); 292 (top and bottom left); 293; 295 (bottom)-William Reagh, Photographer

Madeiros, Monte: pp. 37; 153

Madera County Museum/Historical Society: pp. 208; 209

Marin History Museum: p. 150

Marin Independent Journal: pp. 152 (top); 154 (top two images)

Mariposa County Museum: pp. 19; 88 (bottom); 89; 90; 91 (bottom)

McDevitt, Jessica: pp. 17 (bottom); 91 (top); 113 (bottom, right); 195 (top); 215 (top); 241 (bottom); 243 (top)

McDevitt, Ray: pp. vii; xi (bottom); xii (top); xiii (top); xiv; xv; xvi; xviii; 2 (top); 24; 29; 34; 36; 71 (bottom left and right); 73 (bottom left); 83 (top right); 130; 131 (bottom); 133 (bottom five images); 144 (top three images); 145; 149; 154 (bottom); 155; 158 (bottom); 159; 168; 172 (bottom left); 173 (bottom left); 175 (middle, bottom); 181; 185 (bottom); 186 (bottom); 187; 204 (top right); 207 (bottom center, right); 215 (bottom); 230 (left); 232-233 (bottom series of images); 234; 235; 241 (top); 242; 243 (bottom); 250; 251 (middle, bottom); 257 (bottom); 276 (bottom); 277; 282 (bottom); 283 (top left); 292 (bottom right); 295 (top left and right); 296; 297; 301 (bottom); 303 (bottom left and right); 305; 307 (top); 312 (bottom); 313 (bottom); 318 (three images at left); 319; 324 (top left and right); 325; 326 (top right, bottom) 327 (center, bottom left and right); 332 (top series of four images); 337 (top right); 343; 344 (center)

McHenry Museum: pp. 220; 221; 222; 223 (top)

Museum of Art and History, The McPherson Center, Santa Cruz: pp. 253 (top); 254 (top)

Meamber, Fred & Bernice: p. 69 (bottom)

Mendocino County Historical Society, Robert J. Lee Collection: pp. 54, 56

Mendocino County Museum: p.55

Merced County Museum: pp. 22 (left); 210 (top); 211; 212; 213 (right)

Napa County Historical Society: p. 157

Oakland Museum of California: pp. 141 (top); 143; 167 (top left)

Oakland Public Library: pp. 138; 140 (bottom)

Old Courthouse Museum (Orange County): p.300 (top)

Orange County Register: pp. 301 (top); 302; 303 (top)

Page & Turnbull, Architects: pp. 328; 330; 334 (top and center); 336 (top left and bottom)

Pirkle Jones, Seagram County Courthouse Archives, Library of Congress: pp. 47 (bottom left); 51 (bottom); 65 (lower right); 66 (top); 83 (bottom); 87 (bottom); 97; 109 (bottom); 113 (bottom left); 115 (bottom); 116 (top); 117 (bottom); 118; 125 (top); 126 (left center); 135 (bottom); 186 (top); 199; 201 (bottom); 205 (bottom); 207 (top); 213 (left); 214; 223 (bottom); 227 (bottom); 233 (bottom right); 237 (bottom); 248 (bottom); 249 (bottom); 267 (bottom); 312 (top); 318 (right)

Pisciotto, Cindy: p. ii (Mono County Courthouse)

Placer County Museum: pp. 96; 98; 99

Plumas County Museum: pp. 101; 102; 103 (top)

Porter, William: pp. 323; 332 (bottom right, two images); 333 (bottom); 334 (bottom); 337 (bottom left)

Redwood City Public Library Archives: pp. 170; 171; 172-173 (top)

Riverside California Municipal Museum: pp. 3 (Bob Fitch); 273; 274

Riverside Public Library: pp. 272; 275 (top left)

Riverside Press Enterprise/William Wilson Lewis III: p.2 (bottom)

Rosecranz, Adolph: pp. 172 (center left, right); 173 (center left)

Ross•Drulis Architects: pp. 158 (top); 169; 338; 339; 340; 341; 344 (top, bottom); 345

Sacramento Archives and Museum Collection Center: pp. 120; 122 (top)

Sacramento Bee Photo Morgue, Sacramento Archives and Museum Collection Center: pp. 76; 77 (bottom); 87 (top); 94 (bottom right); 95 (bottom); 105 (bottom); 119 (bottom); 123 (bottom); 124; 125 (bottom four images); 183; 185 (top); 219 (top)

San Benito County Historical Society: pp. 236; 237 (top)

San Bernardino County Museum: pp. 276 (top); 278; 281; 282 (top); 283

San Diego County Historical Society: pp. 306; 307 (bottom); 308; 309; 310; 311

San Francisco Public Library, San Francisco History Center: pp. 67 (top-three photo series); 165 (top left and top right); 166; 167 (top right, bottom); 322; 329 (bottom); 331; 332 (middle); 333 (top)

San Jose Historical Museum: pp. 176 (top); 178 (bottom); 179 (bottom)

San Jose Mercury News: p. xiii (bottom left)

San Luis Obispo County History Museum: pp. 238; 239 (bottom)

San Mateo County Historical Museum: p. 172 (top left)

Sandywood: p.1; 357

Santa Ana Public Library History Room: pp. 298 (bottom); 299; 304

Santa Barbara Historical Society: pp. 228-229; 244; 245; 246 (bottom); 247

Schwering, James: p. xii (middle)

Searls Historical Library: pp. 92; 93 (top); 94 (top right and bottom left)

Seaver Center for Western History Research, Los Angeles County Museum of Natural History: pp. 163 (top); 246 (top); 275 (bottom); 287; 290 (bottom); 291 (top)

Shepard, Mark: p. 21 (right)

Siskiyou County Museum: pp. 68; 69 (top); 70

Skidmore Owings & Merrill Architects: 329 (top); 335; 336 (top right); 337 (top left, bottom right)

Society of California Pioneers: pp. 66 (bottom); 93 (bottom); 216; 279; 288; 290 (top)

Sonoma County Library: pp. 188; 189 (top); 190 (middle); 191 (bottom)

Sourisseau Academy, California State University, San Jose: pp. 176 (bottom); 177 (top, bottom); 178 (middle, bottom); 179; 180

Stewart, Jack: p. xii (bottom)

Stewart, Walter: p. 144 (bottom two images)

Supreme Court of California: p. viii

Sutter County Library: p. 126 (top right)

Symphony Towers: p. 326 (top left)

Tehama County Library: p. 128 (top)

Trinity County Historical Society: p. 72

Tulare County Museum: pp. 224; 225; 226; 227 (top)

Tuolumne County Museum: pp. 106 (top); 108

University of California, Los Angeles, Department of Special Collections, Charles E. Young Research Library: p. 289

University of California Library, Davis, Department of Special Collections: pp. 57; 58-59; 60; 61 (top); 62; 63 (top); 71 (top); 74-75; 103 (bottom); 113 (top); 116 (bottom); 129 (top); 133 (top)

University of California, Santa Cruz, University Library, Special Collections: pp. 31; 141 (bottom); 151; 175 (top); 230 (right); 233 (top); 240 (bottom); 253 (bottom); 255; 256; 258-259; 266; 267 (top)

University of Southern California, USC Library, Department of Special Collections: p. 13, 240 (top); 294.

University of the Pacific Libraries, Holt Atherton Department of Special Collections: pp. 20; 80 (bottom); 88 (top); 192-193; 194; 217; 218; 219 (top- three image series)

Vacaville Historical Society: p. 184

Ventura County Museum of Art & History: pp. 284-285; 314; 315 (bottom); 316; 317

Yolo County Archives and Records Center: pp. 40-41; 132

Yuba County Library: pp. 134 (right); 135 (top)

NOTE: If only one source is listed for a page on which there are several images, all images were furnished through the courtesy of that source.

Biographies

Biographical Information on the Contributors

John Burns

John Burns is an archivist, educator, historian and author. He served from 1981 to 1997 as the state archivist of California, taught history as an adjunct professor at California State University, Sacramento and is now a history-social science curriculum consultant for the State Department of Education. Recent publications include an illustrated history of Sacramento and *Taming the Elephant: Politics, Law and Government in Pioneer California* (coedited with Richard Orsi) to be published this year by the University of California Press for the California Historical Society.

Michael Corbett

Michael Corbett has practiced as an architectural historian for over 25 years. During that time he has worked with architectural and engineering firms (including Dames & Moore/URS), for the New York City Landmarks Preservation Commission, for a preservation foundation, and for numerous private clients. He has also taught at the Department of Architecture at the University of California at Berkeley. Publications include *Splendid Survivors: Downtown San Francisco's Architectural Heritage* (1979) and *Building California: Technology and the Landscape* (1998).

Charles Drulis, AIA

Charles Drulis is a principal in Ross•Drulis Architects & Planners, Inc., in Sonoma, California. A member of the AIA Committee on Architecture and Justice, Mr. Drulis has designed courthouses and other justice system buildings, such as family law centers and juvenile corrections facilities, throughout the United States. Two recently completed projects include the San Francisco Civic Center courthouse and the Napa County criminal courthouse. He is a frequent lecturer at AIA and Justice Management Institute conferences.

Ronald M. George

Ronald M. George is the chief justice of California. He began his legal career in 1965 as a deputy attorney general in the California Department of Justice. While with the attorney general's office, he represented the State of California in six cases before the United States Supreme Court. Thereafter, he served as a trial judge for 15 years, first on the municipal court and later on the superior court in Los Angeles. Appointed to the Court of Appeal for the Second District in 1987, he was elevated to the California Supreme Court in 1991 and has been the chief justice since 1996.

Jessica McDevitt (Researcher)

Jessica McDevitt graduated with honors in history from Pitzer College, Claremont, California. After graduate study in European history at the University of Texas at Austin, she received a Rotary International Fellowship to study at the Université de Bourgogne in Dijon, France. She currently works in the San Francisco office of a New York–based public relations firm.

Ray McDevitt (Editor)

Ray McDevitt is a partner in the San Francisco–based law firm Hanson, Bridgett, Marcus, Vlahos & Rudy, LLP, where his practice emphasizes municipal and environmental law. Prior to joining the firm in 1976, he served as a law clerk to the late Raymond L. Sullivan, an associate justice of the California Supreme Court, and later as an attorney and then associate general counsel for the United States Environmental Protection Agency. He teaches local government law as an adjunct professor at the University of San Francisco School of Law.

Victor Miceli

Victor Miceli is a superior court judge in Riverside County. After two years of service in the United States Army, Judge Advocate Corps, he practiced law, specializing in civil litigation, from 1954 until his appointment to the bench in 1986. He is also president of the Board of Trustees of the Riverside County Law Library. Judge Miceli played a central role in preserving and restoring the historic Riverside County courthouse.

Mark Shepard (Designer)

Mark Shepard is a graphic designer in Marin County. A pioneer in the use of the computer as a design tool, he has over 25 years of experience in designing books, magazines and newsletters for, among others, publishers and local government agencies. He also regularly handles retail design projects for clients ranging from wineries to video game makers, such as LucasArts.

John Gordon Turnbull, FAIA

Jay Turnbull is an architect and urban designer. After serving as Architect of the Foundation for San Francisco's Architectural Heritage, he joined Page & Turnbull, Inc. in 1981. Former chair of the AIA/Heritage Joint Committee on Historic Resources, Mr. Turnbull has published and lectured widely on preservation-related matters. He has served as the preservation architect on many projects involving landmark structures listed on the National Register of Historic Places, including the recent restoration of the Ninth Circuit Court of Appeals, in San Francisco.

Christopher VerPlanck

After receiving his master's degree in architectural history and historic preservation at the University of Virginia, Chris VerPlanck worked at the Foundation for San Francisco's Architectural Heritage. Since 1999 he has been the architectural historian at Page & Turnbull, Inc. in San Francisco. He has published articles in local and national journals, including the *Vernacular Architecture Forum*.

Kings County courthouse.
Drawing © Sandywood.

Acknowledgements

The single most important contribution to this book was that of my daughter, Jessica McDevitt. Taking time off from her own graduate studies in European history, Jessica scoured California for images and written accounts of courthouses. She devoted 14 months to the effort, visiting major research libraries and tiny county historical societies from Del Norte County to San Diego County. The results of her diligence are evident on nearly every page. The book is as much her accomplishment as mine.

Lynn Duncan, a talented and super-efficient legal assistant at Hanson Bridgett contributed at every stage of the project during the past four years. Lynn typed the entire text, as well as countless ancillary documents: letters, brochures, corporate minutes, nonprofit reporting forms, all the while meeting the considerable demands of her position at the law firm. Lynn was, as well, a tactful and reliable point of contact for the many people who played a role in producing the book. Lynn defines grace under pressure.

Mark Shepard, graphic artist extraordinaire, designed and produced the book from cover to cover. Mark accommodated my unpredictable schedule, constant tinkering and unreasonable demands with unfailing good humor and great skill.

My partners at Hanson Bridgett deserve my thanks as well. They allowed me to work a reduced schedule for three years while the book was underway. The firm also made a generous financial contribution. This response is representative of the firm's long-standing tradition of support for public service and *pro bono publico* projects. Special thanks are due to my partners Gerry Marcus and Steve Taber, who served with me on the board of directors of The Courthouse Project, the nonprofit corporation that has been the vehicle for production of the book, and to Fred Weil, Madeline Chun and Patrick Miyaki.

Chief Justice Ronald M. George's early and enthusiastic support for the project opened many doors; his gracious foreword offers a uniquely personal perspective on both the courts and the buildings in which they operate. And Barbara George was most generous in sharing access to the materials she had gathered while assembling the first complete collection of photographs of courthouses from all 58 counties. Those photographs, beautifully printed and framed, may be viewed by the public and are well worth a visit to the State Judicial Council Conference Center at the new Hiram Johnson State Office Building in San Francisco's Civic Center.

Judge Victor Miceli was a gracious and enthusiastic host when I visited Riverside. His love for the splendid old courthouse (which his energy did so much to save) was apparent then and is evident in his warm and personal reflections in this volume.

I am fortunate that the other contributors, all busy professionals as well, made the time to craft individual essays that both delight and instruct. Historians John Burns and Michael Corbett and architects Charles Drulis, AIA, and Jay Turnbull, FAIA, (ably assisted by architectural historian Chris VerPlanck) generously responded to my invitation to participate in this project. Their contributions, each of which exceeded my expectations, bring the special insights of their disciplines and extensive personal experience. I am deeply grateful to each of them.

Some of the most striking images in the book are the product of accomplished contemporary photographers who contributed their work: Alan Balcher, who also practices law in Napa; Robert David of San Francisco, an architect and graphic designer; and Cindy Pisciotto. Adolph Rosecranz, AIA, generously allowed use of photographs recording his firm's work in connection with the recent restoration of San Mateo County's historic courthouse.

So many other people have helped in so many different ways that it would require a small book to describe their contributions and properly express my gratitude. They know best how important their help was and I trust they will not object to my brief expression of public recognition: Hal Cohen, Senior Supervising Attorney of the California Supreme Court; Inez Cohen, Library Director at the Mechanics Institute

This drawing, by the late courtroom artist James Schwering, shows attorney John J. Vlahos addressing San Mateo Superior Court Judge Melvin Cohn in 1979. The picture is included because it illustrates the art of advocacy in a county courthouse as practiced by an outstanding trial lawyer who, coincidentally, also happens to be a partner, mentor and friend of your editor (who is shown seated to John's right).

Library in San Francisco; James Carroll, California Judicial Council staff; Malcolm Margolin, Publisher, Heyday Books; Michael McCone, former Executive Director of the California Historical Society, as well as Stephen Becker, the Society's current Executive Director; James Pfeiffer, Executive Director, State Bar Foundation; McKenzie and Associates in San Francisco; Frank Lopez, Marketing Director, Hanson Bridgett Marcus Vlahos & Rudy; Phil Cronin, County Counsel of Fresno County; Marty Lasden, Len Auletto and Wayne Wedgeworth of the Daily Journal Corporation; Steve Kelly, Clerk/Administrator, and Joyce Nohavec, Assistant Clerk/Administrator, Court of Appeal, Fourth District; Barbara King and Ken Della Penta.

The individuals and organizations who responded to our appeal for support are acknowledged earlier in this volume (page vi). Their generosity helped in obvious practical ways, of course. As important, it provided your editor with encouragement to persevere in a project whose challenges far surpassed those he envisioned. To each of those donors, most of whom I have yet to meet, go my humble thanks.

Finally, there are individuals on staffs of libraries, museums, archives, newspapers, county historical societies, county counsels, courts and judges who took time and energy to share information and correct oversights. Truly, in a work of this kind an editor must depend (as did Blanche DuBois in *A Streetcar Named Desire*) on the kindness of strangers.

ALAMEDA: Harlan Kessel, Alameda County Historical Society; Ronald Overholt, Executive Officer, Alameda County Superior Court

ALPINE: Barbara Jones, County Clerk; Superior Court Judge Harold Bradford; Nancy Thornberg

AMADOR: Larry Cenotto, County Archivist; John Hahn, County Counsel

BUTTE: James Lenhoff, Butte County Historical Society

CALAVERAS: Lorrayne Kennedy, County Archivist

COLUSA: Kathleen Moran, County Clerk and Recorder; Richard Johnson, M.D., Editor, *Wagon Wheels*

CONTRA COSTA: James Marchiano, Associate Justice, California Court of Appeal

DEL NORTE: John Alexander, retired County Clerk and Superior Court Executive Officer

EL DORADO: Marilyn Ferguson, El Dorado County Heritage Association; William Schultz, County Clerk-Recorder

FRESNO: Phil Cronin, County Counsel; Ray Silva, County Librarian; Nancy Ramirez, *Fresno Bee* Editorial Library

GLENN: Susan Rawlins, Colusa County Library Director

IMPERIAL: Superior Court Judge James Harmon; Joanne Yeager, Assistant County Counsel

INYO: Beth Porter, Inyo County Eastern California Museum; Beverly Harry, County Clerk-Recorder

KERN: Stephen Schuett, Assistant County Counsel; William Wilbanks, Kern County Director of General Services; Martin Brantley, Superior County Clerk Supervisor; Kay Beavers, Sr. Secretary-Administrator, Superior Court

KINGS: Denis Eymul, County Counsel; Rose Martinez, Clerk of Board of Supervisors

LAKE: Donna Howard, Curator, Lake County Museum

LASSEN: Tim Purdy, Historian

LOS ANGELES: Joyce Cook and Milan Dragicevich, Los Angeles Superior Court Planning and Research Unit; Carolyn Cole, Curator, Photograph Collection, Los Angeles Public Library

MADERA: Steve Fjelsted, Madera County Librarian; Dorothy Foust, Curator, Madera County Historical Society

MARIN: Lynn Skillings, Office Manager, and Jocelyn Moss, Librarian/Curator, Marin History Museum; Carol Farrand, Librarian, *Marin Independent Journal*; Howard Hanson, County Clerk

MARIPOSA: Karry Lee Self, Curator, Mariposa County Museum & History Center; Leroy Radanovich and Scott Pinkerton, Mariposa Heritage Press

MENDOCINO: Lila J. Lee, Director, Held-Poage Library, Mendocino County Historical Society; Rebecca Snetselaar, Curator, Mendocino County Museum; Marsha Young, County Clerk-Recorder.

MERCED: Andrea Morris Metz, Director, and Sue Sharp, Registrar, Merced County Courthouse Museum

MODOC: Joanne Cain and Peggy Decker, Modoc County Library; Dixie Server, Director, Modoc County Museum

MONO: Marshall Rudolph, County Counsel; Superior Court Judge Edward Denton

MONTEREY: Meg Clovis, Monterey County Parks Department

NAPA: Superior Court Judge Thomas Kongsgaard (Ret.); Superior Court Judge W. Scott Snowden; Georgene Larsen, Assistant Court Executive Officer

NEVADA: Edwin L. Tyson, Librarian, Searls Historical Library

ORANGE: Ann Harder, Orange County History Room, Santa Ana Public Library; Bruce Sinclair, President, Old Courthouse Museum Society

PLACER: Vernon Krause, Auburn

PLUMAS: Robert Shulman, County Counsel; Scott Lawson, Director, Plumas County Museum

RIVERSIDE: William Katzenstein, County Counsel; Robert Fitch; Tom Patterson; Dr. Vincent Moses, Curator of History, Riverside Municipal Museum; William Swafford, Richard Hanks and William Bell, Riverside Local History Resource Center

SACRAMENTO: Stasia Wolfe, Sacramento Archives and Museum Collection Center; Frank Martinez, Assistant Executive Officer, Sacramento County Superior Court

SAN BENITO: Sharlene Van Rooy, San Benito Historical Society

SAN BERNARDINO: Dr. Ann Deegan, San Bernardino County Museum; Wendy Sellnow, Court Services Manager

SAN DIEGO: Jeanne Akin, Museum Curator, California Department of Parks & Recreation; Robert Davis AIA, DavisDavis Architects

SAN JOAQUIN: Superior Court Judge Thomas Teaford, Jr.

SAN LUIS OBISPO: Superior Court Judge Barry Hammer; Jac A. Crawford, Assistant County Counsel; Julie Rodewald, County Clerk-Recorder; Lynne Landwehr and Catherine Trujillo, San Luis Obispo County Historical Museum

SAN MATEO: Superior Court Judge Judith Whitmer Kozloski; John Edmonds, Deputy Sheriff (Ret.); Mitch Postel, Director, San Mateo County Historical Museum

SANTA BARBARA: Michael Redmon and Kathleen Brewster, Santa Barbara Historical Society

SANTA CLARA: Steven Love, County Clerk/Chief Executive Officer; the late Glory Anne Laffey, Executive Secretary, Sourisseau Academy, San Jose State University; Superior Court Judge Leslie Nichols

SANTA CRUZ: Superior Court Judge Robert B. Yonts; Patricia Pfremmer, County Law Librarian

SHASTA: Superior Court Judge Richard B. Eaton (Ret.); Superior Court Judge Steven Jahr

SIERRA: Lee Adams, Sheriff-Coroner

SISKIYOU: Superior Court Judge Robert F. Kaster; Fred & Bernice Meamber; Frank DeMarco, County Counsel; Rita Haas, Office of County Counsel; Siskiyou County Historical Society/Museum staff

SOLANO: Carol Tombarelli, Court Division Manager

SONOMA: Marilyn Josi, Director, Sonoma County Law Library; E.T. Lewis, County Clerk; John & Gaye Le Baron; James Botz, former County Counsel; Steven Woodside, County Counsel; Beth Martinez, Legal Assistant, County Counsel's office

STANISLAUS: June Simas, McHenry Museum

SUTTER: Mazie Mazerrole, Assistant Court Executive Officer; Joan Martin, Assistant Clerk-Recorder; Julie Stack, Director/Curator; Community Memorial Museum

TEHAMA: Nelson Buck, County Counsel; Connie Balmeier, Reference Librarian, and Del Osborn, Tehama County Library

TRINITY: Patricia Hicks; Alice Jones, Trinity County Historical Society

TULARE: Kathy Howell, Curator, Tulare County Museum

TUOLUMNE: Carlo M. DeFerrari, Tuolumne County Historian; Richard Caramena, Tuolumne County Museum and History Center

VENTURA: Charles Johnson, Associate Director, Ventura County Museum of History and Art; Richard D. Dean, County Clerk and Recorder

YOLO: Charles Mack, County Counsel; Mel Russell, Yolo County Archives

YUBA: Mary Robertson, Yuba County Library

Those whose institutions extend beyond a single county and whose assistance was greatly appreciated include Stasia Wolfe, Archivist, Sacramento Archives and Museum Collection Center; Ellen Harding and the other staff members at the California History Section, California State Library; John Skarstad, University Archivist, University of California at Davis; Jennene Ford, Holt-Atherton Department of Special Collections, University of the Pacific; Dace Taube, Curator, Regional History Collection, University of Southern California; William Jones, Merriam Library Special Resources, California State University at Chico; and the staff of the University Library, Special Collections, University of California at Santa Cruz.

Michael Corbett has asked that his appreciation be conveyed to the following people, all of whom helped in the preparation of his essay: Elizabeth Byrne, Environmental Design Library, UC Berkeley; Mary Hardy; Daniel Lane, for research in New York City; Betty Marvin, Oakland Cultural Heritage Survey; Marlene McCall and Ruby Hendryx at Creative Office Services; John Edward Powell; Kerry Samson, Placer County Library; Richard Schwarz, Merced County Department of Public Works; Suzanne Seton, daughter of Russell G. DeLappe; Dell Upton, for research suggestions; Mitchell Van Bourg, architect; Sally Woodbridge, for conversation and comments on the text. In addition, Michael thanks "my father, who first pointed out courthouses to me in Texas in the 1950s and who accompanied my daughter and me on a survey of Sacramento Valley courthouses in 1999… and my wife and children who visited courthouses on every family outing and vacation for the past two years."

Despite help from all of the foregoing, it is inevitable that errors will be discovered in the text. These are the fault of your editor, who regrets them and humbly asks his readers to recall the words of Thomas Noon Talfourd, a 19th-century British judge, member of Parliament and author:

"Fill the seats of justice
  With good men, not so absolute in goodness
  As to forget what human frailty is."

Index

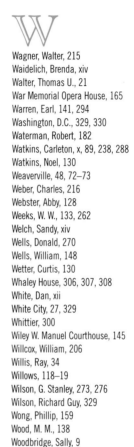